Language ... tice

Michael Vince
Amanda French

English Grammar and Vocabulary

MACMILLAN

Macmillan Education
Between Towns Road, Oxford OX4 3PP
A division of Macmillan Publishers Limited
Companies and representatives throughout the world

ISBN 978-0-2304-1056-5

First published 2011

Designed by Xen
Illustrated by Oxford Designers & Illustrators
Cover design by Andrew Oliver
Picture research by Catherine Dunn

Authors' acknowledgements
Michael Vince: thanks as ever to all the editorial team at Macmillan.
Amanda French: thanks to Liam, Georgia and Joe for support at home, and colleagues and students at Languages International, Auckland for helping trial my material.

The publishers would like to thank Helen Forrest and Christine Dowling.

The authors and publishers would like to thank the following for permission to reproduce their photographs:

Alamy / D Hurst p50 (bl); Alamy / Geog Photos p51, Alamy / Rob Bartree p56, Alamy / Ron Buskirk p110, Alamy / Peter Jordan p211, Banana Stock p108; BrandX p236; Corbis / Michele Falzone p92; Digital Vision p101; Getty pp79,85; Photodisc p208; Photolibrary / Japan Travel Bureau p50 (t); Science Photo Library / Martin Bond p174, Science Photo Library / NASA/JPL p77.

The authors and publishers would also like to thank the following for giving kind permission to have their graphs reproduced by Bonnie Erba:

Howstuffworks.com p10; istrategylabs.com p121; Mapawatt.com / www.epa.gov; Poverty.org.uk pp149,150; Privatehealth.co.uk p161; www.statistics.gov.uk pp11, 23, 24, 37, 38, 49, 135, 136; United Nations.2006. World Urbanisation Prospects: the 2005 revision,Table A17. New York: population Division.Department of Economic and Social Affairs United Nations p36.

Printed and bound in Spain by Edelvives

2016 2015 2014 2013 2012 2011
10 9 8 7 6 5 4 3 2 1

The author and publishers would like to thank the following for permission to reproduce their graphical data:

The Economist Newspaper Ltd p123(Feb/18/2010); Guardian News and Media Ltd pp93(1994/Jan/10), 94(1994/Jan/10),180(2010/Mar/13), 181(2009/Jun/03).

The authors and publishers would like to thank the following for permis sion to reproduce the following copyright material:

Material from 'What is the Channel Tunnel Rail Link – CTRL?' copyrigh © Department for Transport, reprinted by permission of the publisher;

Material from 'Medieval Units of Measure' by John James, reprinted by permission of the author;

Material from 'Don't jump to conclusions', copyright © The Open Universi 2010, reprinted by permission of the publisher;

Material from 'In touch: High pressure jobs linked to depression and an ety' first published in New Zealand Management 01.09.2007, copyright © New Zealand Management 2007, reprinted by permission of the publishe

Material from 'Subliminal advertising really does work, claim scientists' Richard Alleyne, copyright © Daily Telegraph Group Limited 2009, first published in The Daily Telegraph, 28.09.09, reprinted by permission of t publisher;

Material from 'Met Office says new super-computer will give more accura forecasts' by Simon de Bruxelles, copyright © The Times 2009, first published in The Times, 22.05.09, reprinted by permission of the publishe

Extract from 'More How Stuff Works' by Marshall Brain, copyright © Marshall Brain 2002, reproduced with permission of John Wiley & Sons In

Contents

Introduction viii

Grammar

Grammar 1	**Present time** Present simple; present continuous; types of verbs; question and negative forms	1
Grammar 2	**Past time** Past simple; past tense forms without past time meaning; past continuous; participle clauses	6
Grammar 3	**Practice 1**	10
Grammar 4	**Present perfect** Present perfect simple; present perfect simple or past simple?; present perfect continuous; present perfect continuous or present perfect simple?; present perfect simple and continuous uses; present continuous or present perfect continuous?	13
Grammar 5	**Past perfect, *used to*** Past perfect simple and continuous; reports and report verbs; past perfect uses; *used to*	18
Grammar 6	**Practice 2**	23
Grammar 7	**Future time** *Will* and *will not*; *be going to*; *will* or *going to*?; present simple and continuous; future time clauses; future continuous; future perfect simple; formal instructions	25
Grammar 8	**Time words and phrases** *At, in, on*; *already*; *yes, so far*; *for, since, ago*; *still*; *no longer*; *towards*; *by, until, so far, up to*; *during, throughout, over*; *after, afterwards, later, before*; *on time, in time*; *at last, last, finally, in the end, at the end*; *nowadays, these days*; *once, one day, at once*; *formerly, previously*	30
Grammar 9	**Practice 3**	36
Grammar 10	**Direct and indirect questions** Direct questions; indirect or reported questions; noun clauses; subject and object questions	39
Grammar 11	**The passive** Why use the passive?; tense forms; agent *by* and instrument *with*; verbs that cannot be passive	44
Grammar 12	**Practice 4**	49

CONTENTS

Grammar 13	**Conditionals 1** General truths: *If/When* + present simple + present simple; real conditions: *If* + present simple + *will/won't (do)*; general truth or real condition?; other variants; unreal conditions: *If* + past simple + *would (do)*; would; real or unreal?; *unless*	**52**
Grammar 14	**Conditionals 2** Impossible past conditions; mixed conditions; *otherwise*; *providing/provided (that), as long as, on condition (that)* ; *even if*; *if* + *should*; *if* + *were to*; *if (it) were/was not for, if it hadn't been for*	**57**
Grammar 15	**Practice 5**	**63**
Grammar 16	**Modals 1** Modal verbs; assuming that something is true; being certain that something will happen; being certain about something in the present; being certain about something in the past; possibility and uncertainty; past possibility and uncertainty; expectation; annoyance or shock; assuming something is true about the past; *be bound to, be sure to, be certain to*	**65**
Grammar 17	**Modals 2** Ability: *can, be able, could*; obligation: *must, have to, be to*; obligation or necessity: *need, need to*; *it* + *be* + adjective + *that*; recommendation: *should, ought to, had better*	**71**
Grammar 18	**Practice 6**	**77**
Grammar 19	**Articles 1** Context; giving examples; ideas; numbers and measurement; people; cities, towns, streets, places; unique objects; exclamations	**80**
Grammar 20	**Articles 2** geography; academic subjects; nationality; calendar; *home, school, prison, hospital, work, university*; generalized locations and activities; changes of meaning	**87**
Grammar 21	**Practice 7**	**93**
Grammar 22	**Number and quantity** countable and uncountable; *some* and *any*; *how many, how much*; *too many, too few, very few, few* and *a few*; *too much, not much, (only) a little, (very) little*; *a lot of/lots of, plenty, hardly any, not enough*; *no, not any, none (of)*; *many, more, less* with numbers; *enough, hardly enough, just enough*; number and amount; measurement words + *of*	**96**
Grammar 23	**Making comparisons** Comparative forms; comparative + comparative; *the* + comparative or superlative + *of the* + number/quantity; present perfect + superlative; *the* + comparative, *the* + comparative; modifiers; *like* and *as*; *enough* and *too*; *more, fewer, less, not as/ so much/many, too little, most (of the ...)*; *twice, three times* etc + *as much as/as many as*	**103**

Grammar 24	**Practice 8**	109
Grammar 25	**Adverbial clauses 1** Coordinate clauses; subordinate clauses; time clauses; place clauses; manner clauses	112
Grammar 26	**Adverbial clauses 2** Concession clauses; contrast clauses; reason clauses; result clauses; purpose clauses	116
Grammar 27	**Practice 9**	121
Grammar 28	**Relative clauses** defining and non-defining clauses; *which* and *that*; leaving out the relative pronoun; *who* and *whom*; *whose*; prepositions and relative pronouns; *when, where, why, whereby*; reduced relative clauses; *anyone who, those who*; *which*; nominal relative clauses	124
Grammar 29	**Participle clauses** Two actions at the same time performed by the same subject; one action before another performed by the same subject; time clause with *after, before, since, when, while, on*; manner, contrast and conditional clauses; *it* and *there* clauses; *with* and *without* clauses; adjective clauses	130
Grammar 30	**Practice 10**	135
Grammar 31	**Pronouns and determiners** *Every* and *each* + noun; *each (of), both (of), either, neither*; *each other, one another, one ... the other*; pronouns with *some-, any-*, and *no-*; *none, none of, one/ones*	138
Grammar 32	**Prepositional phrases** Prepositions and adverbs; place or position; movement; pairs of adverbs; phrases	143
Grammar 33	**Practice 11**	149
Grammar 34	**Reporting and hearsay** Report verbs; hearsay reports	152
Grammar 35	**Verbs followed by *-ing* or infinitive** Verbs followed by *-ing* + object; verbs followed by *-ing* or *to*-infinitive with change of meaning; verbs followed by *-ing* or *to*-infinitive with no change of meaning; verbs followed by *to*-infinitive or *that* clause; verbs followed by an object and *to*-infinitive; verbs followed by infinitive without *to*; other structures	156
Grammar 36	**Practice 12**	161
Grammar 37	**Organizing text 1** Adding a point; contrast or concession; degree; comparing and contrasting; exceptions and alternatives	163

CONTENTS

Grammar 38	**Organizing text 2** Sequences; summarizing and explaining; making assertions; giving examples; making clear; making statements less direct; comment and viewpoint	**169**
Grammar 39	**Organizing text 3** Reference words: pronouns; reference words: *the former*, *the latter*; emphasis: *It* clauses; emphasis: *What* clauses; emphasis: negatives; emphasis: *very*, *all*; inversion	**175**
Grammar 40	**Practice 13**	**180**

Vocabulary

Vocabulary 1	**Travel and tourism**	**182**
Vocabulary 2	**The natural world**	**185**
Vocabulary 3	**Geography and geology**	**188**
Vocabulary 4	**History**	**192**
Vocabulary 5	**The mind**	**195**
Vocabulary 6	**Technology**	**199**
Vocabulary 7	**Business and marketing**	**202**
Vocabulary 8	**Science and discoveries**	**206**
Vocabulary 9	**The arts**	**209**
Vocabulary 10	**Social issues and the media**	**212**
Vocabulary 11	**The body and health**	**215**
Vocabulary 12	**Attitude and opinion**	**219**
Vocabulary 13	**Academic encounters**	**223**
Vocabulary 14	**Graphs, charts, trends**	**226**
Vocabulary 15	**Synonyms for academic essays**	**230**
Vocabulary 16	**Linking words and phrases for academic essays**	**233**
Vocabulary 17	**The Academic Word List: sublists 1 and 2**	**237**
Vocabulary 18	**The Academic Word List: sublists 3 and 4**	**243**

Words and phrases

1	Family and relationships, ways of dealing with people; expressions with *come*, prefixes *anti-*, *post-*, *pre-*, *pro-*; expressions with *in*	**248**
2	City life; words meaning 'part'; suffixes *-ance*, *-ence*, *-ment*, *-ness*; expressions with *under*; expressions with *give*	**251**
3	Groups; expressions with *take*; time and duration; at work, prefixes *bi-*, *co-*, *mono-*, *semi-*; words with a similar meaning	**253**
4	Traditional events; expressions with *on*; groups; prefixes *cent-*, *pan-*, *multi-*, *tri-*; expressions with *put*	**256**
5	Character traits and emotion; student text types; prefix *in-*; expressions with *make*	**258**

6	Transport and transportation; priority and order; confusing words; prefix *un-*; expressions with *meet*; suffixes *-able*, *-ial*, *-ive*	**260**
7	Rubbish and waste; industry; suffixes *-ify*, *-ize*; expressions with *carry* or *hold*; word formation	**263**
8	Crime; confirming and denying; verbs and nouns with the same form; suffix *-en*; expressions with *life/living*; modifying	**265**
9	Language and communication; importance; relationships and connections; suffixes *-hood*, *-ship*	**268**
10	Forms of authority and government; processes; suffixes *-sion*, *-tion*, *-ity*; adverbs of degree	**270**
	Grammar answers	**272**
	Vocabulary answers	**288**
	Words and phrases answers	**294**

Introduction

This book is designed to revise and consolidate grammar points at the level of Cambridge ESOL IELTS.

Although there is no testing of grammar as such in IELTS, an accurate command of grammar is necessary in order to perform examination tasks successfully. It is assumed that users of this book will have reached a level of at least Council of Europe Common Framework level B2, and many will have reached C1 or C2. The grammar points selected here are those thought to be of most relevance to those planning to take the IELTS exam, and so most worth revising or using for further practice.

Points not included here may be found in the *Language Practice* series and in *Macmillan English Grammar in Context.*

Grammar is explained and practised within contexts and topic areas relevant to the exam and which include the use of information in graphs and tables. There are regular practice units which involve reading and interpreting graphs and tables. These range in difficulty material to reflect the different entry levels of students taking the IELTS exam.

The Vocabulary and Words and Phrases sections expose users to topic-based lexis they are likely to encounter in IELTS Reading and Listening tasks. The Vocabulary section also develops the ability to use language appropriate for Writing tasks 1 and 2, often within the context of various model essays. Language that candidates might use in their Speaking test is made apparent through examples of direct speech in exercises.

Units 17 and 18 of the Vocabulary section focus entirely on the first four sublists of The Academic Word List. The AWL was developed by Averil Coxhead at the School of Linguistics and Applied Language Studies at Victoria University of Wellington, New Zealand. The 570 words in the list are those most commonly used in a wide range of academic contexts. Therefore, they are words which are likely to appear in IELTS and during college and university programmes.

1

GRAMMAR

Present time

Present simple

- For personal routines and habits, often with a frequency adverb (*always, sometimes,* etc):
  I ***always get*** *to work by 9.00.*
  In winter we ***usually go*** *skiing most weekends.*

- For statements of fact, generalizations, or things that always happen:
  This train ***goes*** *to Milan.*
  All cars, except electric ones, ***cause*** *air pollution.*
  A wave ***transfers*** *energy from one place to another.*

- For technical or scientific facts and definitions:
  Inflation ***is*** *an economic process in which prices increase and money loses value.*

- To describe what something does, and how things happen:
  An espresso coffee maker ***forces*** *water through the coffee grounds using the pressure of heated water. When the water* ***boils****, it* ***rises*** *up a tube, through the coffee grounds, and into the container at the top.*

Present continuous

- For actions happening at the moment of speaking and unfinished:
  Jean ***is using*** *the computer at the moment.*

- For actions that continue for some time:
  *We****'re having*** *a lot of problems with the new equipment.*

- With some verbs, e.g. *read, write, work*, the action is generally ongoing, but not happening at the moment of speaking:
  I'm working *on a new project.*

- For changing states, especially with e.g. *increase, change, get* + adjective:
  Most scientists agree that the world ***is getting*** *hotter.*
  In some countries the birth rate ***is falling*** *year on year.*

Types of verb

Some verbs are more commonly found in the simple form. Use a dictionary to check use. Typical examples are:

- Feelings and emotions: *like/dislike, mean, value*

- Believing, thinking, knowing: *assume, believe, consider, estimate, expect, recognize, regard, suppose*

- Preferring: *prefer, want, wish*
- Sensing: *distinguish, observe*
- Being, having, seeming, owning: *appear to be, belong to, come from, comprise, consist of, contain, cost, equal, exist, include, involve doing, own, mean doing, possess, prove, represent, resemble, result from, sound, tend to, weigh*

Other verbs have different meanings in the simple and continuous forms:

- *What do you think?* = Tell me your opinion.
  What are you thinking? = Tell me your thoughts.
- *How much does this weigh?* = its weight.
  I'm weighing myself. = finding my weight.

Question and negative forms

- Questions may be formed using *do* + infinitive without *to* or *be* + present participle:
  ***Do** you **do skiing** most weekends?*
  ***Does** this train **go** to Milan?*
- Questions may also be formed by inverting the verb and subject/object:
  ***Is** Jean **using** the computer?*
  ***Are they** here yet?*
  ***What forces** the water through the coffee?* (subject)
  ***What does** the pressure **do**?* (object)
- Some verbs only refer to subjects:
  *What **happens/occurs**?*
- Negatives are formed by using *do* + *not* + infinitive without *to* or *be* + *not* + present participle:
  *I **don't** always **get** to work by 9.00.*
  *We **aren't having** problems with the new equipment.*

➔ **SEE ALSO**
Grammar 10: Direct and indirect questions

1 Find the best answer a–j for each question 1–10.

1 What do you want to study and why? ...d...
2 What do you spend more time doing – reading or watching TV? ....
3 What sort of music do you generally listen to? ....
4 What kind of transport do you usually use? ....
5 What part of your country do you live in? ....
6 What do most people do there? ....
7 What sort of sport do you like best? ....
8 How do you usually spend the summer? ....
9 What sort of things do you like to do at the weekend? ....
10 Do you rely a lot on your mobile phone? ....

a I sometimes ride my motorbike to college, but I also use public transport.
b I tend to watch TV when I'm tired, but I also like reading when I have the time.
c Quite a lot work in the tourist industry.
d I'm hoping to become an architect and join my father's business.
e I come from a small town by the sea in the north of the country.
f Yes I do, especially for keeping in touch with my friends.
g I generally try to relax and go out with my friends.
h I really love tennis, and play as much as I can.
i I usually take a holiday job and earn some money.
j I download a lot of jazz tracks from the internet.

2 Underline the most suitable verb form in each sentence.

A new approach to traffic control

As our city streets (1) *become/becoming* more congested with traffic, planners (2) *begin/are beginning* to wonder whether previous attempts to control this traffic through parking and stopping restrictions, traffic lights and so on are in fact part of the problem rather than part of the solution. Now as part of a European Union project, in some parts of Europe local authorities (3) *remove/are removing* all traffic signs in city centres. The planners behind this idea (4) *want/are wanting* drivers and pedestrians to cooperate, and they (5) *believe/are believing* that taking away all road signs, line markings and railings, etc generally (6) *encourages/is encouraging* road users to be more responsible towards each other. 'Nowadays people (7) *lose/are losing* the habit of being considerate to each other,' one traffic expert (8) *explains/is explaining*. 'Generally speaking, when there are so many signs telling everyone what to do, any sense of responsibility (9) *disappears/is disappearing*.' Recent research (10) *also shows/is also showing* that most drivers (11) *generally ignore/are generally ignoring* the majority of road signs in any case, so this new approach probably (12) *makes/is making* sense. Initially, seven cities and regions (13) *take part/are taking part* in the project. The centre of Makkinga in the Netherlands, for example, (14) *no longer contains/is no longer containing* any stop signs, direction signs, parking meters or stopping restrictions. And one interesting result so far is that the number of reported accidents (15) *goes down/is going down*.

3 Complete each sentence with the present simple or present continuous form of the verb in brackets.

1 Hello, (you/wait) are you waiting for me?
2 (the price of the room/include) .... breakfast?
3 The word *physics* (come) .... from the ancient Greek term for *nature*.
4 (this laptop/belong) .... to you?
5 It (get) .... cold. Shall I turn on the heating?
6 Look, a lot of people (get on) .... that bus. Is that one ours?
7 I (think) .... we'd better check the figures again.
8 I'm sorry it (take) .... so long, but I haven't had a reply from head office yet.
9 I'm not sure I want to go to university. I (have) .... second thoughts.
10 The word 'it' in line 12 (refer) .... to 'the decision.'

4 Complete each sentence with the present simple or present continuous form of the verbs in brackets.

Working from home

1 Nowadays more and more people (choose) ...are choosing... to work from home.
2 In some companies employees (have) .... the option of spending part of the week working out of the office.
3 But in a changing economy, the number of people who run their own businesses from home (increase) ....
4 Of course, homeworkers (depend) .... heavily on using the Internet and email.
5 According to Karen Holmes, a financial consultant, it (become) .... easier and easier to run your own business from home.
6 'Working at home obviously (save) .... a lot of time, and you can concentrate on what you (work) .... on when you really feel like it.'
7 'I (sometimes/find) .... myself popping out to the shops or doing housework, but on the whole I think it (suit) .... certain kinds of job.'
8 This sounds like a great idea but (it/have) .... any disadvantages?
9 'At the moment I (work) .... on a project with three other colleagues in different parts of the world.'
10 Emails are fine, but we also (feel) .... it's necessary to have video-conferences, just to know that we (all/head) .... in the right direction, and also to keep in touch on a personal level.'

5 Complete the second sentence so that it has a similar meaning to the first sentence, using the verb in bold. Do not change the words given.

1 What do you have to do in your job?
involve
What does your job involve .... ?

2 There are five parts to the examination.
consists of
The examination ....

3 This animal is not the same species as that animal.
belong to
These animals .... same species.

4 African elephants are generally taller than their Asian counterparts.
tend
African elephants ....

5 What is your approximate weight?
do
How much .... approximately?

6 The cost of the meal is part of the ticket price
includes
The ....

7 Professor Sanchez is Spanish.
comes
.... Spain.

8 What's the meaning of this word?
mean
What .... ?

9 I think these two samples are the same.
appear
These ....

10 A chemical reaction in a laboratory caused the fire.
resulted from
The fire ....

2

GRAMMAR

Past time

Past simple

- To describe finished events in the past with a definite time, or a past time context:
  *In 1684 Newton **published** his theory of gravity.*
  *During a storm, the bridge **collapsed**.*

- To describe past conditions, routines and habits:
  *Women and children **worked** in the mines hauling coal along narrow tunnels.*
  *My father **took** the 8.15 train every morning for thirty years.*
  *Whenever they **went** shopping together, they always **had** coffee at the same café.*

  Many common verbs have irregular past forms:
  *A hundred candidates **took** the test.*
  *What events **led** to the American Revolution?*

Past tense forms without past time meaning

- Past tense forms also appear in conditional sentences, but do not refer to past time:
  *If I **knew** the answer, I would tell you.*

Past continuous

- In a narrative context with events in past simple, past continuous describes continuing unfinished actions:
  *The ship **was sinking**, and there weren't enough lifeboats for all the passengers.*

- Continuing unfinished actions describe the background to a sudden event:
  *While they **were getting** into the lifeboats, the ship suddenly went down.*

- Past continuous verbs can describe a number of activities used as background:
  *We looked out across the sea. Passengers **were floating** in the water and sailors **were trying** to pull them into the lifeboats.*

- It is possible to describe two continuing events happening at the same time:
  *While the passengers **were beginning** to lose hope, rescue ships **were approaching**.*

- Describing a changing situation:
  *The weather **was getting** worse by the hour.*

Participle clauses

- Clauses with past continuous are often made into participle time clauses:
  ***While (they were) waiting**, the passengers filled in the forms.*

→ SEE ALSO
Grammar 29: Participle clauses
Grammar 10: Subject and object questions

1 Underline the most suitable verb form in each sentence.

The 'Miracle on the Hudson'

1 First Officer Jeffery Skiles *piloted*/*was piloting* the Airbus A320 when it *took off*/*was taking off* from La Guardia airport at 3.25 pm on Jan 15th 2009.
2 While it *still climbed*/*was still climbing*, and below 1,000 metres, he *noticed*/*was noticing* a flock of birds which *came*/*was coming* towards the aircraft.
3 A few minutes later the plane *collided*/*was colliding* with the birds and the engines *lost*/*were losing* power.
4 The Captain, Chesley Sullenberger, *took over*/*was taking over* the controls at this point, and Skiles *tried*/*was trying* to restart the engines.
5 Sullenberger *got*/*was getting* permission from La Guardia control tower to land back at the airport, but since the plane *rapidly lost*/*was rapidly losing* height, it soon *became*/*was becoming* clear that this would not be possible.
6 With no power in the engines, Sullenberger *made*/*was making* an instant decision, and *decided*/*was deciding* to land the plane on the Hudson River, the only free space available.
7 As office workers *watched*/*were watching* in amazement, he *managed*/*was managing* to make a perfect landing on the water close to Manhattan just six minutes after take-off.
8 The passengers *followed*/*were following* the safety instructions given by the crew, and with their assistance all *left*/*were leaving* the aircraft, including one passenger who *travelled*/*was travelling* in a wheelchair.
9 Nearby boats *quickly rescued*/*were quickly rescuing* the passengers from the freezing water and from the wings of the plane, which *slowly filled*/*was slowly filling* with water.
10 All the passengers and crew *survived*/*were surviving* without serious injury, and the crew later *received*/*were receiving* awards for their conduct.

2 Complete the second sentence so that it has a similar meaning to the first sentence.

1 What were you in my room for?
What were you doing.......................... in my room?
2 The start of the match was at 3.00.
The match .... at 3.00.
3 The temperature was rising.
It .... hotter.
4 After the explosion, what was your next action?
What .... the explosion?
5 We had lunch during our wait.
While .... lunch.
6 On her death, the newspapers described her as the country's greatest writer.
When .... the country's greatest writer.
7 The police do not know the exact cause of the crash.
The police do not know what exactly ....
8 What was your address at the time of the robbery?
Where .... at the time of the robbery?

3 Complete each sentence by writing the past simple or past continuous form of the verb in brackets in each space.

1 When I (hear) ....heard................ the noise I (look) .... out of the window, but I couldn't see what (happen) ....

2 We (wait) .... in a queue for nearly an hour, but after that we (decide) .... to complain because it (take) .... so long to get the tickets.

3 The accused (drive) .... home after a party when he (lose) .... control of his car on a roundabout and (collide) .... with another vehicle.

4 The injured man (not carry) .... any form of identification, and nobody could understand exactly what he (say) ....

5 I (find) .... myself in a rather difficult situation. It (start)............. to rain, and the temperature (fall) .... rapidly, I (wear) .... only light summer clothes and it was a long way back to the road.

6 An archaeological rescue dig (cause) .... further delays to the projects, as engineers (come) .... unexpectedly upon the remains of a 3rd century palace while work on the site (get) .... under way.

4 Complete the text by writing the past simple or past continuous form of the verbs in brackets in each space.

Cholera epidemics in 19th century London

People in London in the mid-nineteenth century greatly (1) ...feared....... (fear) cholera. At this time doctors (2) .... (believe) that cholera (3) .... (circulate) through the air, and (4) .... (not realize) that all the time raw sewage (5) .... (enter) the water supply, and that the disease (6) .... (spread) through the domestic water system. Although in the 17th and 18th centuries London (7) .... (possess) a water supply system and a sewage system which were adequate for a small city, the population (8) .... (now rise) year by year and the authorities (9) .... (do) little to keep pace with the changing situation. Broken water pipes and sewage pipes often (10) .... (flow) into one another, and most sewage (11) .... (end up) in the River Thames, which was the main source of drinking water for thousands. Between 1831 and 1867 a series of severe outbreaks (12) .... (occur). In the outbreak of 1848–49, there were over 30,000 cases of the disease in London, and 15,000 people (13) .... (die). By the mid 1860s the situation (14) .... (improve) mainly because by then engineers (15) .... (work on) the construction of a completely new sewage system, which they (16) .... (complete) in 1875, and which is still in use today.

5 Complete the text by writing a verb from the box in each space.

~~opened~~	died	came	occurred	was getting down	intended
was holding	included	carried	was walking	stopped	
knocked	was attending	decided	entered	was travelling	

The death of William Huskisson

When the Liverpool to Manchester Railway (1) ....opened.... in 1830 the history of transport (2) .... a new phase. As if to underline this fact, the opening ceremony (3) .... what we would now call a celebrity railway accident. While he (4) .... the opening celebrations, William Huskisson, an MP and former member of the government, (5) .... along the line on the same train as the Prime Minister, the Duke of Wellington. At one point the train (6) .... and the distinguished passengers (7) .... to get off and watch a procession of local people. Apparently Huskisson (8) .... to cross the track so as to shake hands with the Duke, but as he (9) .... from the train, a steam engine (10) .... down the other line next to the train. It hit the door that Huskisson (11) .... and (12) .... him under the wheels. Workmen (13) .... him to a nearby house, but he (14) .... a few hours later. Huskisson was not the first casualty of the railway age. This probably (15) .... in 1821 when a train hit a man who (16) .... home along the Middleton Railway in a storm. However the dawn of the Age of Railway Accidents will always be associated with the unfortunate Huskisson.

6 Complete the second sentence so that it has a similar meaning to the first sentence, using a noun formed from the verb underlined.

1 After the Prime Minister <u>arrived</u>, the conference began.
After the arrival of the Prime Minister..., the conference began .

2 After she <u>decided</u> to become a pilot, Amelia took flying lessons.
After her .... , Amelia took flying lessons.

3 After he <u>invented</u> the gramophone, Edison became famous.
After his .... , Edison became famous.

4 Before they <u>discovered</u> America, explorers believed Asia was on the other side of the Atlantic.
Before their .... , explorers believed Asia was on the other side of the Atlantic.

5 While they were <u>flying</u>, the pilot realized something was wrong.
During the .... , the pilot realized something was wrong.

6 After he <u>died</u>, Van Gogh was recognized as a great artist.
After his .... , Van Gogh was recognized as a great artist.

7 While they were <u>constructing</u> the dam, there were several accidents.
During the .... , there were several accidents.

8 While they were <u>investigating</u> the robbery, the police interviewed two men.
During the .... , the police interviewed two men.

3

GRAMMAR

Practice 1

1 Complete the text by writing the correct form of a verb from the box in each space. Sometimes a negative form may be needed.

do	go out	keep	purchase	require
end up	hold back	~~make~~	receive	set

How do banks help the economy?

The banking system (1) ......makes...... money available to fuel the economy. It (2) .... this by lending money to customers. However, banks always (3) .... a certain amount of money in reserve. In some countries a central government authority, such as the Federal Reserve in the USA, (4) .... this reserve figure. The example below shows a 10% reserve figure, although many banking systems (5) .... the banks to keep to a precise figure. The bank either (6) .... this reserve amount in cash, or has credit for this amount at the central bank. When a bank (7) .... a deposit ($100) it can lend 90% of this sum ($90). This sum then (8) .... into the economy, where it (9) .... goods or services, and usually (10) .... in another bank. This second bank can then lend 90% of this deposit, and so on. In this way money circulates through the economy.

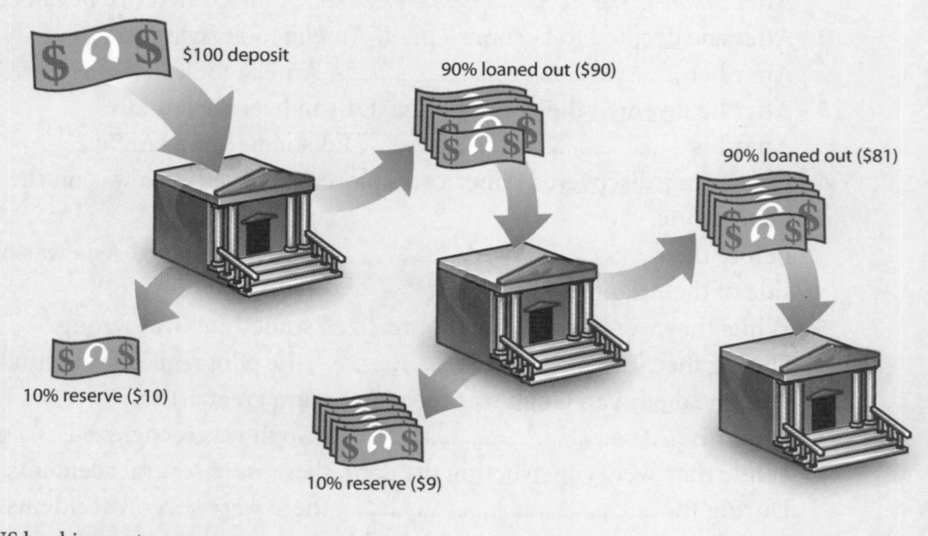

US banking system

2 The graph gives information about UK population figures from 1998–2007. Read the text and complete the questions that follow, using the information in brackets. Make any necessary changes.

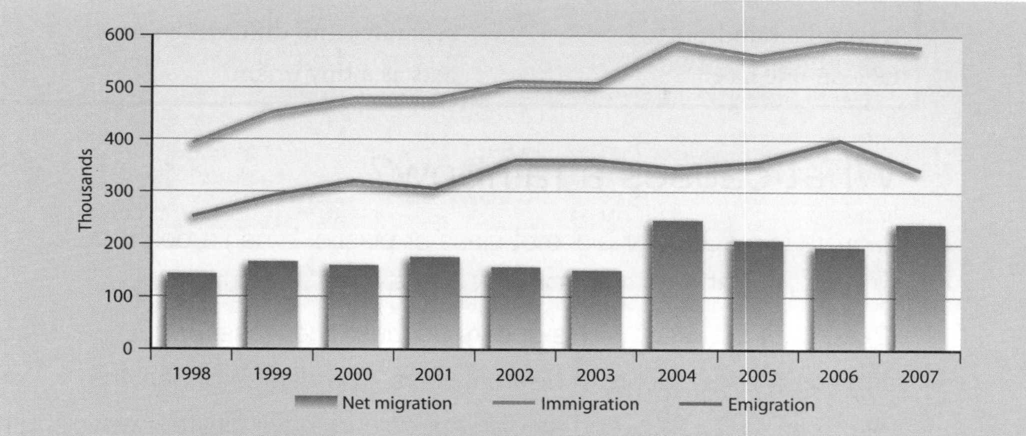

Total International Migration to and from the UK 1998–2007

Every year quite large numbers of people move from their own countries to live in the UK. This table shows the figures for International Migrants, defined as 'someone who changes their country of usual residence for at least a year'. Between 1998 and 2002 there was a steady rise in immigration, from just under 400,000 to over 500,000 per year. Although this figure remained more or less constant for the following year, a steep rise occurred between 2003 and 2004. This trend fell slightly in 2005, returned to 2004 levels in 2006, and now shows a slight downward trend. Of arrivals in 2007, 87% were non-British. They included 96,000 Polish citizens.

At the same time, large numbers of people leave the UK every year, either to return home, or to start a new life elsewhere. This trend peaked in 2006, when around 400,000 people left, but declined steeply in 2007. A fall in British citizens emigrating to Spain and France largely caused this drop in the numbers.

1 What information (the text and table/present) do the text and table present ?
2 How (the text/define) .... an International Migrant?
3 In the immigration figures, what (happen) .... between 1998 and 2002?
4 (this figure/rise or fall) .... over the following year?
5 What (occur) .... between 2003 and 2004?
6 (this trend/continue) .... over the following three years or not?
7 How many Polish citizens (the 2007 arrivals figures/include) .... ?
8 When (the emigration figures/peak) .... ?
9 (this figure/remain) .... the same in the following year?
10 What (cause) .... this change?

3 Now write the answers to the questions.

1 ....
2 ....
3 ....
4 ....
5 ....
6 ....
7 ....
8 ....
9 ....
10 ....

4 Complete the text by writing a phrase from the box in each space.

become visible	depends on the wavelength of the beam
causes the light to bend	sees the range of colours
leaves the raindrop	separates into different colours
~~falls on one face~~	acts as a tiny prism

What causes a rainbow?

A prism is a triangular piece of glass or plastic. When a beam of light (A) (1) ..falls on one face.. of the prism (B), the white light (2) .... This occurs because the glass (3) .... and this affects colours in different ways. The degree of bending (4) .... and as different colours have different wavelengths, the colours spread out and (5) .... We call these separated colours a 'spectrum'.

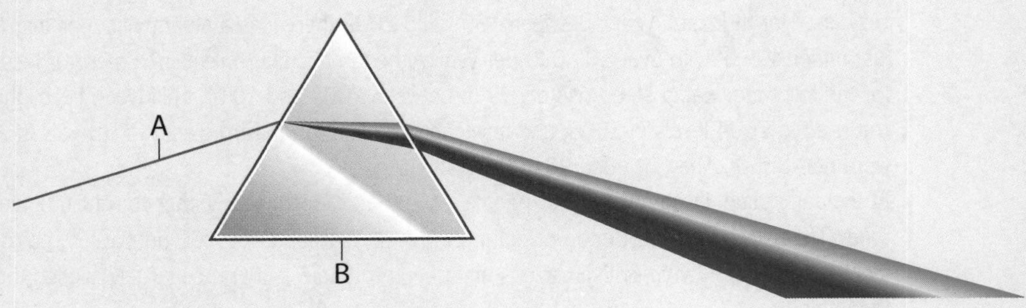

When it rains, each raindrop (6) .... and as light enters and leaves the raindrop, it breaks up into a spectrum. As each colour (7) .... at a slightly different angle, the eye (8) .... as a rainbow in the sky.

4

GRAMMAR

Present perfect

Present perfect simple

- For everyday events connected to the present, without a definite past time. Events may be recent, or part of the current situation:

    What ***has happened?***
    The lights ***have failed!***
    Astronomers ***have discovered*** *three more moons orbiting the planet.*

  The time can be all time up to the present and need not have a time reference:

    No one ***has proved*** *that intelligent life exists on other planets.*

- Time references

  The use of some time expressions is linked with the present perfect simple:

    Recently *the number of car owners has risen dramatically.*
    The situation has worsened ***since the end of 2001.***
    This is the first time *researchers have found this insect in the Antarctic.*
    The authorities have ***already*** *taken measures to deal with the problem.*

Present perfect simple or past simple?

- Indefinite and definite time

  In this sentence the action has happened in a period up to the present, and may well continue:

    This company ***has produced*** *some excellent products.* (present perfect simple)

  In this sentence the action is finished. The company may no longer exist. The events are in a period of time not connected to the present:

    The ABC company ***produced*** *some very successful products.* (past simple)

  Compare these time references:

    So far/Up until now *the ABC company has produced ...* (present perfect simple)
    At that time/Once/In the past *the ABC company produced ...* (past simple)

Present perfect continuous

- For recent continuing activities, emphasizing the length of the activities, and suggesting that the activity will continue.

    They ***have been investigating*** *the same problem for many years.*

Present perfect continuous or present perfect simple?

- With verbs which describe a continuing state, e.g. *live*, *work*, there is little contrast:

    How long has Tom ***worked*** *here?* *How long has Tom* ***been working*** *here?*
    The team ***has been working*** *on this project for the past six months.*

- With verbs which describe events, present perfect simple emphasizes completion:
  *They've **found** some interesting results.* (completed)
  *They've **been finding** some interesting results.* (during a recent period – not completed)

  Use depends on context, and on the choice of the user.

Present perfect simple and continuous uses

- To describe recent trends and developments:
  *The political situation **has now improved**.*
  *A series of poor harvests **has led** to a rise in migration away from the countryside.*
  *Over the past decade, the amount of water consumed **has increased** twofold.*
  *In recent years, the area **has been experiencing** something of a renaissance.*

Present continuous or present perfect continuous?

- In many cases, when we describe uncompleted actions, we can use either present continuous, to show what is happening now; or present perfect continuous, to show that is has been happening for a period of time up to now.

  In these examples, each tense describes the actions of the scientists, but with a different emphasis.

  Using present continuous emphasizes that they are currently studying the data:
  *Scientists **are studying** the data, and hope to publish their results soon.*

  Using present perfect continuous emphasizes the period of time during which they have been studying the data:
  *Scientists **have been studying** the data, and hope to publish their results soon.*

➔ SEE ALSO
Grammar 8: Time words
Grammar 10: Direct and indirect questions

1 Underline the most suitable verb form in each sentence.

Water on Mars

1 Scientists *have recently discovered/recently discovered* that there are traces of water beneath the surface of Mars.
2 Instruments carried by the Mars Reconnaissance Orbiter (MRO) which *has been circling/was circling* the planet since 2006, *have detected/detected* large quantities of ice beneath the surface at the bottom of meteorite craters.
3 The MRO *has found/found* the new craters in August last year.
4 As the ice *has quickly melted/quickly melted* on the planet's surface, the discovery *has been/was* fortunate.
5 Although the research programme *has found/found* traces of water at the poles during its early stages, this is the first time *it has detected/it detected* ice half way between the planet's north pole and its equator.
6 This suggested that there *has been/was* a lot more water below the surface than previously supposed.
7 Scientists *have also believed/also believed* they understood the origins of this ice.
8 Their theory *has been/was* that the climate of Mars was more humid up until a few thousand years ago, and that the water in this ice *has come from/is coming from* this earlier period.
9 Since its arrival in Mars orbit, the MRO *has been monitoring/was monitoring* surface and weather conditions. *It has also studied/It has also been studying* potential landing sites for future Mars programmes.
10 According to experts, this latest discovery *has shown/has been showing* that the MRO is well worth the $720million it *has cost/cost* to build.

2 Complete each short text with the present simple or continuous, present perfect simple or continuous, or past simple or continuous form of the verbs in brackets. Sometimes more than one answer is possible.

Text 1

In a surprise announcement, the Governor of the Central Bank (1) has announced (announce) his resignation. 'I (2) .... (spend) eight years in this post,' he (3) .... (tell) reporters, 'and I (4) .... (feel) that this is the time to move on.' The Governor, who previously (5) .... (hold) the post of Professor of Economics at Cambridge University, (6) .... (now consider) a return to academic life.

Text 2

Since the new flu virus (7) .... (make) its appearance last year, the Health Authority (8) .... (prepare) to respond to a pandemic, and local hospitals (9) .... (already draw up) detailed plans. In March the Authority (10) .... (start) to stockpile essential supplies, and more recently (11) .... (also begin) the process of creating a pool of extra staff from people who (12) .... (already work) for the organization, in order to deal with any possible staff shortages.

3 Complete the second sentence so that it has a similar meaning to the first sentence, using present perfect simple or continuous and a form of the word underlined.

1 The company provides financial services, and was established 14 years ago.
The company ..has provided/has been providing.................. for the past 14 years.

2 Fiona Allan writes the 'Science Impact' books, and there are five so far in the series.
.... of the 'Science Impact' series so far.

3 If there is life on other planets, it is so far undiscovered.
Scientists .... so far.

4 The construction of the Olympic Stadium is now complete.
The construction team ....

5 The company started green vehicle production two years ago.
.... for the past two years.

6 Professor Thompson now lives in Vancouver, where she arrived four years ago.
.... for four years.

7 Ann Smith became chief executive five years ago, and still holds this post.
.... for the past five years.

8 Recent statistics show a rise in the number of young people entering higher education.
The number .... recently.

9 The satellite started circling the Moon two years ago.
.... for two years.

10 The research team's conclusion is that the new vaccine is not effective.
.... the new vaccine is not effective.

4 Complete the text by writing a suitable form of the verb in brackets in each space.

Is a best friend good for your health?

When we (1) ..consider.. (consider) how many thousands of years humans (2) .... (live) with dogs, it is surprising that the serious scientific study of the interaction between animals and humans (3) .... (only recently begin). There (4) .... (always be) plenty of anecdotal evidence, but serious research into this relationship is relatively recent. The question is whether (5) .... (there be) any real health benefits in owning a dog. Recently researchers (6) .... (look) at this in more detail, and results (7) .... (seem) to suggest that dogs can indeed help to improve our health. Dog-owners (8) .... (recover) more rapidly from stress and have lower heart rates and blood pressure. Taking the dog for a walk is good exercise, as you will know if you (9) .... (ever own) a dog, and the social connections made through having a dog are beneficial to older people. As one subject comments in the report, 'Since I got my dog, my life has (10) .... (change) out of all recognition. I (11) .... (meet) new people, and as far as my health is concerned, I (12) .... (never feel) fitter. I (13) .... (never think) a dog could make so much difference!' Some researchers (14) .... (also investigate) links between health and other types of pet, and some (15) .... (believe) their results prove that even a pet snake or rat is good for the health.

5 Write a new sentence with a similar meaning to the first sentence, using the word in bold. Do not change the word given.

1 The project is still continuing.
yet
......The project hasn't finished yet.......

2 There has never been such a serious financial crisis before.
first
....

3 There is no proof that the dinosaurs died in this way.
proved
....

4 The situation is not the same as it was in 2008.
since
....

5 It hasn't stopped raining yet.
still
....

6 This is my first visit to Bulgaria.
been
....

7 Do you know Professor Johnson?
before
....

6 Complete the text by writing the suitable form of the verb in brackets in each space.

It is not generally known that Rudolf Diesel originally (1) ...designed... (design) the engine that (2) .... (bear) his name to use vegetable oil. Now, with increasing oil prices, interest in producing such bio-fuels (3) .... (rise). In recent years, companies in some Pacific nations, where coconut trees are common, (4) .... (experiment) with coconut oil as a fuel. The price of coconut oil (5) .... (soar) lately, so the idea is to export coconut fuel oil to the US and Europe, rather than use it at home. However, use of coconut fuel oil (6) .... (be) common in the past on Pacific islands, especially during World War Two when the islands (7) .... (suffer) fuel shortages, and in recent years there (8) .... (be) more interest in using coconut oil fuel for local consumption. The oil has disadvantages, however, as it (9) .... (begin) to solidify below 25°c and (10) .... (contain) many impurities which can damage diesel engines. However, a company in the Marshall Islands (11) .... (use) the oil in diesel trucks for some years without too many problems. After some earlier experiments, they (12) .... (find) that a blend of coconut oil with diesel (13) .... (work) best, and recently (14) .... (also combine) coconut oil with other fuels, such as kerosene. In Samoa, the electricity company (15) .... (use) a coconut oil blend successfully for some years in its generators. So in the future, coconut oil (16) .... (seem) likely to become an important economic factor in the fuel industry in this region.

5

GRAMMAR

Past perfect, *used to*

Past perfect simple and continuous

- For events in the past which happen before other events in the past:

  *Once **she had decided** to become a pilot, Amelia took flying lessons in California.*
  *She **had been considering** a career in nursing, but now knew what she wanted to do.*

- To make the order of events clear when there is no time expression:

  *She **had thought** a lot about her career and knew she wanted to be a pilot.*

  It may be clearer in a narrative of past events to use a participle clause instead of the past perfect. See Grammar 29.

  ***After deciding to become a pilot**, Amelia took flying lessons in California.*

  Using a past time reference word also makes the narrative clearer and in this case it is not necessary to use the past perfect to show which event came first:

  *Amelia decided to become a pilot, and **then** took flying lessons.*

Reports and report verbs

- Past perfect tenses are common in report structures:

  *She informed the board that **she had already accepted** the other position.*

  Her actual words were:

  'I have already accepted the other position.'

- Past perfect tenses also report past simple statements:

  *He told the police that **he hadn't seen** the other car.*

  His actual words were:

  'I did not see the other car.'

- Past perfect tenses are common with verbs such as *realize, remember, know, understand*:

  *When he looked again, he realized that something unusual **had happened**.*
  *I didn't know **you'd taken** the keys.*
  *At the time we did not fully understand what **had happened**.*

Past perfect uses

- Only use past perfect tenses when necessary, to show that one event in the past happened before another event in the past.

- The past perfect is not used to emphasize that an event happened a long time ago. For this we would use a time expression:

  *His great-grandfather **was** on the Titanic when it **went** down in 1912.*

- In past narrative, what would be present prefect tenses in a present time context become past perfect tenses:

  *Finally they could see the train in the distance. It **had** finally **arrived**!*

Used to

- For habits and states in the past, especially when we make contrasts with the present. Any time reference tends to be general. The pronunciation is /ju:st tə/:
  *Scientists **used to think** that the Galapagos islands were once connected to the mainland, but they now believe that this is not the case.*

- Form questions and negatives using the auxiliary *did*:
  ***Didn't** you **use to live** in London?*
  *I **didn't use to like** him, but we've been married for five years!*

- *Used to* refers only to the past. The construction *be used to (doing) something* has no connection with *used to* and means 'be accustomed to something':
  *Jones **was not used to** running so much, and soon became tired.*

➜ **SEE ALSO**
Grammar 10: Direct and indirect questions

This unit includes tense contrasts with past simple and past continuous (see Grammar 2).

1 Underline the most suitable verb form in each sentence.

The Great Toronto Fire

1 The Great Toronto Fire of 1904 *destroyed/had destroyed* a large part of central Toronto, Canada.
2 A policeman on patrol *first noticed/was first noticing* the fire at around 8.00 in the evening.
3 The flames *had risen/were rising* from the roof of a clothing factory.
4 The local fire brigade did its best, but *was never expecting/had never expected* to have to deal with such a large fire.
5 By the time the fire was under control, *it burned/it had been burning* for nine hours.
6 The situation was made worse by the strong winds which *had blown/were blowing* that night.
7 By the time the fire was put out, it *destroyed/had destroyed* more than a hundred buildings.
8 Fortunately it *had not killed/was not killing* anyone.
9 Later investigations *never established/had never established* the exact cause of the fire.
10 It caused over $10 million of damage, and *put/had put* five thousand people out of work.

2 Complete each sentence by writing the past simple, past continuous or past perfect simple form of the verbs in brackets in each space.

1 While they (examine) were examining.... the results for the second time, the scientists (notice) .... a pattern which they (previously overlook) ....
2 I (stare) .... out of the tent at the worsening weather. The rain (still fall) .... and it (grow) .... colder. Luckily I (pack) ....warm clothes so I (not think) .... that I was in any danger.
3 When I (return) .... to the hospital for a check-up, the doctor who (see) .... me could hardly believe how much I (progress) .... , since he (not expect) .... my condition to improve.
4 Although medieval alchemists were not chemists in the modern sense, they (develop) .... some important chemical skills while they (search) .... for the secret of turning metals into gold.
5 A man (drown) .... while he (try) .... to save a small girl who (fall) .... into a fast-flowing river. He could not be rescued by onlookers because the local council (remove) .... safety equipment, because vandals (repeatedly steal) .... them.

3 Complete each short text with the past simple or past perfect form of the verbs in brackets. In some cases, both tenses are acceptable.

Scientific pioneers

1 Isaac Newton was born in 1643 in a small village in Lincolnshire in England. His father (1) ..had died.... (die) some three months before his birth, and his mother (2) .... (remarry) in 1646. At the age of 18 he (3) .... (enter) Trinity College, Cambridge, even though some years earlier his mother (4) .... (take) him out of school to work on the farm. She (5) .... (became) a widow for the second time by then, but (6) .... (listen) to Newton's schoolmaster, and (7) .... (send) him back to school.

2 On January 7th 1610, Galileo (8) .... (observe) the movements of what he thought were three small stars close to the planet Jupiter. He was using a simple telescope, of a type which he (9) .... (make) for the past two years. When he (10) .... (look) at the three 'stars' on the following nights, he (11) .... (see) that their positions (12) .... (change) and one of them (13) .... (disappear). He then (14) .... (come) to the conclusion that they were orbiting Jupiter. In fact, he (15) .... (discover) three of Jupiter's largest moons, and he (16) .... (find) a fourth on 13th January. His observations would have far-reaching consequences.

4 Complete each sentence using the verbs in brackets. Use a form of *used to* for one verb and *now* + present simple or continuous for the other.

1 Scientists ..used to believe.. that the ancestors of whales were extinct carnivores called mesonychids. However, they ..now think.. that whales are related to mammals such as hippos, cows and giraffes. (believe, think)
2 Some astronomers .... that there were canals on Mars, but they .... that this is not the case. (know, think)
3 Cigarette manufacturers actually .... that smoking cigarettes was actually good for your health, but they .... print health warnings on cigarette packets. (claim, have to)
4 Most Chinese workers .... bicycles to work, but more and more .... cars. (drive, ride)
5 The island of Britain .... part of the mainland of Europe, but the Channel .... it from France.(be, divide)
6 Most people .... letters to friends and family, but more and more people .... e-mail. (write, use)
7 Most families .... at the table and eat meals together, but nowadays family members generally .... in front of the television. (eat, sit)
8 British students .... grants from their local education authority which paid for their university courses, but that system no longer operates, and students .... low-interest loans, and work-part time to finance their studies. (take out, receive)

5 Complete the second sentence so that it has the same meaning as the first sentence, using the word in bold. Do not change the word given.

1 The match started before we got into the ground.
by
The match ...had started by the time we got into the ground... .

2 By then the soldiers knew that the battle was lost.
they
By then the soldiers ....

3 I arrived at the office and realized my keys were at home.
left
When I ....

4 This wasn't my first Japanese meal, so I knew what to expect.
before
I ....

5 Jane left before I phoned her office.
already
When ....

6 It was my first trip to Romania
before
I ....

7 She couldn't understand the meaning of his letter.
what
She ....

8 Having eaten all their of food, they were forced to eat their pack animals.
since
They were ....

9 The injured man seemed to have fallen from the window.
had
It seemed that ....

10 They decided to give him the job before the interview was over.
already
Before ....

6

GRAMMAR

Practice 2

1 Complete the text by writing the present perfect simple, past simple or past perfect form of the verbs in brackets in each space.

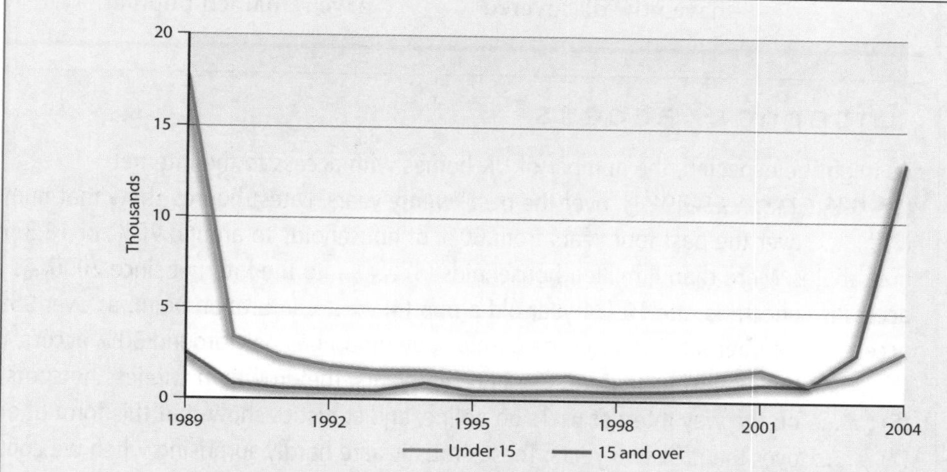

Mumps notifications: by age, England & Wales (ONS)

Mumps in the early 21st century

In recent years in the UK the number of cases of the viral disease mumps (1) ...has risen... (rise) dramatically. In 1988, with the introduction of a new vaccine, the number of infections (2) .... (fall) dramatically, and rates (3) .... (stay) low until 2003. Since that time, there (4) .... (be) a rapid increase followed by another slow fall in the number of cases. Since the publication of the above figures, the rate (5) .... (fall) back again to round about 7,000 cases per year. What exactly (6) .... (cause) the rise in the first place? Although older adults (7) .... (not receive) the new MMR vaccination, they (8) .... (probably have) the disease in childhood, and so (9) .... (already build up) some immunity. On the other hand, those born between 1983 and 1986, before the new MMR vaccine (10) .... (start) to take effect, (11) .... (receive) no exposure to the disease in the community because the vaccine (12) .... (largely eliminate) it from the vaccinated age group, and so this group of young adults, now in their early 20s, (13) .... (not acquire) any immunity. To make matters worse, by the end of the century uptake of the MMR vaccine (14) .... (also begin) to fall, mainly as a result of controversy over its safety. In the 2009 figures it (15) .... (stand) at around 80%, well below the immunity level of 95% recommended by the World Health Organization.

2 Complete the text by writing a phrase from the box in each space.

~~has grown steadily~~	had never been online	has almost reached
has also had an effect	has completely changed	has expanded fourfold
has indicated	has shown	have been complaining
have connected	have continued	have increased
have limited	have now discovered	have remained popular

Internet access

As might be expected, the number of UK homes with access to the Internet (1) ..has grown steadily.. over the past twenty years. Latest figures show that numbers (2) .... over the past four years from 60% of households to around 70%, or 18.3 million households. More than 4 million households (3) .... to the Internet since 2006. As far as access is concerned, the 16–24-year-old group (4) .... saturation point, as over 95% have access to the Internet. Although the 65-plus age group has only around 30% access, it (5) .... the highest increase in use in recent years. The growth in wireless hotspots (6) .... on the way Internet users go online, and statistics show that this form of access (7) .... over the past two years. These statistics are hardly surprising when we consider how the Internet (8) .... the way people work, play and access information. Recently people (9) .... that they cannot easily buy cheap rail tickets, book air fares or find cheaper car insurance without using the Internet. In a 2008 survey, 70% of the 65-plus age group and around 30% of 55–64-year-olds (10) .... and further research (11) .... that those with lower educational qualifications are less likely to own a computer or use the Internet. Interestingly, during the same period despite increased home access to the net, Internet cafés (12) .... Some older people (13) .... that the cafés offer a cheaper alternative to net access from home, and many computer users (14) .... to go there, even though they have home access, because they enjoy the company, or because their employers (15) .... their net use at work.

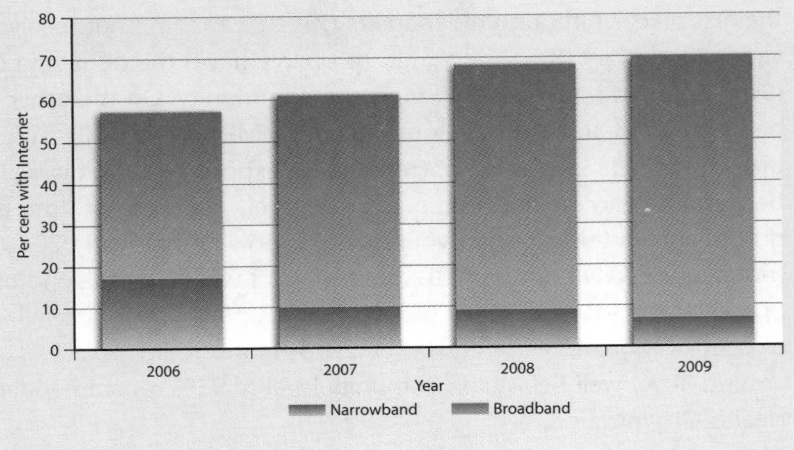

7

GRAMMAR

Future time

Will and *will not*

- For factual predictions, often with a qualifying adverbial:
  *Prices **will increase** by 10% over the next year.*
  *Prices **will almost certainly increase** by 10% over the next year.*
  Other qualifying adverbials: *definitely, probably, no doubt.*

Be going to

- Generally for personal plans and intentions, or when we can see what is going to happen:
  ***I'm going to take** this work home with me.*
  *Look at that egg! It**'s going to hatch**.*

- For decisions about the future:
  *I've decided about next year. **I'm going to apply** to Imperial College.*

- Qualifying adverbials are also common:
  *There **is probably going to be** a revolution in this field within ten years.*

Will or *going to?*

- In formal speech and writing *will* for prediction is more common, but *going to* is common in journalistic writing. It can be replaced by *going to* in everyday speech. This is not true for other meanings of *will*:
  *Prices **will rise** by up to 5% over the next six months.*
  *As I see it, prices **are going to rise** by up to 5% over the next six months.*

Present simple and continuous

- Use present simple for a fixed event, with no personal choice, and the event seen as a fact:
  *The next meeting **is** on March 3rd.*

- Use present continuous for a fixed arrangement, one already definitely made:
  *We**'re leaving** on Saturday. Are you coming with us?*
  Going to in this example gives the same information:
  *Are you **going to come** with us?*

Future time clauses

- Use present simple after *as soon as, after, before, by the time, immediately, the moment, until, when*, etc even though there is a future reference:
  ***As soon as we know** the results, we'll let you know.*

- Use present perfect simple instead of present simple to emphasize completion:
  *When **we've completed** the experiment, we'll have a break.*

Future continuous

- To describe an event or state at a future point:
  *Within a few years, most countries **will be facing** the same problems.*

Future perfect simple

- To describe what we can say when we look back from a future point:
  *By the end of the 21st century, temperatures **will have reached** a dangerous level.*

Formal instructions

- Forms of *will* are all used formally to state what must happen, or must be the case:
  *Students **will leave** all bags, books, documents, etc outside the examination room.*
  *Staff in this category **will have completed** safety training.*

➜ SEE ALSO
Grammar 10: Direct and indirect questions

1 Underline the most suitable verb form in each sentence. Sometimes more than one form is possible.

1 Thanks very much for your help. *I'll let you know/I'm going to let you know/I'm letting you know* how the interview goes.

2 This time next week while we are all hard at work Helen *will lie/will be lying/is lying* in the sun on a beach somewhere!

3 Despite these promising sales results, we expect that profits *will fall/are going to fall/are falling* in the long term.

4 There *will be/is going to be/will have been* another meeting next Friday morning. Do you think you'll be able to come?

5 I don't think that this problem will simply go away. What *are we going to do/will we do/will we be doing* about it?

6 Something's come up, so we *won't be leaving/aren't leaving/won't leave* on Saturday after all.

7 It won't be easy, but I think *we'll finish/we'll be finishing/we're going to finish* the project on time.

8 I'm sorry you're leaving. *We're all going to miss/We'll all miss/We are all missing* you.

9 By the end of the year, interest rates *will probably have risen/are probably rising/will probably rise* sharply.

10 *I'm going to work/I'll be working/I'll work* this weekend, so it's not worth arranging anything.

2 Complete each sentence with the future continuous or future perfect form of the verbs in brackets.

1 Please remember that we (work) will be working in the lab on Tuesday morning. You won't need your laptops as we (put) .... all the data online. Don't forget that we'll be in the Memorial Building, not in the New Block.

2 With the government's plans to be announced next week, the financial sector (soon enter) .... a new era. On Wednesday the speculation will be over, and the finance minister (make) .... further changes to the tax system which he hopes will provide shelter from the financial storm. But with the ferocity of the global crisis, and the massive public deficit, it remains to be seen whether these measures will succeed.

3 We would like to inform customers that engineers (replace) .... the damaged section of pipeline, starting at 7.00am on Monday 21st March. This work should be complete by 8.00pm Monday 21st March, and we hope that water supplies (return) .... by 10.00pm the same evening. During the day we (supply) .... households with bottled drinking water.

4 During the spring the union intends to ask their members to support strike action, though they say they (also talk) .... to management. A spokesman commented, 'Over the next few weeks, we (visit) .... our members to explain our position, and by the end of April either we (come) .... to some agreement with management, or we (start) .... moving more definitely towards strike action.'

3 Complete each sentence with the *will*, present simple or present perfect form of the verbs in brackets.

1 When we (process) process/have processed your application form, we (let) .... you know about the date of your interview.
2 Before you (leave) .... , I (give) .... you the address of that hotel I mentioned.
3 We (begin) .... to market this new product only after we (test) .... it thoroughly in real-life conditions.
4 When the plane (take off) .... and the captain (switch off) .... the seat belt sign, you can use your laptop.
5 As soon as there (be) .... any news, one of our representatives (contact) .... you.
6 The moment I (have) .... the chance I (send) .... you the data you have requested.
7 I (meet) .... you in the cafeteria when the next lecture (finish) ....
8 By the time governments all over the world (come) .... to an agreement on how to deal with global warming, it (be) .... too late.
9 There (be) .... a short meeting in Room 33 for all speakers before the afternoon session (begin) ....
10 Don't worry, I (send) .... you a text message as soon as I (arrive) ....

4 Complete the second sentence so that it has the same meaning as the first sentence, using the the word in bold. Do not change the word given.

1 Doctors expect artificial organs to be commonplace by the end of the century.
will
Doctors expect that artificial organs will be commonplace by the end of the century .
2 Some experts predict a doubling of car use within twenty years.
have
Some experts predict that ....
3 Experts expect most people to be home workers in twenty years' time.
be
Experts expect that ....
4 The future is unknown.
happen
Nobody knows ....
5 Some people expect future technology to be much cheaper.
lower
Some people expect that the price ....
6 Engineers expect to have completed the tunnel by the end of the year.
that
Engineers expect ....
7 Scientists predict 90% mobile phone use by the end of the decade.
be
Scientists predict that ....

8 The forecast predicts rain for tomorrow.
it
The forecast says that ....

9 It is hard to predict future diet exactly.
eating
It is hard to predict exactly what ....

10 Space experts predict human colonization of other planets by the end of the century.
colonized
Space experts predict that humans ....

5 Complete the text by writing a verb from the box in each space.

~~will be introducing~~	starts	will have closed	will pass	will be able
won't really be	will cause	is going to make	will end up	will prove
will record	will get	will no longer be	won't come back	passes
	will receive	will confuse	will result	

New toll system to cause chaos say hire firms

According to city car hire firms, the automated toll system which the government (1) *will be introducing*... on the M36 next year (2) .... difficulties for car rental companies. When the new system (3) .... operating, there (4) .... a chance to pay tolls directly in cash at toll booths, which (5) .... Under the new system, when the car (6) .... through the toll barrier, cameras (7) .... the car registration plate. Motorists (8) .... to pay automatically by signing up to the Tollpass payment system. Those who are not signed up can pay their toll online or by telephone. All tolls must be paid by 20.00 the following day, and non payment (9) .... in a fine of up to €150. This system is not a problem for local residents, but it (10) .... life difficult for customers, such as tourists or business visitors, who are not signed up with Tollpass. It is the driver who is responsible for paying tolls and fines, and car hire firms think that this (11) .... visitors. 'This system (12) .... disastrous to tourism,' said Monica Donovan of FirstUp Cars. 'Three quarters of all cars returned to car rental companies at the City Airport (13) .... through the toll system during their rental period. We think that a lot of visitors (14) .... not paying and it (15) .... their fault. They (16) .... fines through the post, they (17) .... upset, and they (18) .... to the city in the future.'

8

GRAMMAR

Time words and phrases

At, in, on

- *At, in, on* are used with clock time, festivals and definite times:
  at *5.12am/midnight* ***at*** *Christmas* ***at*** *the end of the week* ***at*** *present*

- *In* is used with months, years, seasons, parts of the day and future points:
  in *April* ***in*** *1906* ***in*** *spring* ***in*** *the morning* ***in*** *a week* ***in*** *a moment*

- *On* is used with dates, days of the week and expressions with *day*:
  on *April 18th* ***on*** *Tuesday* ***on*** *my birthday*

Already

- To say that something has happened before now or a time mentioned:
  We've ***already*** *discussed this matter.*

Yet, so far

- *Not yet* means 'not before a certain time'. In British English it is used with perfect tenses. *Yet* can be placed before or after the verb phrase:
  We have ***not*** *finished it* ***yet****.* *We have* ***not yet*** *finished our report.*

- Without *not*, *yet* means 'ever' or 'so far':
  These are our best results ***yet****.*

- *Have yet to do/be yet to do* means that something has not happened yet:
  Scientists have ***yet to confirm*** *these results. The project is* ***yet to begin****.*

For, since, ago

- *For* is used with a period of time:
  We've been working on this project ***for six months****.*

- *Since* is used with a point of time and comes before the time reference:
  We've been working on this project ***since January****.*

- *Ago* describes the time since an event. It comes after the time reference:
  He died ***ten years ago****.*

Still

- *Still* describes a situation that continues to exist:
  Scientists are ***still*** *looking for answers to these questions.*

No longer

- *No longer* means 'not any more':

  *Scientists **no longer** believe that this is true.*

Towards

- *Towards* is used when we need to describe a time more generally. Compare:

  ***At the end of** the 1990s, the problem was solved.* (exactly then)
  ***Towards the end of** the 1990s, the problem was solved.* (round about then)

By, until, so far, up to

- *By* means 'not later than the time mentioned':

  *The new laboratory will be finished **by the end of the year**.*

- *Until* is used for something that happens up to a point in time, and then stops:

  *Helen slept deeply **until the alarm clock woke her**.*

- *So far* means 'yet' or 'until now':

  *We've been examining the samples, but **so far** haven't found any sign of life.*

- *Up to* means the same as *until*:

  ***Up to** the end of the 1970s computers were large and nobody had one at home.*

During, throughout, over

- *During* describes a point in a period of time, or a whole period of time:

  *The castle was destroyed **during** the war.* (point in a period)
  *Electricity consumption fluctuates **during the day**.* (whole period)

- *Throughout* emphasizes 'from the beginning to the end':

  *Explosions continued **throughout the night**.* (all the time)

- *Over* describes what has happened in a period of time:

  ***Over the past five years**, the situation has got worse.*

- *Over* can also mean 'more than':

  *We've been waiting here for **over** half an hour.*

After, afterwards, later, before

- *After* is a preposition and needs an object. *Afterwards* and *later* are adverbials meaning *after that*, and do not need an object. *Before* and *later* can be used to describe times:

  ***After an encouraging start**, the project ran into difficulties.*
  *He wrote a report, but **afterwards/later/after a while** changed his conclusions.*
  ***An hour later** disaster struck, as it had two years before.*

On time, in time

- *On time* means 'at the moment which was arranged'. The opposite is *late*:
  The new bridge was completed exactly ***on time****.*

- *In time* is the opposite of *too late*:
  The paramedics did not arrive ***in time*** *to save the man's life. They were* ***too late****.*

At last, last, finally, in the end, at the end

- *At last* describes the moment when something you have been waiting for happens:
  At last you are here! *I've been waiting for so long to see you!*

- *Last* describe the last time an action occurred.
  It's ages since ***I last saw you/I saw you last****.*

- *Finally* introduces something that happened after a long time:
  The train ***finally arrived*** *more than two hours late.*

  It also begins a sentence, to describe the last in a series of events or process, or introduces the last thing you want to say:
  Finally*, the samples are sealed in plastic and stored at 5°C.*
  Finally*, the article argues that the cost of such a scheme need not be excessive.*

Nowadays, these days

- Both are used to describe general present time:
  Nowadays *more and more people are buying goods online.*
  Most people ***these days*** *are aware of the need to save energy.*

Once, one day, at once

- *Once* refers to a past event, or something which used to exist:
  People ***once*** *believed that the Sun circled the Earth.*

- *Once* can also mean 'as soon as'. *At once* means 'immediately':
  Once *the micro-processor had been developed, cheap computers soon followed.*
  You must start ***at once****! It's very important.*

Formerly, previously

- *Formerly* or *previously* describe a past situation.
  The building was ***formerly*** *used as an aircraft factory.*

1 <u>Underline</u> the most suitable verb form in each sentence.

1 The waterproof coat, or Mackintosh, was invented *since 200 years/before 200 years/200 years ago*.
2 Nuclear physics as a science began *by/towards/throughout* the end of the nineteenth century.
3 Even in the best organized places, trains don't always run exactly *in time/at once/on time*.
4 Unfortunately, we haven't *already/yet/still* obtained any useful results.
5 Halley's comet won't be visible from the Earth *until/up to/yet* it returns in 2061.
6 My ambition is to *one day/once/so far* stand on the Moon and look at the Earth.
7 The volcano hasn't erupted seriously *for/until/since* 1944.
8 The team hopes to complete the project *up to/by/since* the end of the year.
9 *Nowadays/Throughout/Until* the summer there were numerous forest fires.
10 It is more than 10,000 years since the end of the *last/later/after* Ice Age.

2 Complete each short text by selecting from the words in brackets at the end. Not all words will be used.

Theories of evolution

Text 1

(1) .... the middle of the nineteenth century, various theories of evolution had appeared, including that of Darwin, but evolution was not fully understood until (2) .... , when development in genetics (3) .... the 1950s led to the decoding of the human genome (4) .... the beginning of the 21st century.

(*at, during, finally, later, on, since, up to, yet, in*)

Text 2

The science of genetics was (5) .... based on assumptions about what was inherited, (6) .... the plant-breeding experiments of Gregor Mendel, an Austrian monk and scientist. (7) .... 1865 he published an important paper, widely known only (8) .... his death, which used mathematics to describe laws of genetic inheritance.

(*after, at, at last, formerly, in, nowadays, on, throughout, until*)

Text 3

(9) .... April 25th 1953 James Watson and Francis Crick published an article in *Nature* proposing a structure for DNA, the molecule which contains genetic information. This work was based on X-ray data produced the year (10) .... by Rosalind Franklin. Nine years (11) .... , with another colleague, Maurice Wilkins, they received the Nobel prize, and (12) .... 1968 Watson wrote the best-selling book, *The Double Helix*, about the discovery.

(*after, at, in, later, on, over, so far, before*)

Text 4

The Human Genome Project enabled scientists to (13) .... understand our genetic make-up. The project started (14) .... 1990 and lasted (15) .... more than 16 years. (16) .... 2000 an outline of the way the 20–25,000 human genes that make up human DNA had been traced, and the detailed sequence was published three years (17) .... that. (18) .... then, the research has helped to identify more than 30 diseased genes, responsible for human illnesses. (*after, already, by, finally, for, in, later, since, until*)

3 Read the text and decide which option (A, B, C or D) best fits each space.

Blood transfusion

Experiments in blood transfusion were carried out in France (1) .... the 17th century though Australian native people are said to have practised blood transfusion for thousands of years. (2) .... 15th June 1667 a French doctor, Jean-Baptiste Denys, successfully transfused a boy with the blood of a lamb, and (3) .... a short period performed other transfusions. However, several of his patients died and the practice was (4) .... banned, both in France and in other countries. (5) .... the 19th century, blood transfusions became common, but (6) .... that time doctors did not understand that human blood is divided into different groups. It was (7) .... Karl Landsteiner discovered this (8) .... 1901 that transfusions became safe. (9) .... this point, transfusions were still carried out from patient to patient. (10) .... the end of the same decade, it became possible to store blood using refrigeration and by adding anticoagulants, and (11) .... the First World War, blood stored in blood banks was used for the first time. Most countries now have national blood bank systems and receiving blood is (12) .... a dangerous or unusual event. Technical advances (13) .... the past century mean that blood can (14) .... be stored (15) .... about six weeks, and plasma, the liquid component of blood, (16) .... a year.

	A	B	C	D
1	**A** until	**B** since	**C** in	**D** already
2	**A** On	**B** In	**C** At	**D** The
3	**A** since	**B** after	**C** over	**D** from
4	**A** after	**B** these days	**C** previously	**D** later
5	**A** By	**B** In time	**C** Until	**D** During
6	**A** in	**B** at	**C** on	**D** for
7	**A** already	**B** not until	**C** during	**D** since
8	**A** in	**B** at	**C** on	**D** over
9	**A** At	**B** In	**C** Since	**D** On
10	**A** Afterwards	**B** Finally	**C** Formerly	**D** By
11	**A** at	**B** during	**C** since	**D** already
12	**A** so far	**B** already	**C** no longer	**D** at last
13	**A** in	**B** over	**C** until	**D** after
14	**A** yet	**B** now	**C** still	**D** finally
15	**A** since	**B** during	**C** for	**D** by
16	**A** for up to	**B** still	**C** during	**D** not until

4 Complete the text by writing a suitable word in each space.

Traffic lights

Traffic lights only became necessary (1) ......in...... the 19th century, when traffic began to increase. A traffic signal invented by J P Knight, a railway signalling engineer, was installed outside the Houses of Parliament in London as long (2) .... as 1868. It looked like a railway signal of the time but a few weeks (3) .... it blew up, killing a policeman, and signals of this type were no (4) .... used. The modern traffic light is an American invention, the first red and green lights, worked by a policeman, being set up in Cleveland (5) .... 1914 followed a few years (6) .... by three-colour lights in New York. These new lights didn't arrive in Britain (7) .... 1925. A year (8) .... this, the first automatic lights were installed at a road junction in Wolverhampton, where they remained in use (9) .... the next 42 years. Lights of this type had (10) .... appeared in Houston in the USA. (11) .... the beginning of the 1930s, the first vehicle-activated lights were set up in London. (12) .... these early days, traffic light design has developed to cater for different types of road user.

5 Complete the text by writing a suitable word in each space. In some cases there is more than one answer.

An outline history of banking

The first banks were probably established (1) ..around.. five thousand years (2) .... , (3) .... a time when produce such as grain rather than money would have been lent out. Banking (4) .... became common (5) .... the Roman period. (6) .... the Roman Empire in the west had fallen, banking was first restricted by Christian beliefs, and then abandoned, not reappearing (7) .... the Middle Ages. (8) .... that period, the increase in international trade led to a kind of banking linked to trade fairs. (9) .... the early 14th century, for example, Italian banks had branches all over Europe. The oldest bank (10) .... operating today is the Banca Monte dei Paschi di Siena, which was founded (11) .... 1472. This type of bank was in effect a cross between a pawnbroker and a charity to help the poor, a common type of institution (12) .... that time. It has been operating ever (13) .... and today is a bank with 3,000 branches. Modern finance and banking originated in London and Amsterdam (14) .... the 17th century, (15) .... leading to the establishment (16) .... 1694 of the Bank of England to act as banker for the British government. (17) .... the Bank plays a major role in managing the UK economy.

9

GRAMMAR

Practice 3

1 Complete the text by writing a form of a verb from the box in each space.

~~will probably rise~~	will have increased	will be	will be living
will have sprung up	will be struggling	will not have been able	
will be finding	will simply not have	will be facing	will have
will have improved	will have provided	will have to address	

Growth in urban population

Over the next half century, the world's population (1) ..will probably rise.. to around 9 billion. World population (2) .... by nearly 50% compared to the population at the turn of the millennium, and according to a report by the UN agency the United Nations Population Fund, the future for most people in the world (3) .... urban. By 2030 more than 5 billion people (4) .... in towns and cities, and large urban populations (5) .... in Africa and Asia. Most of these people (6) .... to find work and raise families in smaller towns and cities in less-developed regions which (7) .... to keep pace with expansion. Such towns (8) .... it difficult to cope with change, and (9) .... the necessary resources. Most of the inhabitants of these new cities (10) .... a life of poverty. In 2000 the international community recognized that it (11) .... the needs of the growing number of poor people living in cities. The target they set then was an ambitious one. The expectation is that by 2020 the lives of at least 100 million people (12) .... significantly. Governments (13) .... better housing, alongside improved access to basic social and health care. However, nobody is sure what impact the global recession (14) .... on these plans, and whether the 2020 target is now achievable.

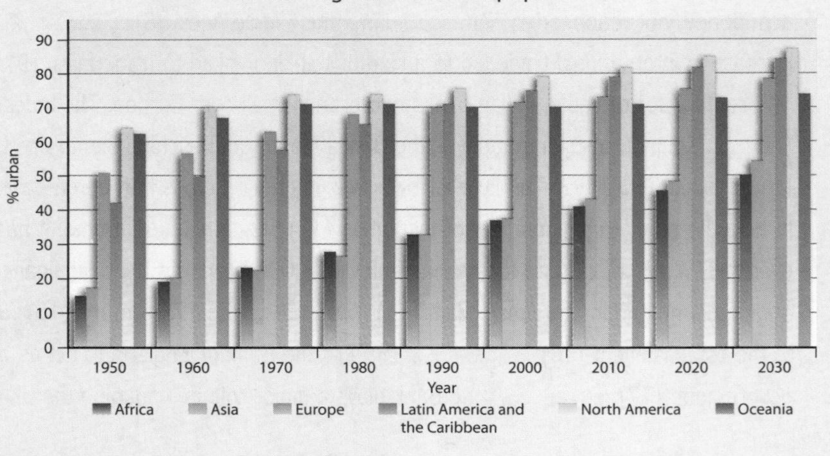

2 **Complete the text by writing a suitable word in each space. More than one answer may be possible.**

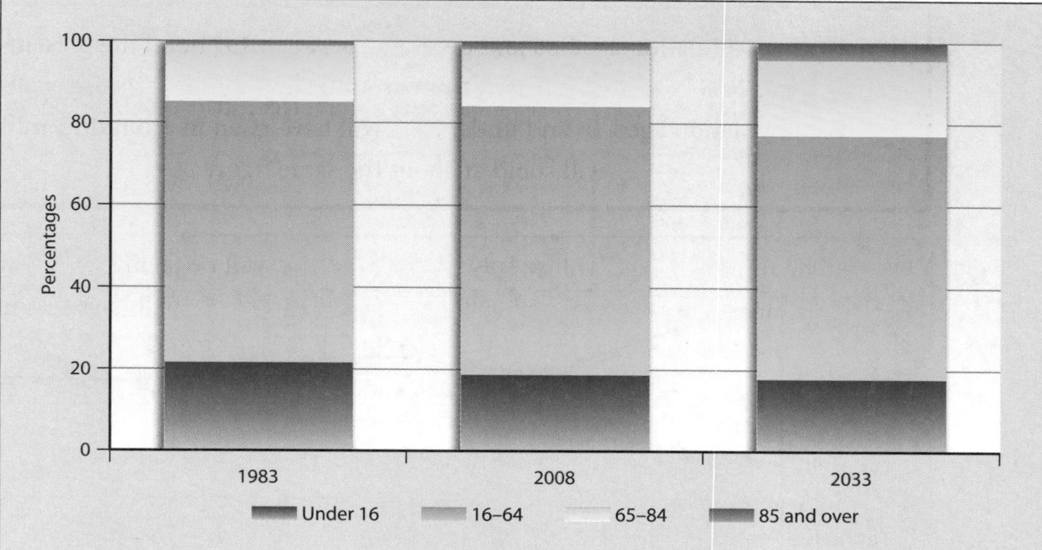

Population by age, UK, 1983, 2008 and 2033

Ageing in the UK

(1) ...Nowadays... the UK population has an increasing number of elderly people. (2) .... the last few decades the percentage of the population aged 65 and over has increased by around 1%, which means that at (3) .... there are more than 1.5 million people in this age group. (4) .... the 1983 figures, the percentage of the population aged 16 and under has decreased by 2%. This trend is projected to continue, and (5) .... 2033, 23% of the population will be aged 65 and over while only 18% will be aged 16 or younger.

(6) .... this period, the fastest population increase has been in the number of those aged 85 and over, the 'oldest old'. Thirty years (7) .... , there were just over 600,000 people in the UK aged 85 and over.
(8) .... then the numbers have more than doubled to stand at around 1.3 million and they are (9) .... rising. (10) .... 2033 the number of people aged 85 and over will have doubled again to reach 3.2 million, and will account for 5% of the total population.

3 Study the table and use the information to complete the text, using the phrases in the box.

~~the population aged 65 and over~~	between 1971 and the present	
fell by about 20%	has increased from around 7.5 million	rose by about 30%
the population aged 16 and under	will have risen to around 13 million	
will stand at about the same figure		

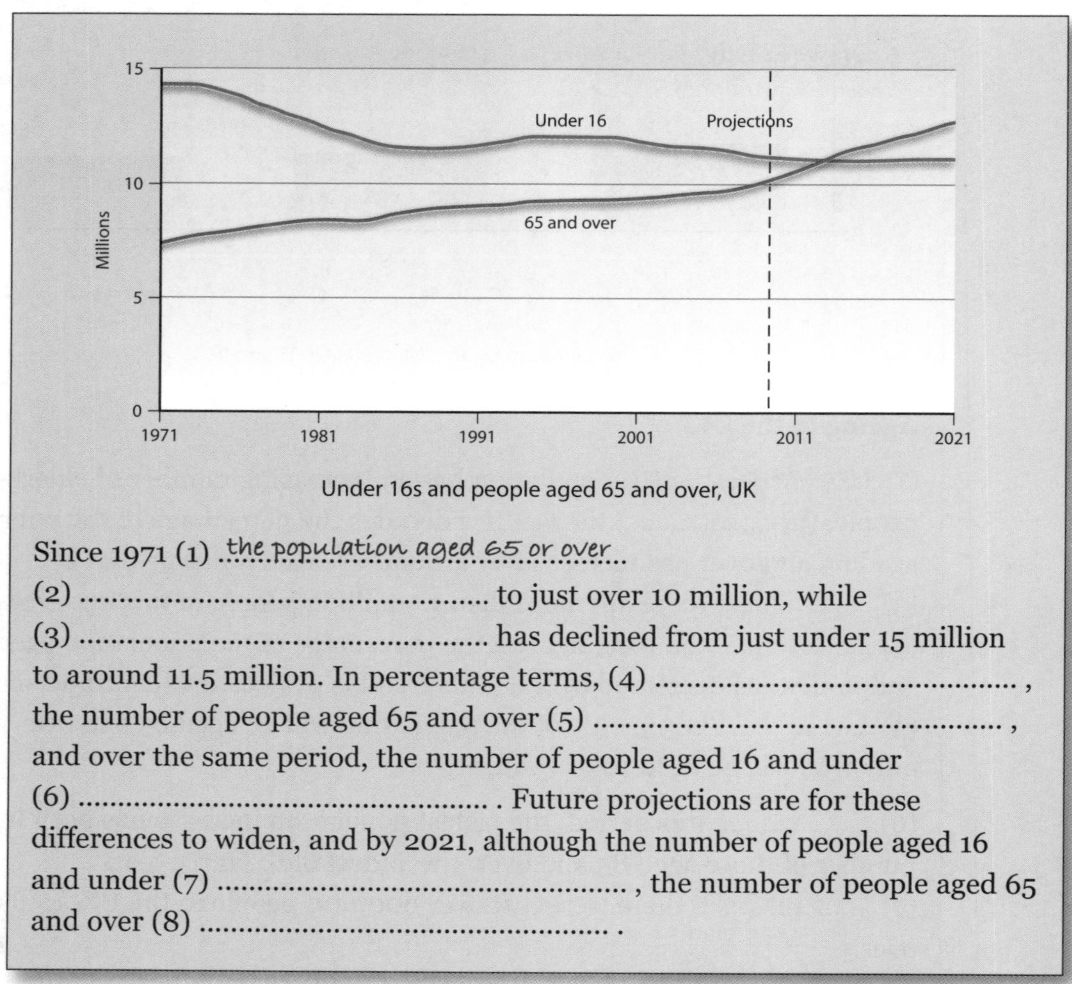

Under 16s and people aged 65 and over, UK

Since 1971 (1) the population aged 65 or over (2) .... to just over 10 million, while (3) .... has declined from just under 15 million to around 11.5 million. In percentage terms, (4) .... , the number of people aged 65 and over (5) .... , and over the same period, the number of people aged 16 and under (6) .... Future projections are for these differences to widen, and by 2021, although the number of people aged 16 and under (7) .... , the number of people aged 65 and over (8) ....

10

GRAMMAR

Direct and indirect questions

Direct questions

- Questions begin either with question words, or with an auxiliary verb. Note the positions of adverbs:

  Present simple

  How (exactly) *does it work?* ***Do*** *they live here?*

  Present continuous

  What *is happening?* ***Are*** *they (**really**) leaving?*

  Past simple

  What *did they find?* ***Did*** *it make any difference?*

  Past continuous

  What *was he trying to do?* ***Were*** *you living there?*

  Present perfect simple

  Have *you (ever) been there?* ***Has*** *it started?*

  Present perfect continuous

  What *have you been doing?* ***Has*** *he been waiting long?*

  Past perfect simple

  What *had they discovered?* ***Had*** *they left?*

  Past perfect continuous

  What *had he been doing?* ***Had*** *you been waiting?*

Indirect or reported questions

- Questions can be introduced by reporting verbs. In this case there is no question form, or question mark. They are called 'indirect' or 'reported' questions. When introduced by a past tense verb, reported questions follow tense rules for reported speech:

  Direct question

  'What time is it?'

  Indirect question

  *I **wonder** what time it is.*

- Questions can also be introduced by expressions formed from *it* + *be* + adjective or *it* + *be* + adjective + infinitive:

  Direct question

  'Who is going to take over from Jan?'

  Indirect question

  It's not clear *who is going to take over from Jan.*

  It's hard to decide *who is going to take over from Jan.*

- Questions can be introduced by other direct questions (with a question mark):

  What size is it? *Where are we going?*

  Do you know *what size it is?* ***Could you tell me*** *where we are going?*

Noun clauses

- Noun clauses beginning *who, what, how, why,* etc often follow verbs such as: *describe, know, understand, realize, explain, reveal, wonder, show*

  and phrases such as:

  it is uncertain/doubtful/not clear

  These are not questions and so are not followed by question forms.

  It is important to describe exactly how this reaction takes place:

  Scientists now understand ***how the birds navigate over long distances.***
  The table shows ***how many 16 to 18 year-olds remain in education.***
  The diagram explains ***what happens under these conditions.***

- In writing it may be clearer to use a direct question:

  But ***how do the birds navigate over long distances?*** *Scientists now think they understand this.*

Subject and object questions

- Object questions with *what* and *who* generally use an auxiliary and inversion:

  These organisms live on carbon dioxide.
  What do *these organisms* ***live*** *on?*

- Subject questions do not use an auxiliary or inversion:

  Strong light kills them.
  What kills *them?*
  Who discovered *this effect?*
  What was *the result?*

→ **SEE ALSO**
Grammar 1: Present time
Grammar 2: Past time
Grammar 4: Present perfect
Grammar 5: Past perfect, *used to*
Grammar 7: Future time

1 Choose the correct sentence (A, B or C).

1 A What was trying to discover exactly the experiment?
B What exactly was the experiment trying to discover? ✓
C What the experiment exactly was it trying to discover?

2 A You have considered ever of applying for the post of lecturer?
B You considered have ever applying for the post of lecturer?
C Have you ever considered applying for the post of lecturer?

3 A Where do I go to renew my library card?
B Where I go to renew my library card?
C Where go I to renew my library card?

4 A Can you tell me how much do I have to pay?
B Can you tell me how much I have to pay?
C Can you tell me how much have I to pay?

5 A What Shakespeare was doing during the years 1585 to 1592?
B What Shakespeare doing during the years 1585 to 1592?
C What was Shakespeare doing during the years 1585 to 1592?

6 A When you are going to let us know the results?
B When are you going to let us know the results?
C When you going to let us know the results?

7 A What particularly makes the birds behave in this way?
B What particularly does make the birds behave in this way?
C What particularly makes the birds do they behave in this way?

8 A What kind of primary education most children did receive at that time?
B What kind of primary education most children did they receive at that time?
C What kind of primary education did most children receive at that time?

2 Write questions using the prompts.

Interview

1 when/you/decide/to be a lawyer? *When did you decide to be a lawyer?*
2 how long/you/have to study? ....
3 how/you/remember/all the facts? ....
4 what/interest/you most about the law? ....
5 what kind of law/you/specialize in? ....
6 what kind of law firm/you work for? ....
7 you/earn/high salary? ....
8 you/ever appear in a murder/trial? ....
9 what/you/ like most about the job? ....
10 what/you/do in ten years time? ....

3 Make questions for which these statements are answers. Leave out any unnecessary words.

1 William Shakespeare died at the age of 52.
How old was William Shakespeare when he died?
2 Teams of scientists have been working on genome projects since the 1990s.
How long..?
3 Thomas Edison developed the first long-lasting practical electric light-bulb.
Who..?
4 The first astronauts on the Moon brought back samples of the lunar rock.
What..?
5 Jacques Monod was a French biochemist born in Paris in 1910.
When..?
6 One reason that birds sing is to show to other birds that they own an area or 'territory'.
Why..?
7 Maria Montessori is best known for her method of educating children.
What..?
8 The entire project will cost something in the region of €50 million.
How much..?
9 The next conference will be taking place in Prague in 2020.
When..?
10 Scientists believe that a black hole exists at the centre of our galaxy
What..?

4 Rewrite each direct question as an indirect question or a statement, following the prompts given.

1 Is this the right answer?
Do you know whether this is the right answer?
2 What time does the train leave?
Do you know ....
3 Where is the entrance?
It's not clear..
4 How does this machine work?
I want to know ....
5 Who is he?
They didn't know ....
6 When does the final examination take place?
Do you know ....
7 Is it going to rain?
I wonder whether ....
8 How do thunder and lightning occur?
Can you explain ....
9 Why did you tell me to wait here?
I'd like to know ....
10 What's the meaning of this word?
Could you tell me ....

5 Complete the text with questions a–j. Some can be included in the text as direct questions, but others must be changed to indirect questions.

- **a** Why do some birds fly thousands of miles?
- **b** How do birds manage to migrate over long distances?
- **c** How do birds find their way?
- **d** Which route should they follow?
- **e** What advantages does migration bring?
- **f** How do these young birds know where to go?
- **g** How are young birds able to follow migration routes?
- **h** How do migration routes become established?
- **i** Why do some birds stay in the same place?
- **j** What strategies do birds use on long trips?

Bird migration

We have all probably wondered why (1) ......*a*...... between breeding and non-breeding areas every year. However, not all birds migrate, and scientists still do not know why (2) .... all the year round. What (3) .... First of all, migration means that birds can find safe places where food is plentiful, and where it is safe to breed, so it is easy to see how (4) .... These migration routes are generally based on weather differences between regions, for example north or south, or higher and lower altitudes. This can involve a lot of flying! In earlier times people found it hard to understand how (5) .... The Arctic Tern, for example, flies up to 30,000 kms when it migrates from the North to the South Pole. We now know what (6) .... These include using high altitude winds as well as resting in convenient places. We also understand how (7) .... using the sun and the stars to navigate, as well as looking out for landmarks. It seems that birds can also sense magnetic north. One interesting question remains. It is not clear how (8) .... for the first time, when they are abandoned by the parent birds as soon as they can fly. How (9) .... Scientists now think that young birds are born with the necessary information about migration genetically imprinted, so they automatically know which (10) ....

11

GRAMMAR

The passive

Why use the passive?

- To place important information at the beginning of the sentence:
  A new bridge across the river ***was opened*** *in 2006.*
- To describe a technical process impersonally:
  The water ***is*** *then* ***heated*** *to 80° centigrade.*
  Finally, ***they are cemented*** *onto the teeth.*
- Without an agent, to avoid mentioning the person who performs the action, because this is obvious from the context, or unimportant or very general:
  Students ***are expected*** *to attend all classes.*
  A new chief executive ***has been appointed****.*
  Her new book ***was well reviewed*** *in the weekend papers.*
  Note that it may be clearer not to use the passive, and writers of scientific reports often use active rather than passive forms in order to focus on the result. The second example below may seem clearer:
  Lack of exercise ***is considered*** *to be a contributory factor in heart disease.*
  Researchers ***have concluded*** *that lack of exercise is a contributory factor in heart disease.*

Tense forms

- All tenses and simple or continuous forms are possible, but some are more common than others:
  Present simple passive
  The parts ***are imported*** *from China.*
  Present continuous passive
  The road ***is being widened****.*
  Will passive
  The project ***will be completed*** *next year.*
  Past simple passive
  The drug ***was developed*** *by a team of scientists.*
  Past continuous passive
  The letters were found while the stones ***were being cleaned****.*
  Present perfect passive
  All work ***has been suspended*** *until further notice.*
  Modal *must/should*
  All doors ***must be kept/should*** *be kept locked.*
  Modal *can/could*
  The door ***can*** *only* ***be opened*** *from the inside.*

Agent *by* and instrument *with*

- It may be important to mention who performed the action:
  *This theory was first developed **by Isaac Newton**.*
  *A new chief executive has been appointed **by the parent company**.*

- In scientific writing, it is common for the agent to be a thing rather than a person:
  *Glucose is used **by the cells** to provide energy.*
  *All social behaviour is determined **by genetic and/or biological factors**.*

- We can describe the instrument used when something was done using *with*:
  *It was removed **with the hand tools that can be seen at the top of the photo**.*

Verbs that cannot be passive

- Only transitive verbs (verbs with an object) can be made passive:
  *They **constructed** the building in the 1980s.*
  *The building **was constructed** in the 1980s.*

- Some transitive verbs cannot be made passive, e.g. *become, get, have, fit* (be the right size) *lack, let, resemble, suit*:
  *That dress really **suits** you!* (*You are suited ...* is not possible)
  *He **resembles** my brother* (*My brother is resembled ...* is not possible)

- Intransitive verbs (verbs with no object) cannot be made passive, e.g. *sleep, arrive*:
  *She **slept** late.*
  *The train **arrived** on time, for a change.*

1 Underline the most suitable verb form in each sentence.

1 Your computer *suspended/has been suspended/has suspended* from the campus network for violation of copyright policy.
2 The report *makes/is made/has been made* no mention of the so-far unexplained departure of the Finance Director.
3 Construction work will begin only after appropriate safety and environmental reviews *were completed/complete/have been completed.*
4 The weight of an atom *is determined/determines/has been determined* by the number of neutrons and protons that are present in the nucleus.
5 Architect Robert de Palma *was choose/is been chosen/has been chosen* to design a new extension for the City Concert Hall.
6 In 2008 a jumping robot *was developed/developed/has been developed* by researchers at the Swiss Federal Institute of Technology in Lausanne.
7 Meteorological data *records/has been recorded/is recorded* globally only for the last 100 years or so.
8 JK Rowling *published/was published/is published* her first novel, 'Harry Potter and the Philosopher's Stone', in 1997.
9 Basque and Lithuanian *are generally considered/generally consider/are generally considering* to be the oldest European languages.
10 The Foreign Minister Magnus Lobo *is being investigated/is investigating/is been investigated* on corruption charges.

2 Complete the second sentence so that it has a similar meaning to the first sentence. Leave out any unnecessary agents.

1 The company is importing the main components from Poland.
The main components are being imported from Poland.
2 Someone invented the magnetic compass about a thousand years ago in China.
The magnetic compass ....
3 The government is increasing the price of fuel oil from tomorrow.
The price ....
4 You must complete all projects by 31st March.
All projects ....
5 Scientists use some radio telescopes to search for extra-terrestrial life.
Some radios ....
6 While the authorities were transporting the painting from Paris to Rome, it was damaged in a train crash.
The painting was damaged in a train crash ....
7 The authorities have suspended both players for the next three matches.
Both players ....
8 The university will publish the test results at the end of the month.
The test results ....
9 Recently scientists have discovered other stars with planets in orbit around them.
Recently other stars ....
10 The authorities are closing the laboratory until further notice.
The laboratory ....

3 Complete the text by writing a passive or active form of the verb in brackets in each space, as appropriate.

Lie detector tests

Lie detectors (1) are known (know) technically as 'polygraph instruments'. A polygraph instrument is a combination of medical devices that (2) .... (use) to monitor changes occurring in the body. While a person (3) .... (question) about a certain event or incident, the examiner (4) .... (check) whether there are any changes in the person's heart rate, blood pressure, respiratory rate, etc . Fluctuations (5) .... (may indicate) that the person is being deceptive. Today most polygraph tests (6) .... (administer) using digital equipment. The familiar scrolling paper lie detector which (7) .... (depict) in so many old films (8) .... (replace) by a computer monitor. When you (9) .... (sit) in the chair for a polygraph test, several sensors and wires (10) .... (connect) to your body in specific locations to monitor your physiological activities. Deceptive behaviour (11) .... (suppose) to trigger certain physiological changes that (12) .... (can detect) by a polygraph and a trained examiner, who (13) .... (sometimes call) a forensic psychophysiologist. Polygraphs (14) .... (limit) in their use in the private sector, but they (15) .... (frequently employ) by government agencies and law-enforcement bodies. Generally speaking, nobody (16) .... (can force) to take such a test.

4 Rewrite each sentence changing the active to passive, or passive to active. Only include an agent if this is needed, and make any other necessary changes.

1 The cells use glucose to provide energy.
Glucose is used by the cells to provide energy.

2 We provided all the athletes taking part with laptops and video cameras.
....

3 Health experts advise everyone to eat 400 grammes of fruit and vegetables per day.
....

4 Nobody knows how the fire began.
....

5 According to reports, coastal areas have been hit the hardest by the storm.
....

6 Worldwide we spent around $400 billion dollars on advertising last year.
....

7 If I were asked to rejoin the project, I would refuse.
....

8 Smith has been forced to abandon the Tour de France after breaking his arm.
....

5 Complete the text by writing a suitable passive or active form of the verb in brackets in each space.

Green hotels

Now that more and more people (1) ...realize....... (realize) the importance of saving energy and other resources, hotels everywhere (2) .... (force) to improve their green credentials. In the UK, a special body called the 'Green Tourism Business Scheme' (3) .... (set up) with just this issue in mind, and (4) .... (become) very popular. The number of hotels assessed by the scheme (5) .... (double) over the past two years as hotel owners (6) .... (persuade) that going green also makes good business sense. Even the least perceptive hotel visitor can spot the problems: energy (7) .... (waste) when lights (8) .... (leave on), rooms are too hot, bathrooms (9) .... (provide) with too many towels and so on. Cutting out waste in areas like these means that business costs (10) .... (can cut), so the scheme helps hotels up and down the country to plan changes. As a result, in some hotels inefficient boilers (11) .... (replace), and better insulation (12) .... (fit), thus saving energy and money. In others, water usage (13) .... (reduce), and some rural hotels (14) .... (collect) rainwater in underground tanks. In one London hotel, beehives (15) .... (install) on the roof as part of a drive to save the threatened bee population. The honey produced here (16) .... (serve) in the hotel's restaurant. As we know, going green is largely a matter of changing attitudes, and this (17) .... (apply) to both hotel owners, and to guests. The latter (18) .... (give) information about green issues in the hotel, but (19) .... (not lecture) in an aggressive way. Everyone (20) .... (encourage) to do their bit, and in some hotels guests even get a discount for not using their car during their stay.

12

GRAMMAR

Practice 4

1 Write questions based on the information given in the graph, using the prompts given and the verb(s) from the box. Add a question word if necessary.

Travel and tourism in the UK

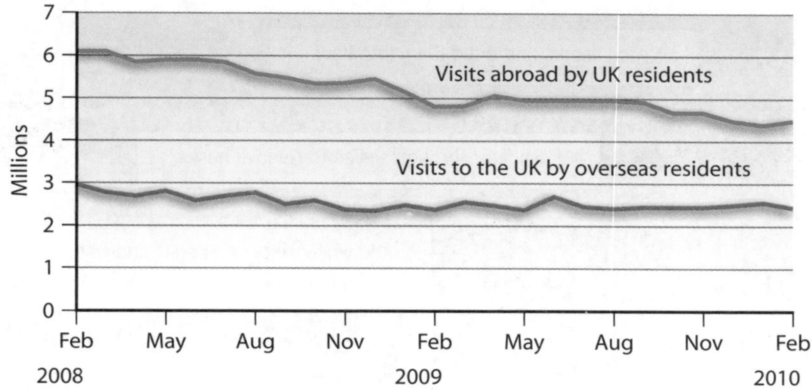

Overseas residents' visits to the UK and UK residents' visits abroad

1 information/graph (show)
What information does the graph show?
2 during this period/UK/visits abroad (rise, fall)
....
3 fall in 2009/as steep/fall in 2008 (be)
....
4 figures for overseas visits/UK/same trend (show)
....
5 figures/any seasonal variations (show)
....
6 approximate difference/millions/February 2008 and February 2010 (be)
....
7 figures for overseas visits to the UK/ the same general trend (show)
....
8 approximate fall/numbers/between February 2008 and February 2010 (be)
....
9 these trends/probably (explain)
....
10 future trends/likely (be)
....

2 Study the diagram and complete the sentences describing how mustard is manufactured, using passive forms where possible. Add any necessary words.

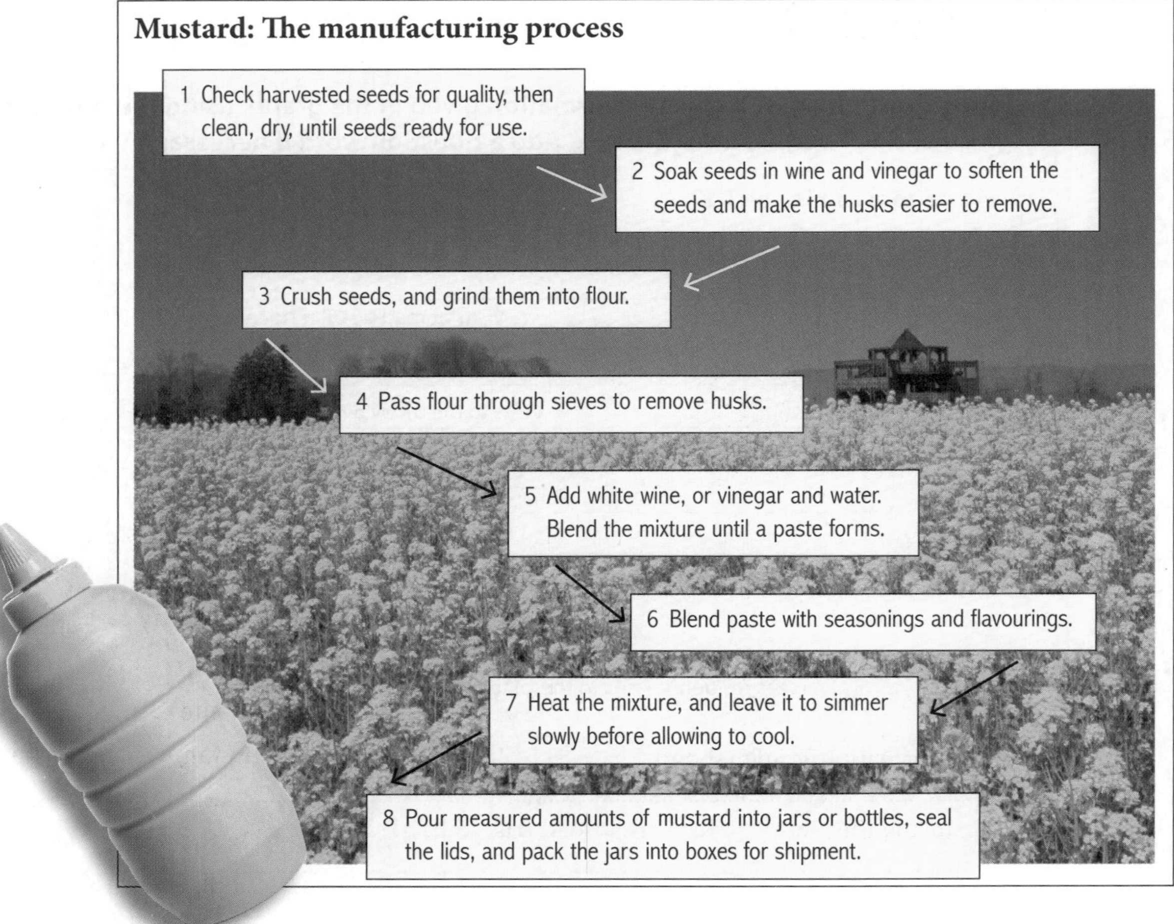

1 First of all, the harvested seeds are checked for quality, ...*then cleaned and dried until the seeds are ready for use*......... .
2 After that, ...
3 In the next stage, ...
4 Then ....
5 Following that, ...
6 Then...
7 In the next stage, ...
8 Finally, ...

3 Complete the text by writing a suitable passive form of a verb from the box in each space.

~~construct~~	achieve	change	distribute	fit out
fund	furnish	give	help	provide
renovate	repair	subsidize	supply	train

From Houses to Homes: our recent accomplishments

From Houses to Homes is a charity which aims to strengthen community harmony in highland Guatemala by building lasting, healthy homes, improving access to health care and education, and inspiring participation between the poor and civil society. Since 2005 around 300 new homes (1) have been constructed. In addition, sixteen homes (2) .... Thanks to voluntary donations, safe and efficient stoves (3) .... to 35 families, and over 100 homes (4) .... with beds, mattresses and bed-linen. In the educational field, more than 1,000 children (5) .... to attend school, several new schools have been built, school buildings (6) .... , and schools (7) .... with new desks and other equipment. Teachers in one school (8) .... with laptops and computer training so that in future their students (9) .... better learning opportunities. Currently, the salaries of some teachers (10) .... and in 2008/2009 two teachers (11) .... entirely by our organization. In 2009, we covered the costs of 30 men who (12) .... to become electricians. A large quantity of food, medicine, clothing and footwear (13) .... All this (14) .... by the hard work of over 700 volunteers from 22 different countries. The lives of many needy people (15) .... for the better, and the volunteers have gained the experience of a lifetime.

13

GRAMMAR

Conditionals 1

General truths: *If/When* + present simple + present simple

This form is often referred to as the 'zero conditional'.

- What always happens as the result of an action. This is a generalization, rather than a description of what will happen in a particular situation:
  If/When *you* ***increase*** *the prices too much, people* ***don't buy*** *the goods.*

Real conditions: *If* + present simple + *will/won't (do)*

This form is often referred to as the 'first conditional'.

- What will really happen as the result of a possible action:
  If *fishing* ***continues****, this species* ***will*** *soon* ***become*** *extinct.*
  If *governments* ***don't take*** *action, the effects of global warming* ***will be*** *disastrous.*

General truth or real condition?

- The choice depends on the attitude of the user.
  This is what happens all the time – a generalization:
  Choosing the right price for your goods is an important part of successful selling. ***If*** *you* ***increase*** *the prices too much, fewer people* ***buy*** *the goods.*
  This is what will happen in a particular situation we are discussing:
  We need to generate more income this year, but we must be careful not to overprice our goods. ***If*** *we* ***increase*** *the prices too much, nobody* ***will buy*** *them.*

Other variants

General truths and real conditions can contain modals *can, could, might, should,* etc. See Grammar 16 and 17.

- General truth
  When *it* ***rains*** *heavily, this area* ***can suffer*** *from flooding.*
  If *the weather* ***changes*** *now, that* ***could cause*** *problems.*

- Real condition
  If *fishing* ***continues****, this species* ***may/might well become*** *extinct.*

Unreal conditions: *If* + past simple + *would (do)*

This form is often referred to as the 'second conditional'.

- An imaginary present result which follows from an imaginary present situation:
  If *the Earth* ***didn't have*** *a Moon, there* ***wouldn't be*** *any tides.*
  If *I* ***knew*** *the answer I'****d tell*** *you. But I don't know it, I'm afraid!*

- The past simple form does not refer to past time. In formal speech or writing we use *were* rather than *was*:
  If *the walls* ***were*** *stronger, they* ***would take*** *a heavier load.*

- *Could*, *might*, *etc* are also possible in the second clause:

  If the walls ***were*** *stronger, they* ***might take*** *a heavier load.*

Would

- We can use *would* to describe imaginary situations with the *if* understood but unstated:

  What ***would*** *you* ***do*** *in that case?* ***I'd resign****, I think.*

Real or unreal?

The difference between real and unreal conditions may be a matter of speaker choice and context. The meaning communicated may be the same.

- The following is a real possibility. You are about to travel – perhaps we are at the station:

  If you ***take*** *the 2.30 train, you****'ll get*** *there before 5.00.*

- In the following sentence, we are only discussing your options. Your journey is in the future, or may not happen:

  If you ***took*** *the 2.30 train, you****'d get*** *there before 5.00.*

Unless

- *Unless* means 'only if not', and is used when we say that if something does not happen, something else will happen (or be true) as a result:

  If the government ***does not help*** *the banks, they* ***will not survive****.*

  The banks ***will not survive unless*** *the government* ***helps*** *them.*

➜ SEE ALSO
Grammar 14: Conditionals 2

1 Underline the most suitable verb form in each sentence.

1 The financial situation is critical, and if we *don't act/didn't act/won't act* now, it *is/would be/will be* too late.
2 If the weather *will improve/improves* by the weekend, the marathon *will go ahead/goes ahead* as planned.
3 The government *increases/will increase/would increase* payments if the money *is available/were available/will be available*, but in the current financial crisis this is just not possible.
4 Carol Smith's work *is/would be/will be* a lot better if she *spends/spent/will spend* more time on it, but she tends to rush and makes too many mistakes.
5 If I *had/have* the time, *I'd help/I'll help* you, but I'm in a hurry and I have to leave now.
6 In a cold spell of this severity, old people suffer a great deal, and if they *are not given/will not be given* help to heat their homes, a number of them *will die/would die*.
7 If human beings *had/have* brains twice their normal size, *would they be/are they* automatically more intelligent?
8 At the moment the lecture is scheduled to take place as normal, but if it *will be postponed/is postponed/were postponed*, it *takes/will take/would take* place on Wednesday 15th February.
9 Don't worry. If you *don't finish/won't finish/didn't finish* the work on Tuesday, *I'll come/I come/I would come* round and help you do it on Wednesday.
10 If bankers *were investing/are investing* their own money, I think they *would/will* take a lot more care of it!

2 Complete each sentence with a suitable form of the verb in brackets.

Taking out a pension

1 If you (be) ....*are*.......... worried about the risks, speak to one of our advisers.
2 If your employer, your partner or some other person also (pay) .... into your pension, their payments (add) .... to the total you can pay in during one year (Annual Allowance).
3 Do not exceed this allowance, as if you (exceed) .... the Annual Allowance, we (not accept) .... the payments.
4 If you (lose) .... your job, you (be still) .... allowed to pay money into your pension.
5 If you (not have) .... enough money to make any payments, you can take a payment break, but we (continue) .... to charge you.
6 If you (stop) .... payment for any length of time, the value of your pension when you retire (be) .... reduced.
7 When you retire you can take 25% of your fund in cash. For example, if your fund (be) .... worth £100,000, you can take out £25,000 as a lump sum.
8 If you (die) .... before you retire, we (pay) .... the value of your plan to the person named as your beneficiary.

3 Write a new sentence with a similar meaning to the first sentence, using *unless*.

1 If you don't water the plants, they won't grow.
The plants won't grow unless you water them.
2 The machine won't start if you don't plug it in.
....
3 The union will call a strike if staff are not given a pay rise.
....
4 If the government fails to act, there will be a water shortage.
....
5 The programme is likely to go ahead if there isn't a last-minute hitch.
....
6 If there is not an examination at the end of the course, some students will not study seriously.
....
7 If they don't enjoy what they are doing, people tend not to succeed.
....
8 Without a valid library card, students cannot use the library.
....
9 If no measures are taken, the situation will get worse.
....
10 If the patient's condition doesn't deteriorate, she should make a full recovery.
....

4 Write an *If*... sentence with the same meaning as the first sentence. Sometimes there is more than one possible answer.

1 I haven't got my driving licence with me so I can't hire a car.
If I had my driving licence with me I would be able to hire a car.
2 Without water, life on Earth would be impossible.
....
3 Everyone speaks different languages, so people don't get on well together.
....
4 We haven't got a computer so it isn't as easy to do the calculations.
....
5 Food isn't distributed fairly so some people don't have enough to eat.
....
6 People don't give up smoking because they probably don't know the risks involved.
....
7 Aliens might land on Earth unnoticed.
....
8 The library doesn't open on Sunday so we can't go there to study.
....
9 Greater use of public transport would cut the amount of pollution from cars.
....
10 People who are overweight eat too much and don't take enough exercise.
....

5 Complete the text by writing a suitable word in each space. Sometimes there is more than one possible answer.

Survival skills

(1) .... you find yourself alone on a desert island, then you (2) .... have to learn how to survive.

This (3) .... be a challenging and disheartening experience to say the least, especially if you (4) .... alone. However, most people in such situations are rescued in the end. (5) .... you remain hopeful and do what you can to survive, there (6) .... a good chance that someone (7) .... rescue you.

Shelter

If you really (8) .... on an island after an accident of some kind, you (9) .... well be exhausted. Many people in this situation spend too long looking for an ideal shelter. If you (10) .... not find the right location straightaway, this (11) .... matter. A temporary shelter will do. If there (12) .... wreckage from the boat, or plane which brought you, this (13) .... give you protection from the weather and from wildlife.

Water

If you (14) .... on an island, there will (15) .... plenty of sea water, which is good for washing and cleaning clothes, but it is not good to drink. If you (16) .... not find clean, safe drinking water within 3 to 4 days, you (17) .... die. Look for a stream or puddles of rainwater. If there (18) .... no suitable container you (19) .... need to make one. You can use plastic sheeting to collect rainwater or morning dew.

Food

(20) .... you have a fire, you (21) .... have to eat raw food, which can be dangerous. Obviously it is difficult to make a fire without matches or a lighter.

Rescue

Nobody will rescue you (22) .... you show that you are there. Light a fire or write an SOS message on the sand using rocks.

14

GRAMMAR

Conditionals 2

Impossible past conditions: *if* + past perfect + *would have (done)*

This form is often referred to as the 'third conditional'.

An imaginary past result which follows from an imaginary past situation. We cannot change the past, so this is an impossible condition:

*If the company **had acted** properly, it **would not have got into** difficulties.*
*If some newspapers **hadn't reported** these problems, nobody **would have known**.*
*If the bank **hadn't helped** the company, it **would not have survived**.*

Could have and *might have* are often used instead of *would have*, as are other modals:

*If the company **had acted** properly, it **might not have got into** difficulties.*

Mixed conditions: *if* + past perfect + *would (do)*

An imagined event in the past with a result in the present:

*If the experiment **had been** successful, Dr Johnson **would be** famous.*

Otherwise

- *Otherwise* is another way of saying *if not*. It can also come at the end of a separate sentence.

  *Make your payments on time **otherwise** this will affect your credit.*
  *If you **don't make** your payments on time, this will affect your credit.*

Note that *otherwise* is also used as an adverbial meaning 'in a different way'.

Providing/provided (that), as long as, on condition (that)

- These are ways of emphasizing *only ... if*:

  *Children aged 5 and under **only** travel free **if** they do not occupy a seat.*
  *Children aged 5 and under travel free **provided/as long as/on condition that** they do not occupy a seat.*

Even if

- *Even if* can also be used in conditional sentences to emphasize *if*:

  ***Even if** we started the project tomorrow, we would not complete it in time.*

If + should

- *If* + *should* emphasizes that an event is not very likely (formal and mainly used in written English):

  *If the expedition **should** discover large amounts of water on the Moon, then the future of space exploration will be different.*

If + were to

- This is often used in writing which speculates about the future:
  ***If** the government **were to** raise taxes, they would certainly lose votes.*

If (it) were/was not for, if it hadn't been for

- This describes how one event depends on another:
  ***If it were not for** the UN, the situation would be worse.*
  ***If it hadn't been for** Hubble, we would not have known that the universe was expanding.*

➜ SEE ALSO
Grammar 13: Conditionals 1

This unit includes contrasts with the conditionals presented in Grammar 13.

1 Underline the most suitable verb form in each sentence.

1 According to a police spokesperson, the weather was so bad yesterday that if they *don't close/hadn't closed/didn't close* the motorway it *will become/would have become/would become* blocked with abandoned cars.
2 If the government *didn't make/hadn't made/doesn't make* a decision soon about a change in the law, then innocent people *would continue/would have continued/will continue* to pay unnecessarily large fines.
3 The project *finished/would have finished* on time if it *wasn't/hadn't been* for industrial action by building workers, which caused a two week delay.
4 We *will certainly carry on/would certainly have carried on/would certainly carry on* with the rescue operation if there *is/had been/were* any chance of finding more survivors, but as far as we knew there was nobody left alive in the area.
5 Even if the school *hadn't collapsed/collapses/didn't collapse* in last month's earthquake, it *would have been/will be/would be* too badly damaged to be used again.
6 In the unlikely event that the city *had flooded/floods/flooded* completely at some point in the future, we *would have had to/have to/would have to* consider evacuating the whole population.
7 The building *will suffer/suffers/would suffer* fewer burglaries if all residents *make/had made/made* sure that the front door remained securely locked at all times, but the caretaker has reported finding it open on numerous occasions. Please lock the door in future!
8 If the engineers *follow/followed/had followed* their instructions, they *will notice/would notice/would have noticed* the cracks in the rails during the inspection of 14th April, and the accident *can be/could be/could have been* avoided.

2 Complete the text by writing a suitable form of the verb in brackets in each space.

History - What if?

Text A

What (1) ...would have happened... (happen) if the Persians (2) .... (successfully invade) the Greek mainland in 490 BC, and (3) .... (conquer) the whole of Greece? Some historians believe that even if the Persians (4) .... (beat) the Athenians at Marathon, they (5) .... (find) it extremely difficult to overcome all resistance in Greece. The Spartans (6) .... (present) a considerable problem, though a political solution (7) .... (might emerge) under which the Greek states accepted the Persian king as their 'ruler', but kept most of their independence.

Text B

Roman military occupation (8) .... (not enjoy) such success, and in some places (9) .... (prove) almost impossible, without the skill of Roman engineers. If the system of Roman roads (10) .... (exist), the movement of troops from one province to another (11) .... (not proceed) with such speed and order.

Text C

Some military historians argue that the First World War (12) .... (end) in a German victory if the USA (13) .... (not enter) the war in 1917. Historians also speculate about what (14) .... (happen) if the Bolshevik revolution (15) .... (not take place) in Russia in the same year. If there (16) .... (be) no revolution, a large German force (17) .... (remain) on the Eastern front, and these valuable reinforcements (18) .... (not be) available for transfer to the West.

3 Write a new sentence with a similar meaning to the first sentence, containing an impossible past condition with *might have*.

1. The company didn't make a profit, so it reduced its workforce.
   If the company had made a profit it might not have reduced its workforce.
2. Rescue teams failed to arrive in time and very few people were rescued.
   ....
3. The government were unprepared for a heatwave, and there was a shortage of water.
   ....
4. The people in the town weren't very friendly, so we didn't stay there long.
   ....
5. We had problems with our computer network so we didn't finish the project on time.
   ....
6. The banks didn't properly understand what they were investing in, so they couldn't avoid the financial crisis.
   ....
7. Neither side was willing to negotiate and the dispute dragged on for months.
   ....
8. The maintenance staff failed to carry out routine checks and a breakdown occurred.
   ....
9. The patient was not given the correct dosage of medication and she did not survive.
   ....
10. An engineer spotted the cracks in the wing and prevented a possible crash.
    ....

4 Complete the sentences using information from the texts.

Business reports

Report A

The company is making progress even though the difficult economic climate last year saw the company on the edge of bankruptcy. It was only after a loan from National Bank, followed by a programme of restructuring that we were able to continue. Assuming that the economic climate does not worsen, we expect to make a profit in the coming year.

1 If the bank hadn't lent the company some money..., the company would not be..... in business now.
2 If it hadn't been for.........................., the company .... bankrupt last year.
3 As long as........................., the company...a profit.

Report B

The rise in the price of oil has boosted company profits this year. Profits are 21% higher than in the previous year, when severe weather in the North Sea forced us to cut production for two weeks. The situation was made more serious after the helicopter crash in November which claimed the lives of sixteen oil workers. This was entirely the result of the bad weather conditions.

4 If it.., company profits .... so much this year.
5 If it hadn't................................., production....................................for two weeks.
6 The situation.......................................if there....................................in November.
7 If ....so bad, ...happened.

Report C

The industrial action called by the Postal Workers Union has now ended. A union representative blamed the strike on the management's unwillingness to negotiate. According to the union, the management's refusal to discuss pensions was largely responsible for the decision to strike. The representative added: 'More responsible behaviour on the part of the management will prevent any future calls for strike action.'

8 If the management...............................with the union, the strike.................. necessary.
9 If the management.............................to discuss pensions, the union.......................to strike.
10 The representative added: 'Provided.. responsibly, there ....in future.'

5 Write a new sentence with a similar meaning to the first sentence, using the word in bold. Do not change the word given.

1 We could catch an earlier train but we still wouldn't arrive before 6.00.
even
Even if we caught an earlier train we still wouldn't arrive before 6.00.

2 If you reconsider our offer, I think you might change your mind.
were
....

3 Thanks to the security officer, the robbery did not succeed.
hadn't
....

4 If you don't use the security code, the computer won't work.
otherwise
....

5 Janet Ward didn't take the job so she isn't head of the company.
had
....

6 Researchers may access this material only if they do not use it for commercial purposes.
condition
....

7 Without government grants many students would be unable to study.
were
....

6 Complete the text by writing a suitable word in each space.

Metal detecting

Many archaeological discoveries (1) ...would..... not be made if it (2) .... for the work of amateur metal detector enthusiasts. In many countries, metal detecting is illegal, and the authorities argue that if they (3) .... to allow unrestricted use of detectors, many antiquities (4) .... be stolen. It is certainly the case that the illegal trade in ancient coins and precious objects (5) .... probably not exist if it were (6) .... for illegal detecting. However, in the UK detecting is allowed, (7) .... that the user has permission from the landowner, and on (8) .... that any finds are reported to local museums. There is then a legal inquiry. Detectorists are usually allowed to keep everyday objects, (9) .... they are of precious metal such as gold or silver. In this case, they belong to the authorities, but the finder and the landowner (10) .... receive shares of the value. The recent discovery in the UK of the Staffordshire Hoard, important gold objects dating from the 7th century and valued at £3.285 million, would not (11) .... been found (12) .... it hadn't been for the efforts of a local metal detector.

15

GRAMMAR

Practice 5

1 Complete the suggestions for saving energy using the information in the text and pie chart.

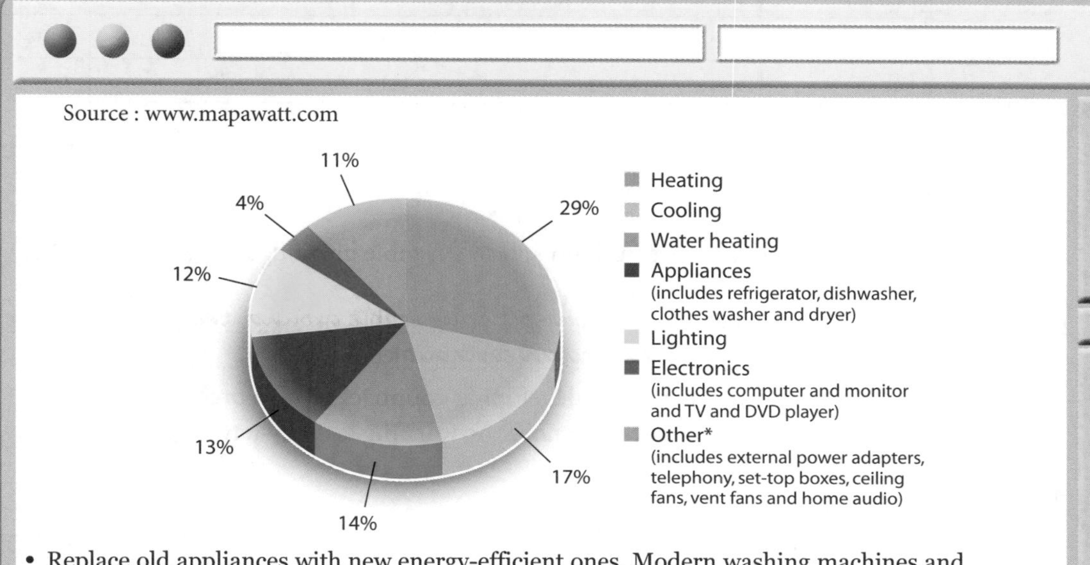

- Replace old appliances with new energy-efficient ones. Modern washing machines and fridges are up to 50% more efficient.
- Installing a home energy monitor helps you see how much energy you are using minute by minute and encourages you to save energy.
- A poorly insulated roof allows up to 30% of the heat in your house to escape.
- A washing machine uses 90% of its energy to heat water, so try using cold only.
- Double-glazed windows are 40% more efficient than conventional windows, so fitting them will keep you warmer and save money.
- Bringing your heating system up to date by fitting a new boiler lowers bills by as much as 15%.
- Leaving appliances on standby is wasteful as many appliances consume 25% of their energy when in this state.
- Setting the thermostat of your heating system too high wastes up to 20% of your heating bill.
- Swapping your old conventional light bulbs for energy-saving bulbs means cheaper and longer-lasting lighting.

1 If you always turn off appliances on standby, you'll save 25% of the energy they use.
2 If you replace ....
3 If you install ....
4 If you use ....
5 If you fit ....
6 If you insulate ....
7 If you bring ....
8 If you turn down ....
9 If you swap ....

2 Rewrite each sentence or pair of sentences as an *If* ... sentence, so that it keeps the same meaning.

Date	Place	Magnitude (Richter scale)	Fatalities
Jan 3rd	Solomon Islands	7.2	0
Jan 10th	Offshore California, USA	6.5	0
Jan 12th	Haiti	7.0	233,000+
Feb 26th	Ryukyu Islands, Japan	7.0	0
Feb 27th	Chile	8.8	800+
Feb 27th	Salta, Argentina	6.1	2
March 4th	Taiwan	6.4	0
2010 Earthquakes			

1 Some houses are built on soft or unstable ground. These are more likely to collapse during an earthquake.
If *houses are built on soft or unstable ground, they are more likely to collapse during an earthquake.*

2 You can ask people in developing countries to take precautions against earthquakes, but they ignore the warning, as they have their daily survival to worry about.
If ....

3 People don't know that an area is situated near a major fault, and so they build their towns and cities there.
If ....

4 Governments sometimes introduce building regulations in earthquake prone areas, and this can reduce fatalities in the event of an earthquake.
If ....

5 In California, building regulations were strictly enforced. In recent earthquakes not many buildings were damaged, and there were few casualties.
In California, if..........

6 Governments don't always make people aware of the dangers of earthquakes, or train them what to do in an emergency, so casualties are often greater than they need be.
If ....

7 People in the Pacific in December 2004 did not know about the effects of tsunamis, so there were many casualties.
If ....

8 There was no tsunami early warning system then, as there is now, so people did not have the chance to move to higher ground.
If ....

9 There was no warning before the Haiti earthquake in 2010. In any case, it might not have made a difference to the number of casualties, as there would not have been enough time to evacuate people.
Even if ....

10 Scientists don't have the same financial and intellectual resources to use in places like Indonesia and Pakistan as are used in the USA or Japan, so they are not able to minimize the effects of more earthquakes.
If ....

16

GRAMMAR

Modals 1

Modal verbs

Modal verbs such as *can, could, might, must*, etc are used with another verb for ideas such as ability, possibility, certainty and obligation. Modal verbs are followed by the infinitive without *to*. They do not have *-s*, *-ing*, or *-ed* forms. They form negatives with *not*, and questions by putting the modal in front of the subject:

*Nobody **can predict** exactly what will happen.*
*It **must be** difficult.*
*The figures **might not be** correct.*
***Could** you **give** me an example?*

These units also include examples of semi-modals, which have some of these characteristics but not all (eg *need*), and some ordinary verbs which have the same meaning as some modal verbs (eg *have to, be able to*).

As modals have more than one meaning they are grouped here according to the way they are used. Other non-modal ways of expressing similar meanings are included. See Grammar 17 for ability, obligation, necessity and recommentation.

Assuming that something is true

- We use *will/won't* and *would* to show that we assume something is true:
  *Most of you **will know** what I am talking about.*
  *You **won't know** the answer.*
  *Not many people **would agree** with you.*
  *That solution **wouldn't work**.*

Being certain that something will happen

- We use *can* and *cannot,* to show a certain belief that something will happen or not happen, often with an explanation of the circumstances:
  *The situation **can** only **improve** in the future.*
  *The government **cannot go on raising** taxes without political repercussions.*

- We use *must* to show we believe that something will happen. A negative is not possible:
  *Directors of companies **must** eventually **recognize** that this is uneconomic.*

Being certain about something in the present

- We use *must* to assert that we believe something is true. It is very common with *be*:
  *This **must be** the answer. Jim **must have** the tickets.*

- We use *can't* to assert that something is not true, very commonly with *be*:
  *This **can't be** the right house.*

- We use *surely* to emphasize that we can't believe what has happened:
  *Surely they **can't live** in a house like that!*

Being certain about something in the past

- For the past we use *must*, *can't* and *couldn't* with the past infinitive *have done*:
  They ***must have taken*** *a wrong turning.*
  You ***can't/couldn't have seen*** *Ann. She's on holiday in Canada at the moment.*

Possibility and uncertainty

- We use *can* and *could* for statements about what is generally possible:
  This type of machine ***can be*** *very inefficient.* (it is sometimes, but not always)

- We use *could* to refer to past possible situations:
  In those days, students ***could depend on*** *a government grant.*

- *May, might* and *could* describe what is possible in particular situations. They are common with *be*:
  This ***may/might/could be*** *the best solution to the problem.*
  The car won't start. The battery ***may/might/could be*** *dead.*

- We can add *well* or *just* between *may/might/could be* and the verb to emphasize the possibility. *Just* makes the possibility less likely:
  This ***may/might/could well be*** *the solution.* (perhaps it's possible)
  This plan ***may/might/could just work!*** (it's unlikely, but possible)

- We use *could easily* to emphasize a possibility:
  There ***could easily be*** *a more serious accident in the future.*

- We use *could always* to point out a possible choice or decision:
  The government ***could always ban*** *the use of plastic bags entirely.*

- We use *may not* and *might not* for negative possibilities. We cannot use *could not* for this meaning:
  I ***may/might not be*** *here tomorrow.*
  I ***may/might not have*** *time to come.*

- We use *may as well* and *might as well* to say that there is no reason for not doing something, usually because we are disappointed something else has not happened:
  Supporting human life on the moon would be dangerous and expensive and so we ***might as well abandon*** *the idea of a moon space station.*

Past possibility and uncertainty

- We use *may have done, might have done*, and *could have done* for possible events in the past:
  The director hasn't arrived yet. She ***may/might/could have missed*** *the train.*

- The negative forms are *may not have done, might not have done*. We cannot use *could not have done* with this meaning:
  Perhaps she's still at home. She ***may not have got*** *our message.*

Expectation

- We use *should* and *ought to* when we describe something we think is probably true, or has failed to happen, especially with *be*:

  There ***ought to be*** *an exit at the end of this corridor.* (I think there is)
  There ***should be*** *an exit here!* (there isn't)

- *Should have* and *ought to have* describe what we believe has failed to happen, or expect has probably happened:

  They ***should have found*** *an answer by now.* (they haven't)
  The plane ***ought to have*** *landed.* (I expect it has)

Annoyance or shock

- We use *might have* and *could have* to show annoyance, when someone fails to do something we feel they should have done:

  You ***might have told*** *me the meeting was cancelled! I went all the way there for nothing!*

- We use *might have* and *could have* when we are shocked because something nearly happened:

  That was a lucky escape. You ***could have fallen*** *down the stairs.*

Assuming something is true about the past

- We use *will/won't have done* and *would have done* to assume something is true about the past:

  You ***won't have heard*** *the news.*
  Nobody ***would have had*** *a chance.*

Be bound to, be sure to, be certain to

- When we need to describe a future event which we are sure will happen, we use the non-modal forms *be bound to, be sure to* or *be certain to*:

  Knowing Peter, he is ***bound to make*** *the wrong decision.*
  The findings of the report ***are sure to be*** *controversial.*

→ SEE ALSO
Grammar 17: Modals 2

1 Underline the most suitable modal verb form in each sentence.

1 The average temperature on Earth *can increase/may increase/must increase* by as much as 7°C by the end of the 21st century.
2 Governments *cannot assume /could not assume /might not assume* that the laws they make will always be enforced.
3 The crisis *must have been/should have been/could have been* much worse, but fortunately the authorities acted in time.
4 Their slogan was 'Things *should only get/can only get/must only get* better'.
5 We're running out of time, I'm afraid. It *can be/must be/should be* nearly three o'clock by now.
6 You won't have to wait for long. There *should be/must be/may be* another bus along in about fifteen minutes, with any luck.
7 You could try looking for the book in that secondhand shop. They *might have/must have/ought to have* a copy, I suppose.
8 The burglars *can't have got in/must have got in/might have got in* through the window. It's still locked.
9 Hello! You *ought to be/must be/could be* Diane Black. Pleased to meet you.
10 There's no point waiting here any longer. We *could as well/should as well/might as well* go home.

2 Choose the answer (A, B or C) that best explains the meaning of each sentence.

1 They can't have realized what would happen in that case.
A Perhaps they didn't realize.
B We can be sure they didn't realize. ✓
C They were not allowed to realize.

2 There can't be two stations with exactly the same name!
A I suppose it's possible.
B I'm certain there are.
C I'm sure there aren't.

3 New technology might provide a solution to these problems.
A I'm sure it will.
B I suppose it's possible.
C It's important to do this.

4 You could have ended up in serious difficulties.
A You didn't do this.
B You did this.
C You wanted to do this.

5 Somebody must know the truth about this matter.
A It's important to do this.
B I suppose it's possible.
C I'm sure this is true.

6 Someone might have started the fire deliberately.
A I suppose it's possible.
B Luckily it didn't happen.
C We know this is true.

3 Write a new sentence with a similar meaning to the first sentence, using the word in bold. Do not change the word given.

1 I'm sure this isn't the way to the city centre.
can't
This can't be the way to the city centre.

2 It's possible that the director won't attend the meeting.
may
....

3 I wish you had told me that the library always closes on Fridays.
might
....

4 It seems certain that the plane struck a flight of birds.
must
....

5 That is possibly why things have been going wrong.
could
....

6 We expect to get some early results by the end of the week.
should
....

7 It's possible that they took the wrong road in the dark.
might
....

8 Be more careful! You nearly gave yourself an electric shock!
could
....

9 I'm sure you are very proud of your daughter's achievements.
must
....

10 I'm sure there will be a lot of traffic on the motorway.
bound
....

4 Complete each sentence with a modal, using the verb in CAPITALS.

1 Are you all right? You could have hurt yourself! HURT
2 Never mind. I suppose things .... IMPROVE
3 Try phoning again .They .... home by now. ARRIVE
4 The door is open. Someone .... to lock it. FORGET
5 Is that really true? Surely they .... more than that! PAY
6 You.............................. me! Now I'm going to be late for work! WAKE
7 I'll try my best but I .... there before six. GET
8 I don't know where it is. I suppose I .... it on the train. LEAVE
9 You'd better take an umbrella because it .... RAIN
10 Do you know, I think you .... the answer. FIND

5 Write ten statements containing a modal form based on the numbered parts in bold.

The Egyptian pyramids

Archaeologists, and others, continue to speculate about the building methods used in the construction of Egyptian pyramids, 138 of which have been discovered so far, built over a thousand year period. **(1) So the first thing we can say with some confidence is that the builders did not construct all the pyramids in the same way or for the same reason.** All theories of their construction **(2) assume that a large labour force dragged huge blocks of stone over long distances** from the quarries where they were cut. **(3) It was originally assumed that slaves performed these tasks**, but recent discoveries suggest **(4) skilled workers probably worked for a salary, or as a way of paying their taxes.** As to the exact methods of construction used, experts are still in disagreement. There is an illustration on a tomb showing a large group of men hauling a giant statue on a sledge. **(5) It is thought that this statue possibly weighed 60 tonnes**, and from these estimated figures, experts have calculated that **(6) it was possible for eight to ten workers to move a typical stone building block** weighing about 2.5 tonnes. During construction the gaps between the stones were filled with gypsum mortar which had to be heated. **(7) We can be sure that the workers used large amounts of wood to do this**, and some experts **(8) are certain that eventually a shortage of wood restricted pyramid construction**. Whatever the precise details of construction, **(9) we can be sure that the ancient Egyptians possessed great organizational skill**, as construction projects required thousands of workers over lengthy periods. Along with advanced engineering skills, **(10) the mathematical knowledge of the builders of the pyramids was certainly considerable.**

1 *The builders can't have constructed all the pyramids in the same way or for the same reason.*
2 ....
3 ....
4 ....
5 ....
6 ....
7 ....
8 ....
9 ....
10 ....

17

GRAMMAR

Modals 2

See Grammar 16 for an overview of modal verbs.

Ability: *can, be able, could*

- *Can, could, be able to* are used for ability. *Be able to* (non-modal) emphasizes that a difficulty has been overcome:
  *Jane **can speak** Mandarin.*
  *Harry **can't walk** at the moment, but he **is able to get around** in a wheelchair.*

- *Will/won't be able to* and *have been able to* are used as tenses of *can*:
  I'll be able to finish.
  *We **haven't been able to decide** yet.*
  *They **weren't able to finish** the project on time.*

- *Could* is used for for past ability. *Was/were able to* describes having the ability and doing something successfully:
  *Jane **could speak** three languages at the age of ten.*
  *I lost control of the car, but luckily I **was able to stop** safely.*

Obligation: *must, have to, be to*

- *Must* is used for:
  A necessary action:
  *You **must turn** it off after use.*
  An order:
  *You **must start** now!*
  Describing a duty:
  *Everyone **must recycle** as much as possible.*
  A strong recommendation:
  *You really **must go** and see that film.*
  Emphasizing an intention:
  *I **must phone** Helen next week.*

- *Have to/Has to* (non modal) is used for:
  A necessary action:
  *We **have to be** there by six.*
  A rule:
  *We **have to wear** a uniform at our school.*

- In many contexts, *must* or *have to* are both possible. Some speakers may use *have to* because it is longer and allows more emphasis:
  *You **have to start** now!*
  *Everyone **has to recycle** as much as possible.*

- *Have/has got to* can be used informally instead of *have to*:
  *We **have got to be** there by six.*

- *Must not* is used for what is not allowed:
  *You **must not remove** any equipment from the laboratory.*

- *Do not have to* is used for what is not necessary:
  *Our department **doesn't have to provide** this service.*

- *Had to, didn't have to* are used as a past forms of *must*:
  *There was a transport strike so we **had to cancel** the meeting.*
  *In the end the company **didn't have to reduce** the workforce.*

- *Be to* (non-modal)
  This is a formal way of saying *must* in instructions:
  *All visitors **are to wait** here.*
  *You **are not to begin** until instructed to do so.*

Obligation or necessity: *need, need to*

- *Need* is a modal verb, so it has no third person form. It is used mainly in questions and negatives. The meaning is similar to *have to*:
  *According to the law, the minister **need not explain** his reasons.*
  *According to the law, the minister **doesn't have to explain** his reasons.*

- *Need to* is a normal verb:
  *The director **needs to be told** about this matter.*
  ***Do** we really **need to go through** the details again?*

- *Didn't need to* describes a past situation, where something was not necessary, so it was not done:
  *The first meeting was a success, so we **didn't need to hold** a second one.*

- *Needn't have done* describes a past situation, where something happened or was done, but it was not necessary:
  *I **needn't have gone** so early to the office. The meeting was cancelled.*

It + *be* + adjective + *that*

- Adjectives such as *necessary, important, vital, crucial, essential* are also used to show what is important or necessary, instead of using *must/have to/need*:
  *You **must turn** it off after use.*
  ***It is vital that** you **turn** it off after use.*

- The subjunctive form of the verb (without -*s* form) or the usual third person -*s* form can be used in formal writing:
  ***It is important that** the meeting **come/comes** to a decision.*

Recommendation: *should, ought to, had better*

- *Should/shouldn't* and *ought to/ought not to* are used when we think something is a good idea, or not a good idea, or when we say what we think is the right thing to do:
  More people ***should cycle*** *to work.*
  They ***shouldn't drive*** *everywhere.*
  I think you ***ought to ask*** *the director for some advice.*
  There is no difference between *should* and *ought to*. In formal writing, *should* is a polite form of *must*:
  All students ***should report*** *to the examination room by 8.30.*
  You ***should not write*** *your name at the top of the letter.*

- *Should have/shouldn't have* and *ought to have/ought not to have* are used when we think someone has made a mistake or done something wrong in the past.
  You ***ought to have put*** *your valuables in the safe.* (you didn't do it)
  You ***shouldn't have left*** *your hotel room unlocked.* (you did do it)

- *Had better (not)* (non-modal) is used to make a recommendation, when we say what we think is the right thing to do. Note that this is often contracted to *you'd better*, etc:
  I think ***you'd better go*** *to the doctor. You look terrible.*

➜ SEE ALSO
Grammar 16: Modals 1

IELTS LANGUAGE PRACTICE

1 <u>Underline</u> the most suitable verb form in each sentence. In some cases more than one form is possible.

1 I *couldn't finish*/*<u>haven't been able to finish</u>*/*cannot finish* my project yet.
2 Visitors *are not to smoke*/*don't have to smoke*/*needn't smoke* anywhere in the hospital.
3 You *shouldn't pay*/*mustn't pay*/*don't have to pay* the bill until the end of the month.
4 It's not far by car, but I think *we must start*/*we'd better start*/*we have to start* now just in case the traffic is bad.
5 I thought I was going to miss the plane, but I *needn't have worried*/*didn't need to worry*/*shouldn't have worried*, because the departure was delayed.
6 You *shouldn't study*/*needn't study*/*don't have to study* all night. You're bound to feel terrible the next morning.
7 Tina left the lecture early because she *had to go*/*must go*/*should have gone* to the doctor's.
8 It's your own fault. You *had better not leave*/*didn't have to leave*/*shouldn't have left* your bike unlocked.
9 At the age of six, Tom *had to swim*/*could swim*/*should have swum* five hundred metres.
10 Warning. You *must not take*/*are not to take*/*ought not to take* aspirin while you are taking this medication, as this may cause serious side effects.

2 Complete each sentence by writing a suitable modal form in each space. More than one answer may be possible.

1 Rather than simply writing down the answer in the examination, you ...should... explain the method by which it is obtained.
2 The government previously expressed concern that this law would have the opposite effect, but they .... worried.
3 So far scientists have not .... to successfully devise a mechanism for accurately forecasting earthquakes.
4 The finance minister .... find an extra £76 billion to balance the books – £2400 for every family in Britain.
5 Fortunately in March it began to rain, and so the authorities .... implement the water rationing scheme.
6 This has been an interesting discussion, but I think we .... move on to something else now.
7 Here are five email tips that everyone .... follow.
8 The new management .... make wholesale changes, but some adjustments were necessary.
9 All students .... provide the telephone number of a contact person.
10 For schools to be successful in this new role, they really .... become full partners in the overall community.

3 Write a new sentence with a similar meaning to the first sentence, using the word in bold. Do not change the word given.

1 It's not a good idea to drink too much coffee.
shouldn't
You shouldn't drink too much coffee.

2 There is plenty of food in the fridge so there's no need to go shopping.
have
....

3 If you want to hire a car a full driving licence is required.
must
....

4 All visitors must report to reception.
are
....

5 It was a mistake for us to travel there by bus.
have
....

6 I can give you more detailed information at the end of the week.
be
....

7 The government must call an election as soon as possible.
important
....

8 If I were you, I'd try to relax for a few days.
better
....

4 Write a new sentence with a similar meaning to the first sentence, using a form of the words in bold.

1 There is surely a better way of encouraging people to recycle more.
have to
There has to be a better way of encouraging .... people to recycle more.

2 It's really important for the government to introduce a scheme that everyone can understand.
must
.... everyone can understand.

3 The prosecutor made a mistake in charging the defendant with murder.
should
.... the defendant with murder.

4 If the management wants a quick solution, then it had better not delay its decision.
ought
If the management wants a quick solution, ...

5 Such injuries are not necessarily a problem provided they are treated promptly.
need
.... they are treated promptly.

5 Complete the text by writing a modal form of the verbs in brackets in each space.

This was an accident that (1) ..*should not have happened*.. (happen). According to our safety guidelines, there (2) .... (be) a qualified instructor with each group, and the group (3) .... (receive) basic safety training before the trip begins. In this case, time was short and the instructor (4) .... (complete) the initial training before the group started the mountain trek. The weather was good, and the instructor felt that he (5) .... (take) any special precautions. However, the group (6) .... (set out).

6 Complete the text by writing a phrase from the box in each space.

~~had to wait~~	needn't have bothered	are only able to	has to monitor
should this be allowed	don't have to be	must not violate	are able to watch
have to think again	should we be	should watch	

Big Brother is watching you

Whereas once the police (1) ..*had to wait*.. before someone reported a crime to them, nowadays CCTV operators (2) .... crimes as they happen. There are almost three million CCTV cameras in Britain, and you (3) .... the owner of a security company to know that it is a growth business. But does CCTV work? Some experts believe that we (4) .... to install so many cameras, as they only reduce a small percentage of crimes – mainly against property. There may be millions of cameras, but in order to make CCTV effective, somebody (5) .... what is happening on the screens. Skilled operators (6) .... all the screens all the time, but in reality, most operators (7) .... watch one screen with concentration for about 20 minutes. When the system is not being used for a particular purpose, in co-ordination with a police operation for example, (8) .... worried that we are all being watched for no reason? This issue extends into questions of personal privacy. Many local councils monitor streets and public places, but (9) .... ? Councils claim that they use CCTV responsibly, but in a recent case where footage was shown on TV, the person filmed made objections. The European Court of Human Rights later ruled that the use of CCTV (10) .... the individual's right to privacy. Perhaps we (11) .... whether we prefer to be a little bit safer – or free to walk along the street without being watched.

18

GRAMMAR

Practice 6

1 Complete the text using a suitable modal form of the verb in brackets in each space.

We (1) ....might suppose.... (suppose) that experts in climate analysis (2) .... (know) what is happening to the climate, but there is a certain amount of disagreement among them. In order to make scientific predictions, scientists (3) .... (use) mathematical models called 'climate models'. These use mathematical techniques to simulate the way that the atmosphere, the oceans, the surface of the earth and the ice caps interact with one another. They (4) .... (use) to make projections of climate change, in particular to predict what the temperature (5) .... (be) in the future. Such models (6) .... (be) quite simple or more complex, and so the results probably (7) .... (agree) exactly. There are so many different kinds of model, that we (8) .... (be) sure that any one prediction is the most accurate. Different approaches (9) .... (produce) different results. In every case (10) .... (take) into account the differences in aim, and use of data, in each model. However, with an issue so important as climate change, it is vital that there (11) .... (be) an accurate figure available. In 2003, Climateprediction.net (CPDN) started a project running hundreds of thousands of different models. In order to do this, they (12) .... (link) thousands of personal computers worldwide. The 2005 results suggest that the highest temperature change (13) .... (be) as much as 11°C, though some experts have said that this figure (14) .... (be) inaccurate. So it seems that we (15) .... (wait) for the final word on climate change. Projections are perhaps just too complex to be totally reliable.

2 Study the leaflet and make recommendations to encourage people to reduce carbon emissions. Use a modal form of the verbs, and make any other necessary changes. More than one answer is possible in each sentence.

Dealing with Global Warming

Improve … Promote … Provide … Introduce … Discourage … Ban …

DO YOU …

... cycle to work, or are the roads too dangerous?

... use public transport , or is it too expensive?

... own a powerful 4x4 vehicle?

... work from home?

... have free car parking at work?

... use disposable batteries?

... receive environmental education in schools?

... buy water in plastic bottles?

... have enough information about the energy efficiency of household products?

... own an electric or non-polluting vehicle?

... take your children to school by car?

... think that companies that have cut carbon emissions get any recognition?

1 The government should *improve roads to encourage bicycle use.*
2 ……
3 ……
4 ……
5 ……
6 ……
7 ……
8 ……
9 ……
10 ……
11 ……
12 ……

3 The phrases in brackets use expressions used to make predictions. Match each one with an expression (a–l).

a could happen
b it could well be
c might have to
d what might be involved
e are bound to
f may well take place
g there could be
h will almost certainly
i could well be a consequence
j might happen to
k they could well suffer from
l will probably

Social implications of climate change

If the climate does get much warmer, what (1) ...*a*..... (are the possible consequences)? While scientists generally restrict their predictions to physical details, and outline what changes of climate (2) .... (are expected to occur) over the next century, other experts have begun to look further at (3) .... (the implications) for human society in general. Rising temperatures (4) .... (are sure to) affect the environment, and other effects (5) .... (are very likely to) follow, especially since the poorest countries (6) .... (are in line to) suffer most. So what exactly (7) .... (lies in store for) the people of the future? First, (8) .... (there is the chance of) poor health, as disease-carrying insects spread into previously immune areas, and fresh food becomes more expensive, or hard to find. Secondly, (9) .... (there is every likelihood) that the impact of increased temperatures on water supplies and agriculture will lead to drought and famine. More people (10) .... (will probably be forced to) migrate to escape worsening poverty. Military conflict (11) .... (is predicted as a result), which would see countries fighting over water rights or to protect their territory. In general, (12) .... (there is the prospect of) social unrest and increased competition for resources.

19

GRAMMAR

Articles 1

The is usually called the 'definite' article, and *a/an* are usually called 'indefinite' articles. 'Zero article' means that an article is not used.

Context

- When we refer to something we have already mentioned, this second reference is definite:

  First, we measure 50 mls of water. Then we put ***the water*** *into a jar.*

- A noun can be made definite by the details which follow it. This is called 'post-modification':

  I attend Sussex University. I attend ***the University of Sussex****.*

- We refer to some things with definite *the* because they are known from context:

  Jim is in ***the lab****.* (the one we all work in)
  Give me ***the keys****, please.* (those ones on the table)

Giving examples

- An instrument or an example of something uses *a/an*:

  A barometer *is used to measure air pressure.*

- We use the zero article with plurals and uncountables when they are used as examples:

  Economists *are divided on this issue.*
  Water *is becoming a scarce resource.*

- We use *the* when these general references are made specific:

  The economists *who believe this put forward powerful arguments.*
  The water *in this glass tastes bitter.*

- We use *a/an* with one of a class of things or people:

  Olga is ***a Russian****.*
  Jan is ***a biologist***
  This is ***an electromagnet****.*

- We use *a/an* with one of a set of named things:

  This is ***a Matisse****.* (a work of art)

- We use *the* with a singular noun to describe a class of things:

  The electric car *is the vehicle of the future.*
  The tiger *is in danger of extinction.*

Ideas

- We use zero article with abstract ideas:
  In some respects, ***war*** *has no winners and losers.*

- We use *the* when an abstract noun is made specific by what comes after it:
  The war *between the North and the South continued for four years.*

Numbers and measurement

- We use *a/an* (or *per*) for rates and speeds:
  A skydiver falls at the rate of approximately ***195 kms an hour****.*
  It costs over ***€5 million a year*** *to run the project.*

- We use *a/an* for large numbers, fractions with singular nouns, weights and distances:
  a *hundred*   ***a*** *million*   ***a*** *third*   ***a*** *fifth*
  two and ***a*** *half*   ***a*** *kilo*   ***a*** *metre and a half*

- Fractions with plurals have zero article:
  We are already ***two thirds*** *of the way there.*

People

- Names of people have zero article but can be made definite:
  Angela Thomson runs the Biology Department.
  Is she ***the*** *Angela Thomson who used to work in Leeds?*

- We can use *a/an* with names when we mean 'a person called ...':
  Is there ***an*** *Angela Thomson staying here?*

- We use *the* with the names of specific groups of people:
  the *Liberal Democrats* (the party we know about)

- However, if the group is more general we use zero article:
  Euro MPs *tend to claim large sums of money for expenses.*
  Manchester United *supporters are usually well-behaved.*

- Names of music groups vary a great deal, and may not fit general rules:
  The *White Stripes*
  Radiohead

- Many groups of people are described by *the + singular adjective*:
  the *unemployed*
  the *dead*

Cities, towns, streets, places

- We use zero article with proper names, but use *the* if there is post-modification with *of*:
  Alan lives in ***North Road*** *in London in an area called Highbury.*
  Have you been to ***the Museum of Childhood****?*

- We use *the* with the names of shops and places with a general reference:
  *at **the** cinema/**the** supermarket/in **the** garden/in **the** mountains/at **the** beach*
- Other places vary. If they begin with the name of a place or person, then they tend to use zero article:
  London Bridge *Waterloo Station* *Madame Tussaud's*
  (But: ***the** London Eye*)
  Otherwise they use *the*:
  ***the** Golden Gate Bridge* ***the** Hard Rock Café* ***the** Odeon Cinema*
- Note that a place name can also be used as an adjective, in which case we can use *the*:
  ***The Paris** rush hour can cause long delays.*

Unique objects

- We use *the* with some familiar objects when we think of them as the only one:
  ***The sun** was setting over the sea. **The moon** rose into the sky.*
- We use *a/an* with *a headache, a cold*, etc.
  *Have you got **a** cold/**a** headache/**a** toothache/**an** earache?*
- Most illness words use zero article:
  I've got flu. *She's suffering from appendicitis.*

Exclamations

- We use *a/an* in the expressions *What a ...! such a ...!*
  ***What a** huge animal!*
  ***What an** incredible result!*
- We use *such a/an* ... for emphasis with singular nouns:
  *Newton was **such a** great **man**!*

➔ SEE ALSO
Grammar 20: Articles

This unit also contains general practice in the use of articles.

1 Underline the most suitable options. A dash (–) means that no article is included.

1 *An/The/–* agronomist is *an/the/–* expert in *an/the/–* agricultural sciences.
2 *An/The/–* agreement of 1994 finally brought *a/the/–* peace to *an/the/–* eastern region.
3 In *an/the/–* engineering, *a/–* foundation is *a/–* structure that transfers *the/–* loads to *the/–* ground.
4 *The/–* dolphins are *the/–* marine mammals that are closely related to the/– whales and *the/–* porpoises.
5 *The/–* murder, as defined in *the/–* common law countries, is *an/the* unlawful killing of another human being with *the/–* intent.
6 In *an/–* election, *a/–* population chooses *an /–* individual to hold *the/–* public office.
7 *A/The/–* vacuum gauge is used to measure *a/the/–* pressure in *a/the/–* vacuum.
8 *A/The/–* term 'dialect' can mean *a/the/–* language of *a/the/–* particular group of *a/the/–* speakers in *a/the/–* particular society.
9 In *an/the/–* economics, *a/the/–* recession is *a/the/–* general slowdown in *a/the/–* economic activity over *a/the/–* period of *a/the/–* time.
10 *A/The/–* subliminal message is *a/the/–* signal or message designed to pass below *a/the/–* normal limits of *a/the/–* perception.

2 Write a new sentence with a similar meaning to the first sentence and containing the words in bold.

1 Giorgio comes from Italy.
an
Giorgio is an Italian.

2 Does someone called Jane Smith live here?
a
....

3 My head is aching.
a
....

4 This painting is by Renoir.
a
....

5 Maria has been studying French wines.
the
....

6 Elephants are herbivores.
the
....

7 The head of the bank has an annual income of over £10 million.
a
....

3 Complete each short text by writing *a/an, the* or – (no article) in each space.

Dieting and writing

In (1) ..a.. study published in 2008 in (2) ..... American Journal of Preventive Medicine, (3) ..... authors showed that (4) ..... person on (5) ..... diet who keeps (6) ..... daily food diary loses twice as much weight as someone who does not do this. This shows that writing down what is eaten seems to act as (7) ..... encouragement to consume (8) ..... fewer calories.

Deserts

In (9) ..... Arabic, (10) ..... word *sahra* describes (11) ..... flat area without (12) ..... water. In fact, (13) ..... Sahara, (14) ..... largest hot desert in (15) ..... world, is (16) ..... combination of (17) ..... sandy or stony regions and (18) ..... rocky mountains, (19) ..... highest of which, Emi Koussi, has (20) ..... altitude of 3415 metres. It also includes low-lying areas called depressions which are below (21) ..... sea level, such as (22) ..... Qattara depression in (23) ..... Egypt.

4 There are twelve necessary uses of *a/an* and *the* missing from these texts. Write a correction in the space at the side.

Irrigation

Three basic types of irrigation are flood irrigation, drip irrigation 1 The three
and spray irrigation. Names are self-explanatory. In flood irrigation, 2 ....
which is cheap and does not require expensive machinery, water simply 3 ....
flows among the crops, and while this is easily administered system, 4 ....
a lot of water is wasted. Much of it evaporates, either on ground or 5 ....
from the leaves of plants in process known as 'transpiration'. In drip 6 ....
irrigation the water is channelled along plastic pipes with holes in them 7 ....
that are laid along the rows of crops or under the soil close to roots 8 ....
of the plants. Compared to flood irrigation, there is 25% saving of 9 ....
water, but against this saving is cost of the pipes and any necessary 10 ....
equipment. Spray irrigation, where water is sprayed into air and 11 ....
falls on the crops like rain, is even more expensive. Lot of water 12 ....
is blown away, but main advantage of these systems is that they 13 ....
are easily moved, and more modern systems do this automatically. 14 ....

5 **Underline the most suitable options. Sometimes more than one option is possible.**

Work-related stress

Work-related stress is **(1)** *a/the/–* cause of clinical depression and anxiety among **(2)** *a/the/–* young adults, according to **(3)** *a/the/–* new research from Dunedin. **(4)** *A/The/–* study of almost nine hundred 32-year-olds, found that 14% of women and 10% of men experience stress at **(5)** *the/–* work. **(6)** *The/–* findings, published in **(7)** *a/the/–* UK journal Psychological Medicine, come out of the Dunedin Multidisciplinary Health & Development Study at **(8)** *a/the/–* University of Otago, which has followed one thousand Dunedin-born people since their birth in 1972–73.

At **(9)** *a/the/–* age 32, study members were asked about **(10)** *a/the/–* psychological and physical demands of their job, **(11)** *a/the/–* level of control they had in **(12)** *a/the/–* decision-making, and social support structures in their working environment. **(13)** *The/–* women who reported high psychological demands of their job, such as working **(14)** *a/the/–* long hours, working under **(15)** *a/the/–* pressure or without clear direction, were 75% more likely to suffer from **(16)** *a/the/–* clinical depression or general anxiety disorder than women who reported **(17)** *a/the/–* lowest level of psychological job demands. **(18)** *The/–* men in **(19)** *the/–* similar situations were 80% more likely to suffer with **(20)** *the/–* same problems, and men with low levels of social support at work were also found to be at **(21)** *an/the/–* increased risk of depression, anxiety or both. **(22)** *The/–* researchers found that almost half **(23)** *the/–* cases of depression or generalized anxiety disorder newly diagnosed were directly related to workplace stress and high job demands.

6 Underline twelve unnecessary uses of *a/an* and *the*.

Text A

What is the Channel Tunnel Rail Link – CTRL?

The CTRL is the first major new railway to be constructed in the UK for over a century and the first high-speed railway. The 109 km track of the CTRL will stretch from the St. Pancras, central London, to the Channel Tunnel complex at Cheriton in Kent, connecting Britain directly with the Europe's expanding high-speed rail network and significantly reducing a journey times. The CTRL has been built in two separate sections. Section 1 runs for 70km from the Channel Tunnel through the county of Kent. Section 2 links to Section 1 and continues for a further 39km to London. The CTRL will serve the new international stations along its route at Stratford in the east London and Ebbsfleet in Kent and the existing Ashford International station. CTRL will provide the catalyst for the substantial redevelopment around the several stations on the route.

Text B

Subliminal advertising really does work, claim scientists

The phrase 'subliminal advertising' was coined in 1957 by the US market researcher James Vicary, who said he could get the moviegoers to 'drink Coca-Cola®' and 'eat popcorn' by flashing those messages onscreen for such a short time that viewers were unaware.

His claims led to fears that the governments and cults would use the technique to their advantage and it was banned in many countries, including the UK. Vicary later admitted he had fabricated his results. But more than 50 years on the British researchers have shown messages we are not aware of can leave a mark on the brain. A team from University College London, funded by the Wellcome Trust, found that it was particularly good at instilling the negative thoughts. 'There has been much speculation about whether the people can process the emotional information unconsciously, for example pictures, faces and words,' said Professor Nilli Lavie, who led the research.

'We have shown that people can perceive the emotional value of subliminal messages.'

20

GRAMMAR

Articles 2

See Grammar 19 for other uses of *a*, *an* and *zero* article.

Geography

- We use *the* with the names of oceans, seas, rivers, geographical areas:
  *The ship sailed across **the Pacific/the Atlantic/the Mediterranean**.*
  *The sun rises in **the East**.*
  *Our company sells air conditioning equipment in **the Middle East**.*
  *The Danube is the longest river in **the European Union**.*

- We use *the* for locations, but zero article for general directions:
  *The sun rises in **the east**.*
  *The road runs from **north to south**.*

- We use zero article with continents, countries, lakes:
  ***Lake Geneva** borders **France** and **Switzerland**.*
  ***Morocco** is a country in the north-west of **Africa**.*

- We use *the* with plural or collective names:
  *The road crosses **the Alps** through a series of tunnels.*
  *She lives in **the Philippines/the Netherlands/the United Kingdom/the USA**.*

- Names of mountains vary:
  *He's climbed **Everest** and **Mont Blanc** but not **the Matterhorn**.*

- Islands are normally with zero article unless part of post-modification with *of*:
  *I've been to **Crete/Majorca/Cuba**.*
  *I haven't been to **the Isle of Wight**.*
  *They lived for many years on **the island of Crete**.*

- We use *the* with deserts:
  *Parts of **the Sahara** can be cultivated.*

Academic subjects

- We use zero article for academic subjects, such as geography and history:
  *I'd rather study **physics** than **biology**.*

- Note that these words can be used as adjectives. In this case the use of articles depends on the noun:
  *I've started **a physics course**.*
  ***The biology teacher** is really good.*

Nationality

- We use *the* with nationality adjectives that end *-ese, -ch, -sh, -ss* to refer to all the people of that nationality, e.g. *Chinese, Japanese, French, Spanish, British, Swiss, Dutch*:
  ***The Japanese** eat a diet that includes a lot of fish.*
- We use *the* with plural nationality nouns in same way e.g. *Russians, Americans, Poles, Greeks, Turks, Germans, Belgians*:
  ***The Russians** and **the Poles** are used to cold weather.*
- We use *a/an* with singular examples:
  ***a** Swiss, **an** Australian, **a** Greek, **a** Turk, **a** Chinese, **a** Japanese, **a** Russian, **a** Pole, **a** Romanian, **a** Bulgarian, **an** Egyptian, **a** Jordanian*
- Some nationalities end in *-man/-woman*, and others have unique names:
  ***an** Englishman, **an** Irishman, **a** Scotsman, **a** Welshman, **a** Frenchman, **a** Dutchman, **a** Spaniard, **a** Cypriot, **a** Thai, **a** Pakistani, **an** Iraqi, **a** Saudi, **a** Filipino*

Calendar

- We use zero article when we refer to days, months or parts of the day:
  *I'll see you on **Monday** at **midday**.*
  *The course begins in **September**.*
- *The* with a day of the week refers to a day in a particular week, and with a month to a month in a particular year:
  *During the week the weather worsened, and on **the Friday** it rained all day.*
- *A/an* with a day of the week refers to the day as a typical example:
  *It was **a Tuesday** afternoon in August and nothing much was happening.*

Home, school, prison, hospital, work, university

- We use zero article with *at home, at school, in hospital, in prison, in bed, at university* when we speak about the use or purpose of the place:
  *Maria is in **hospital**.* (she's ill)
  *Alan is at **university**.* (he's a student)
- We use zero article with verbs of movement, e.g. *home, to school, to bed*:
  *Are you going **home**?* *No, I'm going **to school**.*
- We use *the* when we refer to the building, place, etc:
  *The bus stops outside **the university**.* (the building)
  *Leave the towels on **the bed**.* (the item of furniture)
  *I was walking past **the hospital**.* (the building)
  *There was a riot in **the prison**.* (the building)

  Compare:
  *Alan's in **bed**.* (he's asleep)
  *There's a beetle in **the bed**!* (the item of furniture)

Generalized locations and activities

- We use zero article in these phrases when we are more interested in what people are doing than where they are:

  on ***holiday****, on* ***tour*** (performers), *on* ***location*** (place where a film is shot), *on* ***stage****,*
  on ***duty****, at* ***work***
  We're **on holiday** *for three weeks.* (we're not working)
  He's **on stage** *for eight performances a week.* (he's performing)

- For specific instances we use *a/an* or *the*:

  They decided to take ***a holiday*** *abroad.*
  He ran onto ***the stage****.*

Changes of meaning

- Uncountable nouns can change meaning in context as shown by the use of the article:

a/an: ***a*** *coffee,* ***a*** *cup of coffee*	*Can I buy you* ***a*** *coffee?*
the: ***the*** *coffee* (a definite example)	*Put* ***the*** *coffee on the table.*
zero: *(some) coffee* (in general)	*Do you like coffee?*

- Many names of substances have a change of meaning when referring to objects:

  glass (a glass for holding liquid)
  glasses (for helping the eyes)
  iron (for smoothing clothes)
  paper, a paper (a newspaper, or a piece of technical writing)

- Some food names which usually have no plural have a technical use as a singular noun with *a/an*:

  I try to eat as much fresh ***fruit*** *as I can.*
  This is ***a fruit*** *that only grows in the tropics.*

  Others are: *wine, beer, cheese, meat, oil*

➜ SEE ALSO
Grammar 19: Articles 1

This unit also contains general practice in the use of articles.

1 Underline the most suitable option in each sentence.

1 There are many interesting geological formations on *Greek island of Milos/the Greek island of the Milos/the Greek island of Milos*.
2 From here you can observe *moon rising above the Alps/the moon rising above the Alps/the moon rising above Alps.*
3 In order to complete this course, all students will need *physics textbook /the physics textbook/a physics textbook.*
4 The festival usually takes place on *first Tuesday in August/the first Tuesday in August/the first Tuesday in the August.*
5 Generally speaking, at breakfast I prefer *a coffee to a tea/coffee to tea/the coffee to the tea.*
6 Mrs Adams is *on a holiday/on the holiday/on holiday* at present but she will be back next Monday.
7 Norway is not *a member state of the European Union/member state of the European Union/a member state of European Union.*
8 Does this bus go in the direction of *a British Library/the British Library/British Library?*
9 Have you finished with *paper/the paper/a paper*? I'd like to read it.
10 An ugli fruit is *a citrus fruit/citrus fruit/the citrus fruit* produced by crossing a grapefruit, a tangerine and an orange.

2 Write a new sentence with a similar meaning to the first sentence, using the word in bold. Do not change the word given.

1 Susan comes from Australia.
an
Susan is an Australian.

2 I'm afraid that George is still asleep.
bed
....

3 Anna studied to become a doctor.
medicine
....

4 The sun is hottest at midday.
middle
....

5 Helen is at the office, but I can give you her number.
work
....

6 We get paid at the end of the month on a Friday.
last
....

7 Inspector Gorse is working at the moment.
duty
....

3 Complete each short text by writing *a/an, the* or – (no article) in each space.

1 ....–..... Psycholinguistics is .... study of .... psychological factors that enable .... human beings to acquire, understand, use, and produce .... language. Developmental psycholinguistics is .... branch of psycholinguistics which studies .... process by which .... children learn to speak.

2 .... hurricane is .... large-scale storm system which rotates around .... area of .... very low pressure. Its strong winds have .... average speed of more than 120 kms .... hour. .... whole system can have .... height of 15 kms and may be 800 kms wide on .... average.

3 In .... UK general election, 650 Members of .... Parliament are elected to .... House of Commons. .... longest period .... parliament can sit for is five years, and .... election is usually called before .... end of this term. .... general elections generally take place on .... Thursday.

4 .... Sydney Harbour Bridge, opened in 1932, is .... road and rail bridge which crosses .... Sydney Harbour. It is .... steel structure with .... length of 1.15 kms and height of 134 metres above .... water. For 35 years it was .... tallest structure in .... city of Sydney. Its local nickname is '........... Coat Hanger'.

5 '........... Times' is .... British newspaper which was first published in 1785 as '........... Daily Universal Register'. .... widely-used typeface (font) .... Times New Roman was developed in 1932 by Stanley Morison, ... English typographer, for .... use in .... newspaper.

4 Complete the text by writing *a/an* or *the*, or – (no article) in each space.

What is a jury?

(1) ..A.. jury is (2) ..... group of (3) ..... people who attend (4) ..... court hearing, consider (5) ..... evidence presented and then decide whether (6) ..... defendant is (7) ..... guilty or not guilty. (8) ..... jury trial usually involves (9) ..... more serious criminal cases. (10) ..... members of (11) ..... jury are known as jurors. Jurors do not have legal training. In (12) ..... UK, jury members are selected from (13) ..... electoral register and represent (14) ..... cross-section of (15) ..... society. (16) ..... twelve jury members are then chosen at (17) ..... random. The jury attends (18) ..... court and follows (19) ..... case as presented by (20) ..... prosecution and (21) ..... defence. The jury members are not allowed to discuss their case or talk to (22) ..... people about it. At the end of (23) ..... case, (24) ..... judge gives (25) ..... case summary and also gives (26) ..... instructions about possible decisions, based upon (27) ..... law. Then the jury discusses (28) ..... case in (29) ..... private until they reach (30) ..... decision, known as (31) ..... verdict. On their return to the court, one of (32) ..... jury members, usually called (33) ..... foreman, is asked to give their verdict.

5 There are twelve necessary uses of *a/an* and *the* missing from these texts. Write a correction in the space at the side.

A Mayan City

Palenque is a ruined city of ⁄ Maya civilization which reached its 1 the Maya
height around 700 AD, and was abandoned within the next 2 ....
150 years. It is located in the foothills of Tumbalá Mountains in 3 ....
the Mexican state of Chiapas. For centuries ruins of the city lay 4 ....
hidden in a tropical forest, until they were examined by Europeans 5 ....
in 18th century. The site contains over 200 buildings. It has now 6 ....
been excavated and restored and attracts tourists from all over world. 7 ....
Archaeologists have deciphered the hieroglyphic inscriptions 8 ....
in the city, and from them learned much of the history of city and its 9 ....
rulers. The most important buildings in Palenque are the Palace and 10 ....
the Temple of Inscriptions, and there is also aqueduct and a stone 11 ....
bridge. The Palace is actually complex made up of several buildings, 12 ....
and includes sculptures and carved reliefs, and a striking tower. In 13 ....
the Temple of Inscriptions was discovered the tomb of Pacal the Great, 14 ....
most famous ruler of Palenque. He came to power in 615 AD and was 15 ....
buried in 683 in a sarcophagus within the temple. His body was found 16 ....
still inside this sarcophagus, his face covered in a mask made of jade 17 ....
mosaic, and his body clothed in jade suit. The sections of jade are 18 ....
joined together with gold wire. In 1994 in another temple, archaeologists 19 ....
discovered a secret door. This led to series of underground rooms, 20 ....
in one of which was a sarcophagus containing the remains of a woman 21 ....
painted red with cinnabar, and known as 'Red Queen'. 22 ....

21

GRAMMAR

Practice 7

Two exercises in this unit form one continuous text.

1 Complete the paragraph by writing *the* or – (no article) in each space.

A Time series graphs

(1) ....–.... time-series graphs are popular with (2) .... newspapers for suggesting and comparing (3) .... trends. However, showing how a single quantity varies with (4) .... time is not the same as showing how two quantities vary, and then suggesting a link between them.

(5) .... graphs showing the variation of two things with (6) .... time often use two different vertical scales. Figure 34 shows an example taken from a national newspaper.

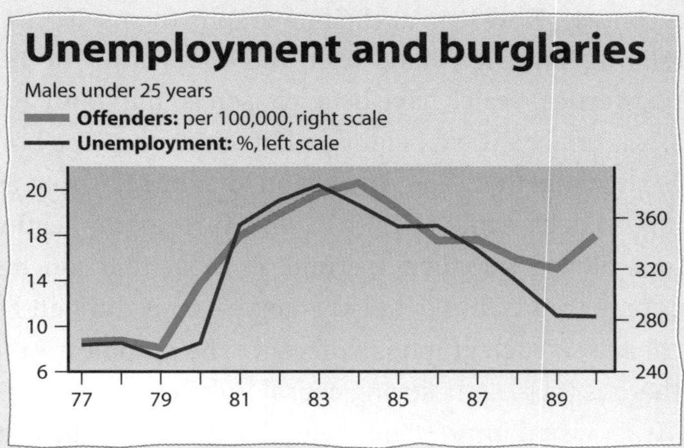

Figure 34: Unemployment and burglaries

This graph was included in a front-page article suggesting that there is a link between (7) .... level of unemployment among (8) .... young men and (9) .... number of offenders committing (10) .... burglaries.

(11) .... way the graph has been drawn seems unambiguously to support (12) .... claim that when (13) .... unemployment rises so does (14) .... crime and, by virtue of (15) .... closeness of (16) .... shape of (17) .... two curves, carries (18) .... strong implication that indeed (19) .... unemployment causes (20) .... crime.

2 Complete the paragraph by writing *a* or *the* in each space.

B Examining the data

However, you should not jump to conclusions. First, look carefully at what Figure 34 shows and read out (1) ..the... information that is actually there. Along the bottom, the scale represents the years 1977 to 1990. The vertical axis on the left-hand side shows the level of unemployment among men under 25 years old expressed as (2) .... percentage. Notice that the scale divisions are 4%, except for the top one which is 2%, although this may be (3) .... misprint and '20' should have been printed as '22'.

On (4) .... right-hand side, the scale shows the number of offenders per 100,000. Note that the graph on its own does not make it clear just what this scale means. Is it (5) .... number of offenders per 100,000 men under 25, or might it be (6) .... number of offenders per 100,000 unemployed men under 25? The graph gives no clues, so you would have to look elsewhere for clarification, emphasizing the point that all graphs are part of (7) .... wider context. Now look at the line graphs themselves. There are two lines, one relating to the left-hand scale and one relating to the right-hand scale. The two vertical scales have been chosen so that both graphs occupy roughly (8) .... same vertical height and, if you look at the bottom left of the graph, start together. The conclusion, of course, is that as unemployment goes up, so does crime, with (9) .... further implication being that it is the unemployed who turn to crime. To make that conclusion you are asked to compare trends, but detailed comparison is difficult because (10) .... vertical axis of each graph is different. The graphic encourages you to think that there is (11) .... strong causal link between two different trends, by (12) .... visual impression created by the way it has been drawn.

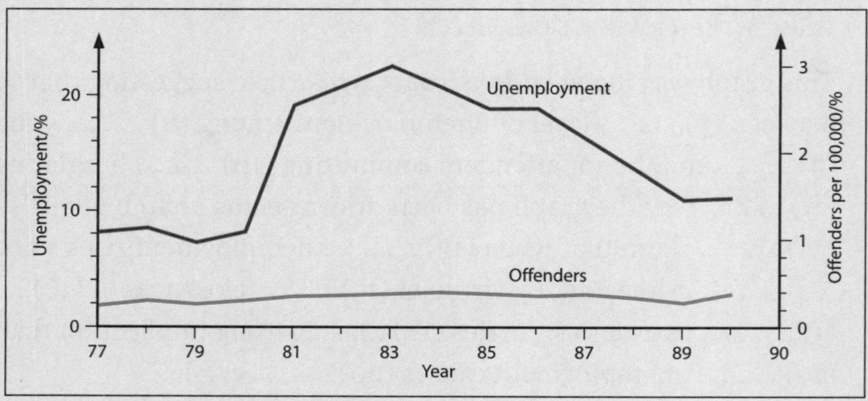

Figure 35: A different perspective

3 Complete the paragraph by writing *a/an, the* or – (no article) in each space.

C Same data, different graph

Figure 35 shows (1) ..the.... the same data, with both vertical axes scaled in percentages. The left axis still shows (2) .... percentage level of unemployment, but now the right axis shows the number of (3) .... offenders expressed as (4) .... percentage. You could argue that this graph tells (5) .... different story – that (6) .... level of crime is hardly affected by unemployment. In spite of a significant increase in (7) .... joblessness between 1979 and 1983, the number of offenders increased by under 0.2%. Even the original graph starts to tell (8) .... different story towards the end of the 1980s, revealing that in 1990 the level of unemployment had fallen almost to the level of 1980, while (9) .... crime was not far below its 1984 peak. The strong visual impression of the two overlaid graphs and (10) .... apparent close match between 1977 and 1983 works to divert (11) .... attention from (12) .... last years of the decade. What the graphic actually shows is two separate time-series graphs that have been drawn in the same place. There may be (13) .... causal link between crime and unemployment, but graphical similarity alone does not tell you about (14) .... cause. For that you need additional knowledge about (15) .... factors and forces that influence a real situation.

4 Put *the* (twice) and *a* (five times) into the text.

D What does this tell us about graphs?

Comparing trends requires notion that variables plotted against time are somehow related, but any such relationship must be established elsewhere – graph itself cannot do it. Graph is presentational device, and all it can do is display data in chosen format. Graphs are drawn by people, and it is people who decide what graph shows and how it shows it. There is nothing inevitable about graph.

22

GRAMMAR

Number and quantity

Countable and uncountable

- Countable nouns have singular and plural forms:
  book/books   *child/children*
- Uncountable (or mass) nouns do not have a plural form:
  milk   *information*
- Some nouns can be countable or uncountable with a change of meaning.

a chicken (an animal)	*some chicken* (food)
a glass (container)	*some glass* (substance)
damage (something broken)	*damages* (money a court orders to be paid)

Some and *any*

- We use *some* with plural countable nouns, and uncountable nouns in positive sentences:
  *There are **some glasses** in that cupboard.*   *I need **some information**.*
- We use *some* in questions that are invitations, offers or requests:
  *Would you like **some help**?*
- We use *some* rather than *any* in questions about plural nouns or uncountables when we expect the answer 'yes':
  *Have you got **some information/some results** to give me?*
- We use *some* to mean 'not all':
  ***Some** of the/**Some** experiments were successful, but others failed.*
- We use *any* with plural countable nouns, in questions and negatives:
  *Are there **any glasses** in that cupboard?*
  *There aren't **any glasses** in this one.*
- We use *any* with uncountable nouns in questions and negatives with a singular verb:
  *Is there **any information** about this subject?*
  *There isn't **any money** left.*
- We use *any* to mean 'whichever one you like':
  *You can use **any desk**.*

How many, how much

- We use *how many* to ask questions about quantity with countable nouns:
  How many planets *are there in the solar system?*

- We use *how much* to ask questions about mass with uncountable nouns:
  How much oxygen *is there in the atmosphere?*

- We use *not many* to make a negative statement about countables:
  There ***aren't many*** *good* ***restaurants*** *around here.*

- We use *not much* to make a negative statement about uncountables:
  Hurry up, there ***isn't much time*** *left.*

- We use *many* and *much* in positive statements in formal or written language:
  Many *people travel everywhere by car.*
  Much *damage was caused by the storm.*

Too many, too few, very few, few and *a few*

- We use *too many, too few, not many, (only) a few, (very) few* with countable nouns:
  There are ***too many employees*** *for a building this size.*
  We've had ***very few complaints*** *about this.*

- *Few* is negative, *a few* is positive:
  We invited ***a few*** *friends for a meal.* (some)
  I have ***few*** *friends in this part of the country.* (not many)

Too much, not much, (only) a little, (very) little

- We use *too much, not much, (only) a little, (very) little* with uncountable nouns:
  *We have**n't** got* ***much time****.*
  I need ***a little*** *help.*
  There is ***too much noise*** *in here.*
  There's only ***a little water*** *left.*

A lot of/lots of, plenty, hardly any, not enough

- We use *a lot of/lots of, plenty of, hardly any, (not) enough, hardly enough* with countable and uncountable nouns:
  We've got ***lots of friends****.*
  There was ***a lot of noise****.*

  There are ***hardly any seats****.*
  There's ***hardly any water****.*

  *We have**n't** got* ***enough employees****.*
  *There are**n't*** ***enough seats****.*

- *A lot* and *lots* can stand alone as pronouns in answer to *how much/how many* questions:
  How many *animals are there on the farm?* ***A lot/Lots!***

No, not any, none (of)

- We use *no* and *not any* with countables and uncountables:
  *There's **no time** to finish.*
  *There **isn't any time** for lunch.*

- *None* stands alone as a pronoun, often with *at all*. *None of* is used with nouns, with either a singular or a plural verb, though many users prefer a singular verb:
  *There might be lots of people there, or there **might be none** (at all).*
  ***None** of the suggested proposals **was/were accepted**.*

Many, more, less with numbers

- We use *many* as an intensifier with *hundreds of/thousands of*, etc:
  ***Many thousands of** people took part in the survey.*

- *A good many* means a large number:
  ***A good many** people have left the area.*

- We use *as many as* or *up to* when we estimate the highest number:
  ***As many as/Up to a hundred** people were injured.*

- We use *more than/less than* or *in excess of* to estimate numbers:
  ***Less than/More than/In excess of €5 billion** has been spent already.*

Enough, hardly enough, just enough

- We use *enough* with countables and uncountables when we want to show that the number or amount is acceptable or sufficient:
  *We'll have **enough time** to check the results.*

- *Hardly enough* means *almost not enough*. *Just enough* means the right amount or number. *More than enough* means the amount or number is sufficient:
  *There is **hardly enough** room for so many new buildings.*
  *There are **just enough** lifejackets for everyone.*
  *Don't worry, there is **more than enough** money to pay for this.*

Number and amount

- We use *a number* with *large/small* to describe how many, and *a large/small amount* to describe how much. We use a singular or a plural verb:
  ***A small number** of companies have/has already closed down.*
  ***A large amount** of gold is missing from the warehouse.*

Measurement words + *of*

- Measurement words such as *litre, ton, kilometre*, etc are followed by *of*:
  *Millions of **litres of** water are wasted every day.*
  *There were several **kilometres of** wiring in each machine.*

1 Underline the most suitable option in each sentence. Sometimes more than one option is possible.

1 There isn't *some money/any money/a money* in the drawer.
2 I'm afraid there is *little hope/not much hope/none hope* left of any survivors.
3 There are *too many containers/many containers/large numbers of containers* to fit into one van.
4 Do you need *help/some help/a help*?
5 I'm sorry, but you are making *enough/much/too much* noise.
6 Do you think we have *any/very little/enough* paint to do all the rooms upstairs?
7 Could you give me *an advice/some advice/advices* about my application?
8 Sit here, there's *just enough room/too much room/a few room.*
9 There *isn't very much/isn't a lot/is hardly enough* we can do about that, I'm afraid.
10 *Millions litres of wine/millions of litres of wine/millions of litres wine* are drunk every year.

2 Complete each short text by writing one suitable word in each space.

Global warming and business

(1) .... business leaders agree with politicians and scientists that too (2) .... has been done to limit global warming. However, too (3) .... companies are only enthusiastic about the profits they can make when governments start handing out large (4) .... of taxpayers' money.

Languages

Do we know how (5) .... languages there are in the world? Estimates suggest that there are (6) .... to 7,000 living languages, with (7) .... experts quoting the precise figure of 6,909. Interestingly, Europe has relatively (8) .... languages – fewer than 3.5% of the world total – though (9) .... millions of people speak them as it has about 25% of the world's population.

Exercise

A recent study shows that (10) .... any men and women do the amount of exercise recommended. Only a (11) .... do 30 minutes' exercises five times a week, although most of the people interviewed thought that they were taking (12) .... of exercise. When researchers measured exactly how (13) .... exercise was taken by a sample of people, they found that most of the sample were not taking (14) .... useful exercise and were getting out of breath when walking or running.

3 Write a new sentence with a similar meaning to the first sentence, using the word in bold. Do not change the word given.

1 The earthquake made many people homeless.
large
The earthquake made a large number of people homeless.

2 How long have we got left?
time
....

3 There is not much point in carrying on.
little
....

4 We've been thinking, and we've come up with some suggestions.
few
....

5 Too little interest has been shown in the project to make it viable.
not
....

6 The emergency fund hasn't got any money in it.
there
....

7 No patients reported any side effects.
none
....

8 There are very few remaining options.
any
....

9 The bridge has been badly damaged.
done
....

4 Complete each short text by writing one suitable word in each space.

Endangered species

There is not (1) much that can be done to save some endangered species. When a species is (2) .... in number there may be (3) .... chance of keeping it from extinction, mainly because (4) .... a few of the species at risk are protected by law, and (5) .... of them simply do not get (6) .... public attention. It is not even clear how (7) .... endangered species either vanish or manage to recover. A small (8) .... of species, such as tigers and elephants, receive a (9) .... of publicity, but even they are still at risk. In the future there may be (10) .... any of these animals left in the wild, and their survival may depend on captive breeding in zoos.

Taxation policies

In (11) .... ways there is a (12) .... of difference between the taxation policies of the two parties. While the Liberal Party believes that there are too (13) .... high earners who are paying (14) .... little income tax, and proposes raising millions (15) .... pounds of tax revenue by increasing tax rates for higher earners, the Centre Party believes that in fact (16) .... of us has been paying (17) .... tax, and proposes steep rises for higher earners and an overall rise for all earners, apart from the small (18) .... of people earning less than €10,000. However, as the Liberal Party also proposes an increase in VAT, very (19) .... of us would avoid paying (20) .... more for goods and services.

*VAT = Value Added Tax, a tax on goods and services

An enquiry into how local councils dealt with winter weather

The report concluded that while (21) .... of the agencies involved made every effort to respond to the emergency, very (22) .... (only 2 out of 14 in fact) managed to clear the main roads within 24 hours. A large (23) .... (12 out of 14) reported that they did not have (24) .... warning of the change in weather conditions. There were too (25) .... snow-clearing vehicles available, and (26) .... valuable time was wasted in moving equipment from other areas. Because of the severe weather conditions, a large (27) .... of staff were unable to reach depots, and there was (28) .... evidence of adequate planning for such emergencies.

5 Complete the second sentence so that it has a similar meaning to the first sentence.

1 Not many companies specialize in this product.
Very...few companies specialize in this product........ .

2 Could you advise me about what I should do?
Could you give.. ?

3 This area lacks open spaces.
There aren't.. .

4 Whenever you need a break, there's a cafeteria on the next floor.
Any.. .

5 What proportion of the atmosphere is nitrogen?
How.. ?

6 This model doesn't require much more maintenance than the earlier model.
This model requires only.. .

7 This condition does not have a cure.
There is.. .

8 Up to a hundred police officers were involved in the security operation.
As.. .

6 Write a new sentence with a similar meaning to the first sentence, using a word or phrase from the box.

~~not enough~~	none	how much	hardly enough	a few
many	plenty	a little	a large amount	too few

1 There is insufficient time to deal with this issue properly.
...There is not enough time to deal with this issue properly...

2 Thousands and thousands of people remain homeless.
....

3 There was barely room to fit everyone in.
....

4 Considerable damage has been reported from the capital.
....

5 A small number of troublemakers was arrested.
....

6 There is more than enough time before the plane leaves.
....

7 Add a small amount of salt, and stir well.
....

8 Nobody I spoke to knew where the college was.
....

9 There is an insufficient number of parking places.
....

10 What volume of water does the reservoir contain?
....

23

GRAMMAR

Making comparisons

Comparative forms

Comparatives may be formed in various ways.

- comparative adjective + *than*:
  *This experiment is **longer/better/more detailed than** the last one.*

- *Not as, just as*:
  *This experiment is **not as detailed as** the last one.*
  *This computer is **just as fast as** the other one.*

- *Not as/so* + adj + *to*-infinitive + *as*:
  *It's **not as/so** easy to explain **as** I thought.*

- *As* + adjective + *a* + noun + *as*:
  *We asked for **as large a car as** possible.*
  *It's not **as long a journey as** I used to have.*

- *Too* + adjective (+ *a* + noun) + *to*-infinitive:
  *Failure at this stage is **too terrible even to think** about.*

- *Sufficiently* + adverb + *to*-infinitive:
  *Some students are unable to write **sufficiently well to pass** the test.* (formal)

- *More* + adjective + *than* + adjective, *not so much* + adjective + *as* + adjective:

- To make a distinction between adjectives which are close in meaning:
  *I was **more surprised than angry**.*
  *I wasn**'t so much angry as surprised**.*

- (subject) + *be* + comparative +*to*-infinitive *(than ...)*
  ***It's more/less convenient** to use public transport.*
  ***A computer is easier** to use **than** a typewriter.*
  ***It's easier** to learn some languages **than** others.*

Comparative + comparative

- Two comparatives are often used with verbs of becoming, changing, etc:
  *The project is **becoming more and more interesting**.*
  *Computers are **growing faster and faster**.*

The + comparative or superlative + *of the* + number/quantity

- A comparative can be used to compare two things:
  *This is **by far/easily the most dangerous of the two** methods.*

- A superlative is used to compare one thing with many things:
  *The second proposal seems to be **the best of the three**.*

Present perfect + superlative

- We often use the present perfect with a superlative:
  This is ***the most interesting*** *research* ***I've*** *ever* ***done***. (I'm still doing it)
  That was ***by far/much the worst*** *film* ***I've seen*** *this year.*

The + comparative, *the* + comparative

- To describe an action and its consequences:
  The longer *we postpone the decision,* ***the more serious*** *the situation will become.*

- Adjectives and adverbs can be mixed:
  The more effort *we put into this project,* ***the more slowly*** *it seems to progress.*

Modifiers

- Comparisons can be modified to make them less extreme:
  This is ***probably the best*** *solution.*
  We've done ***just about as much as*** *we can.*
  *This is****n't quite as easy as*** *I thought.*
  The new one is ***not nearly/half/nowhere near as good as*** *the old one.*

- Comparisons can be made stronger:
  This is ***easily the best*** *solution. It's the* ***most popular*** *sport in the world* ***by far***.
  Tennis is ***far/a lot/much more demanding***.
  It's ***a lot/much more interesting***.

Like and *as*

- *As ... as*:
  Her hands were ***as cold as*** *ice.*

- *Like*:
  A caravan is ***like*** *a house on wheels.* (it is similar)

- *Look like, smell like, sound like, feel like*:
  The college ***looks like*** *a factory.* (it is similar)
  This ***smells like*** *a rotten egg!* (they smell the same)
  That ***sounds like*** *the postman.* (it sounds is if he has arrived)
  The pain ***felt like*** *a red-hot needle.* (it was similar)
  I ***feel like*** *going out tonight.* (that's what I want to do)

- *As* and *like*:
  Sue works ***as*** *a lab assistant.* (that's her job)
  They worked ***like*** *slaves to get the project finished.* (that's how they would)

- *Look as if/as though* + present simple/unreal past simple:
  You ***look as if you need/needed*** *a rest. You must be really tired.*

Enough and *too*

- *Not* + adjective/adverb + *enough* + *to*-infinitive:
  *I was**n't** **quite old enough to get** into the film.* (I was nearly old enough)
  *He did**n't** work **hard enough to win**.*

- *Too* + adjective + *to*-infinitive:
  *The police arrived **far/much too late to catch** the robbers.*
  *It was **too great a problem** (for him) **to solve** on his own.*

More, fewer, less, not as/so much/many, too little, most (of the ...)

- We use *more, not a/so many* with countables and uncountables, and *fewer, less, not as/so much, too little* with uncountables. We use superlative *most* with countables and uncountables:
  *We need **more paper**.*
  *There is **less time** than we thought. There is **too little money**.*
  *There have been **fewer storms**/there have**n't** been **as many** this year.*
  *Most people try to save money **most of the time**.*

Twice, three times, etc + *as much as/as many as*

- We use *twice as much, three times as much*, etc to make comparisons between a larger and smaller quantity or number:
  *There has been **twice as much** rain this year compared with last year.*
  *There are **ten times as many** students here as in my old college.*

- *(Just) as much/many* means 'an equal amount or number':
  *This machine uses **just as much** electricity as that one.*

1 Underline the most suitable option in each sentence.

1 In city areas a motorbike can be *faster as a car/faster than a car/as fast than a car.*
2 This is easily the worst film *than I've ever seen/I've ever seen/as I've ever seen.*
3 Your laptop is *twice as fast as mine/twice faster than mine/faster than mine twice.*
4 That kind of job is *too difficult than to do/too difficult doing/too difficult to do* on your own.
5 The more I think about this proposal, *more appealing it becomes/the more appealing it becomes/it becomes more than appealing.*
6 Ann hasn't worked *too hard/the hardest/hard enough* to qualify for a bonus.
7 There isn't *too much money left/as much money left/more money left* as I thought.
8 The work I'm doing is becoming *a more demanding/the more demanding/more and more demanding.*
9 This looks *like/as/than* an interesting old village.
10 I've had *more and more that I can take/just about as much as I can take/easily the most I can take* from you!

2 Complete the text by writing a suitable word in each space.

The popularity of football

Football is generally considered to be the (1) ....most.... popular sport in the world. It doesn't require very much in the way of equipment, so it's (2) .... as easy for a group of children to play football in the street (3) .... it is for an organized team to play on a proper pitch. For many people, playing in a team is (4) .... interesting and (5) .... demanding (6) .... playing other kinds of sport, such as tennis or golf. At the professional level, football probably attracts (7) .... spectators and television viewers (8) .... any other sport, but it is here that the situation is perhaps (9) .... as healthy (10) .... it might seem. According to some, the profit motive has begun to dominate the game, and the more that clubs and players earn, the (11) .... they care about football as a game. In other words, winning at all costs and making as much money (12) .... possible are beginning to overwhelm the sport. For some fanatical fans, in any case, football has become more of a religion (13) .... a sport. Winning is (14) .... more important than anything else, and they are happy to insult rival teams or fight with other fans. Of course it's (15) .... easier to watch a game than it is to play in one, so perhaps what football needs is (16) .... spectators and more participants. One way or another, the 'beautiful game' is perhaps not (17) .... beautiful (18) .... some people would like to think.

3 Complete the second sentence so that it has a similar meaning to the first sentence using a comparative or superlative form.

1 It's not as difficult a problem as we thought.
It's an *easier problem than we thought it was* .

2 The finances have never been in such a bad state.
This is the.. .

3 James is less likely to change his mind.
James is not.. .

4 This method is more dangerous than that one.
This method is the.. .

5 Our profits have doubled compared with last year.
We have made.. .

6 By the time the fire brigade arrived to put out the fire, it was too late.
The fire brigade arrived.. .

7 I think this is the bus now.
This sounds... .

8 It costs a lot more to travel by air.
Travelling by air is.. .

4 Write a new sentence with a similar meaning to the first sentence, using the word in bold. Do not change the word given.

1 This research paper is a lot more detailed than the other one.
not as
The other research paper is not as detailed as this one.

2 At weekends, Harry has a cleaning job.
works
....

3 This problem is a lot harder than I thought it was.
easy
....

4 This book is more interesting than that book.
the two
....

5 We haven't had a summer as wet as this for ten years.
wettest
....

6 This year there are fewer students on the course.
not
....

7 If he'd felt stronger, he would have carried on.
enough
....

8 She couldn't try any harder.
tried
....

5 Complete the text by writing a word or phrase from the box in each space.

~~just as~~	a little richer	a lot more	as much	than
as simple as	drier	harder	higher	the longer
less water	minute less	more and more	more sense	
more surprising	shorter and cooler	twice as much	the best	

Saving water

Climate change in the UK may not be obvious, as to most people it seems (1) ...just as..... wet a place as ever. And everyone complains that gas and electricity is costing them (2) .... as their bills get bigger. In fact, there isn't (3) .... water available in southern England as there used to be, mainly because new housing and light industry is increasing demand. Some of the facts about the situation are (4) .... than you might suppose. For example, London is actually (5) .... than Istanbul and the South East of England has (6) .... available per person than the Sudan and Syria. This is why everyone needs to try (7) .... to avoid wasting water supplies, especially hot water, because consumers are having to pay (8) .... prices for it. Easily (9) .... solution is to change your bathroom habits! It's said that a typical bath uses around (10) .... hot water as a five-minute shower, and therefore uses (11) .... energy to heat the water. If you already do this, then remember that (12) .... you stay under the shower, the more water (and energy) you use. So try making your showers (13) .... A (14) .... in the shower could save as much as 11 litres of water, and it obviously makes (15) .... to save water (16) .... to waste it. This way everyone can make themselves (17) .... by cutting energy bills. The less water we use, the more money we save, it is (18) .... that.

24

GRAMMAR

Practice 8

1 Complete the text by writing a suitable word in each space.

The table below shows how (1) .... people in total were employed in Alabama in 1990, with the various employment sectors expressed as percentages. Of 1,741,794 people in employment, by far the highest (2) .... were employed in manufacturing of both durable and non-durable goods. Slightly (3) .... people were employed in the durable goods sector (4) .... in the non-durable goods sector. Taken together, the two sectors accounted for around 23% of the total, thus providing (5) .... of the state's employment, nearly ten (6) .... as many as worked in agriculture. Over recent years far (7) .... had found employment in traditional industries such as mining and agriculture, forestry and fisheries, these sectors eventually accounting for not much (8) .... than 3% of employment. Retail and wholesale trade combined employed almost as (9) .... people as manufacturing at 20.4%. Both health and educational services employed (10) .... people than construction.

Alabama: Occupations 1990

Employed persons 16 years and over	total 1,741,794 percentage%
Agriculture, forestry, and fisheries	2.4
Mining	0.7
Construction	7.1
Manufacturing, non-durable goods (eg food, fuel, clothing, etc)	11.3
Manufacturing, durable goods (eg cars, computers, toys, etc)	11.5
Transportation	3.8
Communications and other public utilities	3.2
Wholesale trade	4.2
Retail trade	16.2
Finance, insurance, and real estate	5.0
Business and repair services	4.0
Personal services (e.g. cleaning, domestic care, child care, etc)	2.9
Entertainment and recreation services	0.9
Health services	8.2
Educational services	8.1
Other professional and related services	5.2
Public administration	5.3

2 Complete the text by writing a phrase from the box in each space.

~~most populous~~	greater extent	busiest	considerable
dominant	extensive	highest	large quantities
largest	major	many	mostly	not even
large numbers	significant amounts	substantial	

The state of Alabama, US

Alabama, with about 4.6 million residents, is the 23rd (1) ...most populous... in the United States. In 1810 its population was (2) .... 10,000, but its (3) .... city, Birmingham, now has a population of about 1.25 million. Until the late 19th century, Alabama's economy was (4) .... agricultural but from then on manufacturing became the (5) .... sector. Until the 1960s (6) .... quantities of iron ore were mined in the state. However the agricultural sector still produces (7) .... of soya beans, cotton and peanuts, and (8) .... of beef cattle and chickens. Over the last thirty years the economy has been transformed, with information technology, bio-technology and medical research expanding to a (9) .... compared to other sectors. Alabama also now has the 4th (10) .... level of motor manufacturing output in the US. In addition, Alabama has a (11) .... tourist industry, and (12) .... tourists visit Alabama's historic sites, state parks, and national forests. The state's (13) .... forests also produce (14) .... of pulpwood and lumber. Mobile, the only port, is the 10th (15) .... (by tonnage) in the United States. There are also (16) .... road, rail and canal systems.

3 Complete the text by writing one word in each space.

Britain's universities are producing more and (1) ....more........ graduates, but there aren't (2) .... graduate level jobs to go round. According to a recent report, there are now (3) .... many graduates for the UK jobs market, and their work skills are not quite good (4) .... According to the latest figures, more (5) .... a million graduates are in jobs for which they are over-qualified, and there are too (6) .... graduate level jobs (9 m) to provide for the number of graduates currently available (10.1 m). To make matters worse, by 2020 there will be even (7) .... graduate jobs, with the figure for graduate jobs as low as 42%. And this situation is not being improved by government policy, which is to encourage an even greater (8) .... of young people to enter higher education. In fact the intention is for as (9) .... as 50% of all young people to be on degree courses. But does producing (10) .... graduates mean that the quality of their education will not be as high (11) .... it should be? The report, by the Confederation of British Industry (CBI), goes on to say that current graduates are (12) .... as well qualified as they might be, and lack 'people skills'. (13) .... many young graduates, they say, are not able to communicate (14) .... well for today's workplace. Some are (15) .... skilled enough in teamwork and time management, and a (16) .... , it is suggested, even find it hard to get up in the morning. The CBI report points out that there is (17) .... great a need for graduates to be good employees as there is for them to be scholars. At the same time, the CBI expressed concern that universities were not producing (18) .... graduates in maths, science, technology and engineering subjects. The report also criticized employees, saying that too (19) .... of them provided students with high quality work experience to prepare them before they apply for a job. The government too came in for criticism, with evidence showing that the UK spent proportionally (20) .... on higher education than other European countries.

25

GRAMMAR

Adverbial clauses 1

Coordinate clauses

- A coordinate clause can make sense on its own. A coordinating conjunction, such as *and, but, because* joins the clause to another clause and makes a longer sentence. This kind of sentence is sometimes called a 'compound' sentence:
  We reduced the temperature of the oil, ***but*** *the results stayed the same.*

Subordinate clauses

- A subordinate clause gives more information about a sentence, but does not make sense on its own. A subordinating conjunction introduces a subordinate clause, and joins on to the main part of the sentence:
  Although *the experiment was successful, the results were not as expected.*
  This section deals with a range of subordinate clauses called 'adverbial' clauses. Most adverbial clauses can be placed after or in front of the main clause. Note the changes below:
  Although the experiment was successful, *the results were not as expected.*
  The results of the experiment were not as expected, ***although it was successful.***

- It is sometimes possible to place the clauses in the middle of another clause:
  The results of the experiment, ***when you consider them in context,*** *were unusual.*

Time clauses

- Time clauses are introduced by time conjunctions: *when, after, as, as soon as, before, by the time, at the same time, during the time, immediately, the moment, now, once, since, till/until, whenever, while.* If the time clause comes first, we usually put a comma after it:
  As we were leaving, *I noticed that something was wrong.*
  The moment the news leaked out, *we received a flood of offers.*
  The company ran into difficulties ***when the factory was burned down.***
  Take the medication ***for as long as is stated on the label.***

- In adverbial time clauses referring to the future we do not use *will*, but use present simple, or present perfect to emphasize completion:
  As soon as there ***is*** *any definite information, we'll make a decision.*
  *Let me know as soon as you****'ve left*** *the building.*

Place clauses

- Place clauses are introduced by *where* for a particular place and *wherever, anywhere,* or *everywhere.* They normally come after the main clause:
  There is a warning sign on the cupboard ***where poisons are kept.***
  You can leave your bicycle ***wherever you like.***
  Everywhere scientists look, *they are finding the same results.*

Manner clauses

- Manner clauses are introduced by *as*, *like*, *just as*, *much as* and *normally* come after the main clause:
  *I used brown sugar, **as/like it said in the recipe**.*
  *The village remains **much as it was in the 18th century**.*

- We also use *how* or *in the way (that)*:
  *He makes coffee **just how I like it**.*
  *They didn't perform the task **in the way that we wanted them to**.*

- We use *as if* and *as though* to describe something which seems to be true:
  *The company acted **as though there was nothing wrong**.* (there was)
  As if and *as though* with a past tense have an imaginary or 'unreal' sense, as in a conditional sentence:
  *Most people treat this problem **as if it were just a matter for scientists**.* (it isn't)
  As if and *as though* are common with *be*, *act*, *appear*, *behave*, *feel*, *look*, *seem*, *smell*, *sound*, *taste*. Using a past tense shows that the matter is an imaginary or 'unreal':
  *He acted **as if he had seen a ghost**.* (imaginary)
  *It sounds **as though they are having a good time.*** (real)

➜ SEE ALSO
Grammar 26: Adverbial clauses 2
Grammar 29: Participle clauses

1 Underline the most suitable option in each sentence.

1 When the inquiry *completed/will complete/has completed* its investigation it will publish a report.
2 You can park *as though/what/wherever* you like in this street.
3 *During the time/Immediately/While* he spent in intensive care, he was not allowed visitors.
4 The tests differ *as if/like/in the way* they measure potential performance and aptitude.
5 We've been living in temporary accommodation *while/since/when* we moved here in September.
6 We can find you a ticket for *just as/as soon as/anywhere* you want to go.
7 The technicians replaced the safety mechanism *as/whenever/while* they had been instructed.
8 We'll let you know *anywhere/when exactly/just as* you need to come for your interview.
9 Give me a call as soon as you *arrive/arrived/will arrive* at the airport.
10 A bell will ring three times five minutes *before/until/as soon as* the library closes.

2 Complete each short text by writing one suitable word in each space. Sometimes more than one answer is possible.

Natural cleaning

A research team in the US is looking at a method of removing pollution from the environment in the (1) ....way......... that it occurs in nature – by using bacteria. (2) .... scientists look – at the bottom of rivers and in the Antarctic ice – they find microbes feasting on materials in their environment. (3) .... they feed on toxic chemicals, some bacteria convert these substances into useful compounds.

Rebuilding work

(4) .... construction begins in South Court, the Student Centre will remain open on its regular schedule. The cafeteria will be usable (5) .... the first phase of work is taking place, but will be closed from June 30th. (6) .... this work has been completed, the cafeteria will reopen. This is scheduled for November 1st. (7) .... access to the Student Centre from North Road is closed, use the fire exit at the rear of the building. This will be kept open (8) .... this occurs and warning signs will be placed outside.

George Orwell in Spain

(9) .... the Spanish Civil War broke out, Orwell decided to go to Spain and fight on the Republican side (10) .... he was needed. (11) .... the time his wife Eileen joined him in Spain the following year, he had been involved in fighting in the Aragon area. (12) .... he had spent a short period in Barcelona, he returned to the fighting (13) .... he was wounded in the throat and was lucky not to be killed. (14) .... he had recovered sufficiently, he and his wife left Spain later that summer.

3 Write one new sentence with a similar meaning to the two sentences, using the word in bold.

1 The instructions said I should use glue. I did use glue.
as
I used glue as it said I should in the instructions.

2 The match finished. There was a huge cheer.
moment
....

3 The tomb was discovered, and the archaeologists were astounded.
when
....

4 The operation had started. It could not be interrupted after that.
once
....

5 They fitted the windows, but not as we wanted them to be fitted.
way
....

6 I always imagined the village would be just like this.
how
....

7 I'll leave home at six. I'll be here until then.
before
....

8 The refugees found shelter in any place they could.
wherever
....

9 The way of life of the people in the mountains hasn't changed a lot since the last century.
much as
....

10 They are not telling the truth. That is the way it sounds.
if
....

26

GRAMMAR

Adverbial clauses 2

See Grammar 25 for an overview of coordinate and subordinate clauses.

Concession clauses

- Concession clauses add information which seems to oppose the information in the rest of the sentence and are typically introduced by *although, though, even though*:
  The expedition pressed on, ***although everyone was tired.***
  Even though it had rained all night, *they were able to cross the river.*
  They were in good spirits, ***considering how bad conditions were.***
- *Even if* explains that although something may happen, another situation stays the same:
  Even if the price of the product is reduced, *we are unlikely to buy it.*
- *Despite* and *in spite of* can only be followed by noun forms:
  In spite of /Despite the bad conditions, *they were in good spirits.*
  In spite of /Despite feeling tired, *they pressed on.*

Contrast clauses

- Contrast clauses are typically introduced by *although* or *though*. In formal speech and writing *while, whereas, whilst* are used:
  Although/While they accepted his theory in part, *they rejected his conclusions.*
  The study found that ***although/whereas the total number of cancer deaths had increased by 22%,*** *cancer of the respiratory tract had increased 120%.*
- *Much as* is a formal way of saying *although*:
  (As) Much as I would like to believe you, *I find your explanation hard to accept.*

Reason clauses

- Reason clauses are introduced by *as, because, since, seeing that*:
  I won't be able to attend the meeting ***as I have another appointment.***
  Since you refuse to answer my letters *I am referring this matter to my lawyers.*
- *Seeing how/as/that* are spoken forms:
  Seeing that I am paying, *I think I should decide which film we see.*
- *For* is a formal and often literary use:
  He did not check again, ***for there was no reason to expect any change.***
- When *in case* and *just in case* refer to a future situation which explains the reason for doing something in the present, we use a present tense to refer to future time:
  We use safety gloves ***just in case the liquid spills.***

- In past situations, we use two past tenses:
  They all ***wore*** *heavy clothing* ***in case the weather turned cold.***

Result clauses

- Result clauses are introduced by *so* + adjective/adverb + *that, such (a)* + (adjective) + noun + *that*. It is not possible to reverse these clauses:
  The plane is so small/It is such a small aircraft that *it can take off from a road.*
  The weather changed so rapidly that *everyone was taken by surprise.*

- We also use *so much/many/few/little + that*:
  The company made ***so much profit that it was able to expand rapidly.***

Purpose clauses

- Purpose clauses are introduced by *so (that)* usually followed by a modal auxiliary:
  They filmed the experiment ***so (that) they could be sure of what happened.***

- We use *in order that* in formal speech and writing:
  Legislation is needed ***in order that this problem may be dealt with effectively.***

- *So as (not)* + *to-* infinitive also describes the purpose of the subject in the main clause:
  I closed the door quietly ***so as not to disturb anyone.***

➜ SEE ALSO
Grammar 25: Adverbial clauses 1

This section includes practice of adverbial clauses in Grammar 25.

1 Underline the most suitable option in each sentence.

1 *Whereas/As/Much as* finance is no longer available, this project has been postponed.
2 It is *so/such a/so that* powerful engine that it requires a great deal of fuel.
3 You should wear warm clothing *in case/although/since* the weather changes for the worse.
4 *Despite she took/In spite of taking/In spite she took* the medication, she still developed malaria.
5 *Whereas/Such as/Seeing as* the concert tickets are free, we might as well go along.
6 The organism grew *such rapidly/so much rapidly/so rapidly* that it doubled in size within two days.
7 *Although/Despite/Even if* supplies of gas are suspended, there is enough in the country to last the winter.
8 *Although/In order that/Since* your application for funding can be considered, please complete and return this form.
9 There was *such/so little/so* hope of finding any more survivors that the search was abandoned.
10 The year ahead will be difficult for wind power, *despite/whereas/as much as* sales of solar energy equipment should do well.

2 Complete each short text by writing one suitable word in each space.

Are robots dangerous?

Scientists, and film-makers, have wondered whether robots might become (1) ....so............ sophisticated that they will become a threat to human life. (2) .... it seems unlikely that robots will ever become self-aware, more advanced robots could be dangerous (3) .... they might become more independent of human control. In other words, they might become so 'intelligent' (4) .... they start to take decisions on their own. However, (5) .... if robots started to think and act for themselves, these abilities would be extremely limited and in any case robots are (6) .... complex that they nearly always require human controllers.

Radon gas

(7) .... most people are aware of the dangers of radiation, not many consider that they might be at risk in their own homes from radon, a naturally occurring radioactive gas. (8) .... it is colourless and odourless, home owners may not be aware of potential problems. However, radon is (9) .... dangerous that in the USA alone it is the second most common cause of lung cancer. (10) .... there are no immediate symptoms of exposure, which may take years to surface, it's as well to have your house tested if you are in a risk area.

Tea with milk?

Research has found that (11) .... drinking black tea can have a relaxing effect on the arteries, (12) .... they expand and protect the heart, the tea has no effect at all if milk has been added. Tea without milk relaxes the arteries (13) .... it produces nitric oxide, (14) .... tea with milk has no effect at all. (15) .... tea is the second most popular drink in the world, after water, its health effects are of considerable importance. Researchers also suggest that other foods with known health benefits, such as olive oil and red wine, are looked at in context, (16) .... it can be determined whether they too lose their effects in combination with other foods.

3 Write a new sentence with a similar meaning to the first sentence, using the word in bold. Do not change the word given.

1 As the headwind was strong, the flight was delayed.
that
........The headwind was so strong that the flight was delayed.........

2 Your application has not been accepted because you have failed to provide any references.
since
....

3 The meeting was poorly attended so no vote was taken on the proposal.
as
....

4 The computer programme had a lot of errors and it had to be rewritten.
that
....

5 The building work was completed on time, despite the bad weather.
although
....

6 I'll give you my phone number because you may change your mind.
just
....

7 I appreciate your offer but I have to decline.
as
....

8 Classes finished early to allow students to attend rehearsals for the play.
could
....

9 It is a dangerous substance so it has to be kept in a special container.
such
....

10 They had been advised to turn back, but the expedition went on.
even though
....

4 Rewrite the two sentences as one sentence with a similar meaning, using the word in bold. Leave out any unnecessary words.

Living in a tax free country: The Cayman Islands

1 The Islands are a tax-neutral jurisdiction. No one there pays income tax.
as
As the Islands are a tax-neutral jurisdiction, no one there pays income tax.

2 The Islands do not produce manufactured goods. Everything has to be imported.
since
....

3 The government can pay for essential services. It does this by levying a special tax on all imports.
so
....

4 The government is also able to raise large amounts of revenue from work permits and port fees. A lot of people want to work there and there is a lot of tourism.
many
....

5 This policy has been very successful. The Islands are one of the wealthiest places in the world.
that
....

5 Complete the text by writing one suitable word in each space.

Why buy organic food?

(1) Although organic food is more expensive, it has some important environmental benefits. (2) .... animals are raised organically, they live under better conditions. They are not given growth hormones or antibiotics, (3) .... you will not have to worry about these chemicals being passed from the meat you eat into your body. (4) .... conventional farmers uses pesticides which contaminate the soil and the air, organic farming avoids these. Farmers also have to keep increasing the strength of pesticides (5) .... they can control pests which have become resistant. So when the authorities insist that all meat products are 'safe', what they really mean is that the levels of chemicals in the meat is (6) .... small that it is not considered to be a risk. However, you may prefer to eat organic meat (7) .... you can be absolutely sure that it is not contaminated. (8) .... it has not been proved that organic food is healthier than non-organic food, it can safely be said that non-organic food carries more risks. And (9) .... organic farms are safer places for those who work there, (10) .... you buy organic food you are protecting farmers' health as well as your own.

27

GRAMMAR

Practice 9

1 Complete the text by writing a phrase from the box in each space.

~~a as has often been observed~~
b as sites like Facebook
c before long the adults start
d despite the fact that Facebook
e so rapidly that people began
f while the figures might
g although the number
h as the new figures showed
i when Facebook users see
j even if the figures are wrong
k so striking that some commentators
l while the number of users

Who uses Facebook?

(1) ...a..... , once kids start doing something, then (2) .... to do it too. Recent figures from IStrategy Labs in the US suggest that this is happening to the personal networking site Facebook. (3) .... of Facebook users aged 18–24 rose by 4.8% in the first half of 2009, the number of older users grew much more. (4) .... aged 25–34 grew by 60.8%, users aged 35–54 showed an increase of 190.2%, and the number of users aged 55 or above rose by 513.7%. This rise in older users was (5) .... suggested that Facebook had become mainly a site for older people. (6) .... was considered a site for young people, most of its users (28.2%) in July 2009 fell into the 35–54 age group. (7) .... , the 18-24 age group had dropped to third place with 25.1% of users, just behind the 25–34-year-olds. The rise in users aged 55 from under a million in January 2009 to nearly 5.9 million six months later took place (8) .... to see Facebook in a different way. (9) .... seem to show a decline in younger users, in fact what they show is that the overall number of users is growing, but at different rates. (10) .... rely on advertising, this is significant. (11) .... an advertisement, they react differently, because the audience has changed. (12) .... (if for example younger users didn't enter their data into the site), older users are still making a big impact.

	As of 1/04/09		As of 7/04/09		
Gender	**Users**	**Percentage**	**Users**	**Percentage**	**Growth**
US Males	17,747,880	42.2%	29,090,240	40.5%	63.9%
US Females	23,429,960	55.7%	39,246,680	54.6%	67.5%
Unknown	911,360	2.2%	3,564,480	5.0%	291.1%
Total US	42,089,200	100.0%	71,901,400	100.0%	70.8%
Age	**Users**	**Percentage**	**Users**	**Percentage**	**Growth**
0–17	5,674,780	13.5%	7,050,320	9.8%	24.2%
18–24	17,192,360	40.8%	18,017,480	25.1%	4.8%
25–34	11,254,700	26.7%	18,102,320	25.2%	60.8%
35–54	6,989,200	16.6%	20,285,640	28.2%	190.2%
55+	954,680	2.3%	5,859,160	8.1%	513.7%
Unknown	23,480	0.1%	2,586,480	3.6%	10915.7%
Geography	**Users**	**Percentage**	**Users**	**Percentage**	**Growth**
New York	1,622,560	3.9%	2,179,400	5.2%	34.3%
Chicago	797,040	1.9%	1,068,660	2.5%	34.1%
Los Angeles	636,160	1.5%	1,250,920	3.0%	96.6%
Miami	627,840	1.5%	825,280	2.0%	31.4%
Houston	560,520	1.3%	955,500	2.3%	70.5%
Atlanta	535,300	1.3%	1,297,420	3.1%	142.4%
Washington DC	526,460	1.3%	749,400	1.8%	42.3%
Philadelphia	498,220	1.2%	706,940	1.7%	41.9%
Boston	440,500	1.0%	605,600	1.4%	37.5%
San Fransisco	264,460	0.6%	387,280	0.9%	46.4%
Current Enrollment	**Users**	**Percentage**	**Users**	**Percentage**	**Growth**
High School	5,627,740	13.4%	4,697,780	6.6%	-16.5%
College	7,833,280	18.6%	6,133,600	8.7%	-21.7%
Alumni	4,756,480	11.3%	3,997,880	5.7%	-15.9%
Unknown	23,871,700	56.7%	55,927,000	79.0%	134.3%

2 Complete the text by writing a word or phrase from the box in each space. Use each word or phrase once only.

~~when~~	although	as	as if	as soon as	as though	by the time
even though	in case	such	since	the moment	whenever	while

How many Facebook friends should you have?

(1) ......When...... everyone you know starts using Facebook, it's time to wonder how many friends you should have. Facebook friends, that is. (2) .... someone boasts to me that they have 500 or 1000 friends, I become sceptical. (3) .... it's good to have lots of friends, can these electronic contacts really be worthy of the name? According to a recent book by Robin Dunbar, a professor of evolutionary anthropology, (4) .... you reach the number 150, you've arrived at the optimum number of people the brain can deal with. The professor argues his case at some length, (5) .... nobody could possibly deal with more than that number of people. Well, it is (6) .... an appealing idea that a lot of people have jumped on the bandwagon and declared that Dunbar's number, 150, is about the maximum number of Facebook friends anyone should have. (7) .... I heard about this idea, I started asking people how many Facebook friends they had. (8) .... you're wondering, no, I'm not on Facebook myself, so I needed to ask around. (9) .... I had to use normal conversational means, this took me some time. (10) .... it became rather a slow process, I considered signing up to Facebook, just so that I could ask people about this. Anyway, (11) .... I'd spoken to a few people about this, I began to think that 150 simply wasn't enough. For a start, (12) .... Facebook contacts are called 'friends', a lot of them turned out to be business contacts, or companies, or people the user had been at primary school with years ago. (13) .... these contacts are not close friends, people who are contacted often, it's useful to keep in touch with them. So if you have thousands of Facebook friends, it might sound (14) .... you have an over-active social life, but it depends on how often you contact them and why. It seems that you can never have enough friends, after all.

3 Rewrite the sentences as one sentence containing an adverbial clause.

1 Many people in the developing world now use or have access to mobile phones. Mobile technology is now a major contributor to economic growth.
So many people in the developing world now use or have access to mobile phones that mobile technology is now a major contributor to economic growth.

2 It seems that mobile phone use will just keep on rising. The entire world population owns or has access to a mobile phone.
....

3 Puerto Ricans top the list of mobile phone chatters. Many mobile phone plans in Puerto Rico include unlimited calls to the US where many people have relatives.
....

4 However, people in developing countries may come lower on the list as far as minutes per month are concerned. Mobile use is still booming.
....

5 Many people using mobile phones subscribe to money transfer services. They can send money easily by text message.
....

6 Sales of mobiles have rocketed. Sales of landline connections have remained at the same level for some time.
....

7 In the developing world, which now accounts for over 60% of mobile use, people choose not to have landlines. They are more expensive and harder to acquire.
....

8 Traditionally, effective communications infrastructure has been poor in developing countries. They have been held back economically, but mobile technology has changed everything.
....

9 You travel. It is now possible to use your mobile phone.
....

10 Even though there are a few parts of Britain where there is no mobile coverage, it is possible to use your mobile on Mount Everest. There is a China Telecom mast at the bottom of the mountain!
....

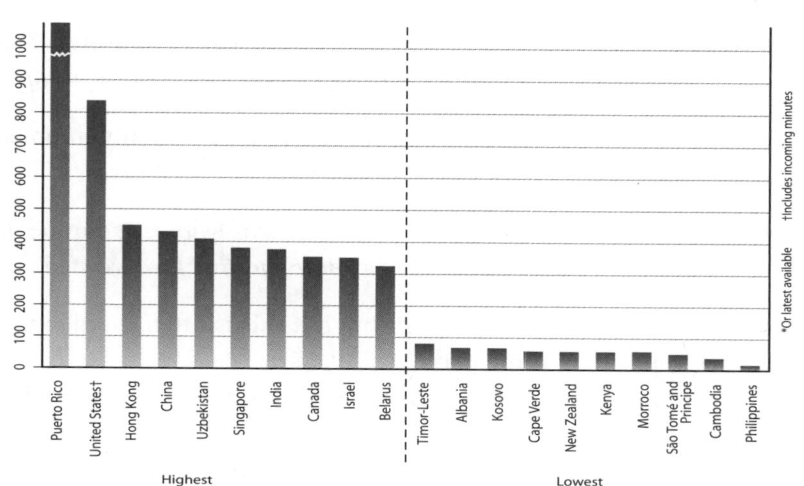

28

GRAMMAR

Relative clauses

Defining and non-defining clauses

- A defining relative clause gives specific information about a person or thing. It comes immediately after the noun it describes and is not separated from it by a comma:
  There are several matters ***that/which we need to discuss.***
  The book ***that/which I ordered*** *has not arrived yet.*

- A non-defining relative clause gives extra information which does not identify the person or thing it follows. It is separated from the main clause by commas:
  Paris, ***which I've visited several times,*** *is my favourite city.*

Which and *that*

- We can use *which* or *that* in defining clauses. In British English, *which* is more formal, while *that* is more common in American English:
  This is the equipment ***that/which gave us a lot of problems.***

- *Which* is more usual than *that* in a non-defining clause. *That* cannot be followed by a preposition:
  It is subject ***about which Professor James knows a great deal.***

Leaving out the relative pronoun

- We can leave out *that/which* if it is the object of the defining clauses:
  There are several matters ***(that/which) we need to discuss.***

- We cannot leave out *that/which* if it is the subject:
  This is the equipment ***that/which gave us a lot of problems.***

Who and *whom*

- *Who* is often replaced by *that* in everyday use in defining clauses:
  The people ***who/that lived there*** *had no idea what was happening.*

- *Whom* is the object form of *who*, and is used formally in object clauses:
  There were several people ***whom I did not recognize.***

- *Who* or *that* are used informally instead of *whom*, or can be left out:
  She was exactly the person ***(whom/who/that) we wanted for the job.***

- *Whom* is used after a preposition, but this is often avoided in everyday use by putting the preposition at the end of the clause:
  In the survey subjects were asked to describe a person ***to whom they had spoken earlier.*** (formal)
  They were asked to describe ***someone they had spoken to earlier.*** (less formal)

Whose

- *Whose* is the possessive form of *who*, and is used in both defining and non-defining clauses. It can apply to both people and to things:
  The police want to interview anyone ***whose car has been vandalized recently****.*
  One of the cars, ***whose wheels had been removed****, had to be taken to a garage.*

Prepositions and relative pronouns

- In everyday use we often put the preposition at the end of the clause to avoid over-formality, unless there is a long clause between the relative pronoun and the preposition:
  The goods, ***for which we had already paid****, had to be returned to the factory.*
  The goods, ***which we had already paid for****, had to be returned to the factory.*

  The professor ***with whom I attended the conference*** *offered me a research post.*
  The professor ***I attended the conference with*** *offered me a research post.*

- We do not split phrasal verbs in this way:
  All the extra responsibilities ***which she has taken on*** *are proving to be a worry.*

When, where, why, whereby

- In defining clauses, *when* and *where* follow general words for time or place:
  The office ***where my brother works*** *is near here.*
  Monday was the day ***when the results were expected.***

- In non-defining clauses, the place or time is usually much more exact:
  I stopped at the top of the stairs, ***where there was a window.***
  The accident occurred at around 4.30, ***when it was starting to get dark.***

- We can use *why* or *reason why* to explain reasons:
  This lack of preparation was ***the main reason why the project was a failure****.*

- *Whereby* is used after words such as *method, arrangement, regulation*, etc:
  The company operates an arrangement ***whereby employees can choose*** *their own working hours.*

Reduced relative clauses

- In defining clauses we can leave out the relative pronoun and part of the verb phrase to leave a past participle or a present participle acting as an adjective to define the noun, or we can omit a relative and *be*, leaving an adjective or adjectival phrase:
  This is the only painting ***(which was) not sold during the exhibition****.*
  Most of the people ***(who were) waiting for tickets went away disappointed****.*
  The house ***(which is) on sale*** *includes more than 10 hectares of land.*

- In non-defining clauses reduced clauses often occur in descriptive writing:
  The police officer, ***(who was) covered in blood,*** *staggered back to the car.*

Anyone who, those who

- We can use relative clauses after *anyone, something,* etc, and after *this/that/these/those*:
  I am looking for ***someone who can help me.***
  I think there is ***something (that) we need to discuss.***
  Those who know her well *say she is the ideal person for the job.*

Which

- We can use *which* to relate a non-defining clause to the main clause, and act as a comment upon it as a whole:
  The train was over an hour late, ***which was extremely annoying.***

- We can use other phrases in the same way: *at which time/point, by which time, in which case, in which event*:
  The symptoms may become worse, ***in which case contact your doctor***.

Nominal relative clauses

- In this kind of clause, *what* can mean 'the thing or things which':
  I don't know ***what to do***.
  What we really need *is a larger lab.*

- *Whatever* and *whoever* meaning 'anything/anyone at all' can be used in the same way:
  You can do ***whatever you want***.
  Whatever you do*, do it now!*
  You can bring ***whoever you like***.
  Whoever gets most points*, wins the prize.*

- *Whichever* is used when there are more than two items to choose from:
  There are three desks. You can use ***whichever one you prefer.***

- *All of, most of, some of, (number) of, none of,* etc can combine with *which* and *whom*:
  There are three castles, ***one of which*** *has Roman origins.*
  Ten people were rescued from the crash, ***none of whom*** *was badly injured.*

1 Underline the most suitable option in each sentence. Sometimes more than one option is possible.

1 There are a few details in this agreement *what/–/whom/that/which* are causing us problems.
2 Professor Smith is an expert for *what/who/–/whom/that/which* we all feel the highest regard.
3 Students *whose/who/–/whom/that/which* mobile phones are not switched off run the risk of expulsion from the examination room.
4 There are two other matters *what/who/–/whom/that/which* we need to discuss.
5 Did you take the name and address of the person *whose/what/who/–/whom/that/which* car you crashed into?
6 Helen is the kind of student *whose/what/who/–/whom/that/which* will succeed at the highest level.
7 There was only one college *what/–/whom/that/which* asked me to attend an interview.
8 I'd like to hear from anyone *whose/who/–/whom/that/which* flat will be available for rent in July and August.
9 The official *who/–/whom/that/which* issued the report later admitted that its conclusions had been wrong.
10 There is something *what/who/–/whom/that/which* the first witness said that doesn't really make sense.

2 Underline uses of *who, whom, which* or *that* which can be left out.

1 The last thing that we expected was to discover a species that nobody had previously recorded.
2 The hall into which we were led was full of children who were all shouting and screaming.
3 The inquiry that we set up heard evidence from a number of residents whose homes had suffered damage in the floods.
4 The person who I spoke to told me that the goods which I had bought online could not be exchanged.
5 The scientist who is in charge of the project is the one whose opinion matters most.
6 The tomb that we have recently discovered is the one that everyone has been looking for.
7 There is somebody here whom I'd like you to meet, somebody whose research I think you will find interesting.
8 The second expedition, which took place in 1932, found no traces of a city, which was disappointing.
9 The period that I find the most interesting, and one which is rightly getting a lot of interest nowadays, is that between 800 and 1000 AD.
10 The entry which wins the competition will be the one which shows most originality.

3 Complete each sentence by writing one suitable word in each space, or leave it blank.

1 ...What...... we really need now is some help from the government.
2 William Golding, ... won the Nobel Prize in 1983, is best known for his novel *Lord of the Flies*.
3 Five people were interviewed for the position, none of .... were suitable.
4 There was no one .... opinion was so sought after.
5 I am uncertain to .... I should address my letter.
6 If you cannot open the document you may not have the appropriate software, in .... case you should download a viewer from the Magnosoft website.
7 It is a subject on .... some people hold very strong views.
8 What was the main reason .... the company chose Paris as their headquarters?
9 Everyone .... knows my father thinks very highly of him.
10 The earthquake occurred during the night .... most people were at home in bed.

4 Write a new sentence with a similar meaning to the first sentence by placing the word in bold at the end of the sentence and leaving out unnecessary relative pronouns.

1 I need someone **on** whom I can rely.
...I need someone I can rely on...
2 The doctor phoned back all the patients **with** whom she had already had interviews.
....
3 This is exactly the kind of material **for** which we have been looking.
....
4 There are two or three matters **with** which I want to take issue.
....
5 A phenotype contains the genome **from** which it originates.
....
6 His third film, *Last Time*, is **for** what he will be remembered.
....
7 It was not the experiment **with** which they were most satisfied.
....
8 The sale of its old offices was the transaction **from** which the company profited most.
....
9 Such a substance can be broken down into the elements **of** which it is composed.
....
10 Shakespeare is one of those writers **for** whose personal life there is very little evidence.
....

5 Complete each short text by writing one suitable word in each space, or leave it blank.

The Penny Post

The postal service (1) ....which.... existed in the UK up to 1840 was expensive. All charges, (2) .... varied according to the distance the letter travelled and the number of pages (3) .... it contained, were paid by (4) .... received the letter, something (5) .... seems odd from a modern perspective. The person (6) .... can be called the father of the modern postal system was Sir Rowland Hill, (7) .... reforms were based on pre-payment, and (8) .... introduced the postage stamp, the Penny Black, (9) .... became one of the most famous stamps in the world.

Belém, Portugal

The Portuguese port of Belém, (10) .... name is derived from the Portuguese word for Bethlehem, is part of the city of Lisbon. It is the port from (11) .... many Portuguese ships set out on voyages of exploration, (12) .... established it as a profitable trading port (13) .... spices and other goods were imported from India, the far East and from South America. The Belém Palace, (14) .... is now the residence of the President of Portugal, is a former royal palace built in the 16th century. The city's most famous image is the Torre de Belém, (15) .... was originally built as a fortress to protect the port, and (16) .... image often appears in tourist literature.

Commuting in Britain

Research in Britain has found that British commuters, (17) .... spend an average of 45 minutes commuting to work, have the longest commute in Europe. People (18) .... work in London use public transport most, but outside the capital 70% of commuters use cars to get to work, a situation (19) .... the researchers say should convince the government to improve Britain's road system. The conclusion of their report, (20) .... will come as no surprise to anyone (21) .... has travelled on British roads at peak times, is that Britain is a nation (22) .... the car is king. Many people (23) .... drive to work do it because they have no other choice, and the poor state of public transport is something else to (24).............. the report draws attention.

29

GRAMMAR

Participle clauses

Participle (or non-finite) clauses use a participle instead of a full verb. They can be either defining or non-defining.

Defining: *Anyone* ***parking without permission*** *will receive a penalty fine.*
All those ***interested in attending the meeting*** *should arrive by 7.30.*

Non-defining: ***Closing the door behind her****, she walked quickly down the road and out of sight.*
Sold at auction*, the painting fetched £10 million.*

Two actions at the same time performed by the same subject

- The participle clause can come at the beginning or end. If at the beginning it is usually followed by a comma:
  Using a compass, *they calculated the area affected by the quake.*
  They calculated the area affected by the quake ***using a compass.***

One action before another performed by the same subject

- The subject of both clauses must be the same:
  After reading the report, *she changed her mind.*

- We cannot use a participle clause when the subject of each clause is different:
  After I gave her the report, she changed her mind.
  (*After giving her the report, she changed ...* is not possible as this would mean she gave herself the report.)

- *Having* + past participle is used to show that one action is the consequence of the other:
  Having used up all the money we had, *we asked for a loan from the bank.*

- Using the present participle can refer to past time:
  Leaving the door open, *I went outside to see who was there.*

- A passive participle clause can also be shortened:
  (Having been) introduced to the President, *he could think of nothing to say.*

Time clause with *after, before, since, when, while, on*

- The participle follows the time word:
  Clean it thoroughly with warm soapy water ***before using it for the first time.***
  Since examining the data, *I've come to a different conclusion.*

- *On* describes an event immediately followed by another event:
  On hearing the fire alarm, *we evacuated the building.*

- *Be* is not changed to a participle, but left out:
  While in the laboratory, *she noticed that something was wrong.*

Manner, contrast and conditional clauses

She waved her arms about, ***as if (she was) swatting a fly.***
Although feeling ill, *I went to the meeting.*
If studying full-time, *expect to spend 20 hours a week outside of set lectures.*
(Being) interested in animals, *she took a job at Bristol zoo. (As she was ...)*

It and *There* clauses

- *It* or *there* can also be used as a subject in formal speech or writing:
  There being no further time today, *the meeting will continue in the morning.*
  It being a Sunday, *there were fewer trains than usual.*

With and *Without clauses*

- These are used in descriptive writing. We can leave out *with* in many cases:
  (With) blood pouring from his wounds, *he staggered into the room.*
  Without making a sound, *she opened the door.*

Adjective clauses

- A present or past participle can be used as an adjective, making an adjectival clause:
  There were several people in the room, ***looking*** *closely at the paintings.*
  They found the wreckage of the aircraft ***scattered*** *over a wide area.*

1 Correct any errors in these sentences.

1 Taking a deep breath and she dived into the water.
Taking a deep breath, she dived into the water. ....

2 After considered the new evidence, the judge dismissing the case.
....

3 They removed the fragments, carefully having photographing each one first.
....

4 Driving to work, a tree fell across the road in front of him.
....

5 Accepted the recommendations of the committee, the principal has now resigned.
....

6 Foster on checking the figures again, he realized there had been a mistake.
....

7 It was being a public holiday, all the banks were closed.
....

8 Since becoming president O'Hara, he has been forced to change his plans.
....

9 Suffered from a paralysis of the right hand, although Leonardo was still able to draw.
....

10 Forcing to leave Vienna, Freud spent his last years in London.
....

2 Complete the second sentence so that it has a similar meaning to the first sentence.

1 She took a holiday and then she felt much better.
After taking a holiday she felt much better ....

2 It was badly damaged but the plane managed to land safely.
Although ....

3 He didn't think and deleted the document.
Without ....

4 She arrived in Paris and went directly to her hotel.
On ....

5 He removed his shoes and walked through the metal detector.
Having ....

6 JK Rowling wrote the first *Harry Potter* book and then became a top-selling author.
Since ....

7 He hardly dared to breathe and pressed the button.
Hardly ....

8 The doctor examined the patient and decided she should be admitted to hospital.
Having ....

9 The archaeologists used carbon-dating and established the age of the sword.
Using ....

10 She was trapped in the wrecked car and was not discovered for several hours.
Trapped ....

3 Complete the text by writing a suitable participle in each space, using a form of a verb from the box. More than one answer may be possible.

~~retain~~	abandon	concern	investigate	notice	study
attract	continue	leave	develop	return	succeed
carry out	go	make	publish	spend	turn out

Leonardo and flight

Leonardo da Vinci was also an engineer, (1) retaining a professional interest in various kinds of machinery, while (2) .... his career as an artist. He was especially fascinated by flight, (3) .... many drawings of flying machines, most of them, however, (4) .... to be impractical. After (5) .... the way that birds moved their wings, Leonardo drew detailed plans, (6) .... these in the *Codex on the Flight of Birds*. Despite (7) .... much of his life (8) .... himself with the problem of flight, he only produced one workable flying machine, a hang glider, which has actually been constructed in modern times.

Fleming and penicillin

While (9) .... the properties of staphylococci, Fleming stumbled upon penicillin by chance. In September 1928, on (10) .... to his laboratory after (11) .... on holiday with his family, he checked the cultures of staphylococci (12) .... for several weeks in a corner on the bench. (13) .... that one of them had grown a fungus and that the surrounding staphylococci had died, he showed it to an assistant, and after (14) .... research on this fungus for a year or so, published an article about it in 1929, (15) .... little interest at the time. (16) .... his research as there seemed little chance of anyone (17) .... a drug from the fungus, he concentrated on other work. Two other researchers, Florey and Chain, took over, and (18) .... in producing a usable drug, were awarded the Nobel Prize, along with Fleming, in 1945.

4 Write one new sentence with a similar meaning to the two sentences, using a non-finite clause and the word in bold. There may be more than one possible answer.

1 We locked all the doors. Then we left.
before
Before leaving, we locked all the doors.
We locked all the doors before leaving.

2 She checked the photographs. She made an interesting discovery.
while
....
....

3 He received the news of his appointment. Then he called a press conference.
on
....
....

4 I started to take this medicine in June. I have had no recurrence of symptoms.
since
....
....

5 She picked up the papers. Then she ran out of the room.
picking
....
....

6 Some students do not wish to attend on Friday. There will be a session for them next Tuesday.
wishing
....
....

7 Jackson was forced to resign. He was accused of falsifying the bank's accounts.
having
....
....

8 The castle is thought to be of timber construction. There were no traces of masonry.
being
....
....

9 We have been burgled twice. We have decided to install a new alarm system.
having
....
....

10 Trains leave this station. All of them stop at Euston.
leaving
....
....

30

GRAMMAR

Practice 10

1 Put one suitable word in each space.

Walking and cycling in Scotland

Recent research in Scotland focused on the number of adults (1) ......who...... walked or cycled in 2008. There are several conclusions (2) .... can be drawn from the figures, though it is stressed that the report, (3) .... was based on a small sample of people, gives indications only. 53% of adults (4) .... were questioned had walked more than 400 metres in the previous seven days, (5) .... might seem a low figure considering the distance involved. Unsurprisingly, the people (6) .... had walked the most were in the 16–19 age group. Older people walk far less, (7) .... is also unsurprising. The proportion of those (8) .... had walked for pleasure or to keep fit (47%) tended to rise with income. The figures for cycling, (9) .... were much lower than those for walking (5%), seem disappointing. More generally, it is men (10) .... do most of the walking and the cycling, though there are age variations. For example, the walking figures show significant numbers of women (11) .... are in their thirties. Not shown in the graph are other trends, (12) .... suggest that people are generally walking less and walking shorter distances than they were twenty years ago. The figures for cycling, (13) .... show that cyclists now make longer average journeys, were based on too small a sample to be significant. (14) .... would also be useful would be more information on people's reasons for taking part or not taking part in these activities.

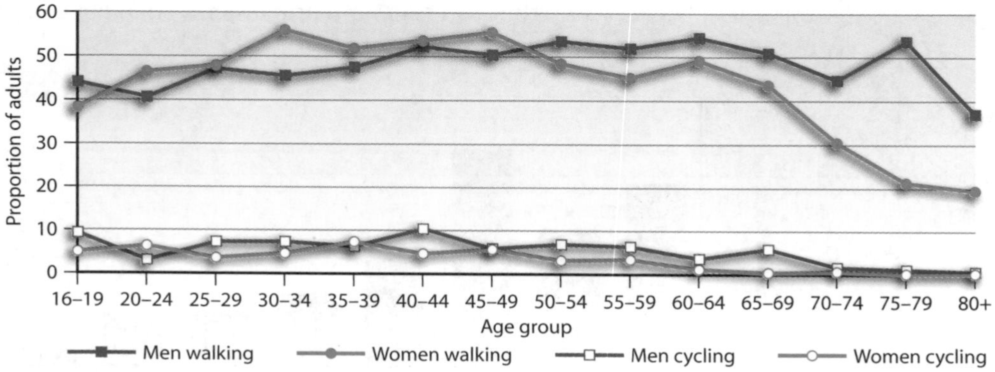

Scottish Government statistics

2 Rewrite the numbered clauses as participle clauses where possible.

Your carbon footprint: travel and transport

If you study this table (1) showing.... (which shows) the carbon emissions (CO_2) per passenger kilometre (CEPPK) made by different kinds of transport, it is clear that anyone (2) .... (who chooses) to travel by train has a much smaller 'carbon footprint' than someone (3) .... (who uses) a car. Obviously, anyone (4) .... (who travels) by car alone is responsible for more emissions than someone (5) .... (who carries) passengers. The more people being transported, the lower the emissions per passenger kilometre, as becomes clear when you look at the information (6) .... (which gives) the CEPPK figures for domestic air travel. A plane of course carries a large number of people, (7) .... (which means) that the figure per passenger is lower than that for a car with a single passenger. Both trains and planes, (8) .... (which tend) to travel long distances, show lower rates than cars, (9) .... (which may be used) only for short range commuting. What this kind of table shows clearly is that relative to domestic flights and rail journeys, cars are the form of transport (10) .... (which cause) the most pollution.

What do these figures really tell us, however, about (11) .... (what we should do) if we want to reduce our personal carbon footprint? There are number of issues (12) .... (that are not mentioned) in the table. For example, what about people whose journeys can only be made by car? There are many regions where there are poor public transport links, or none at all. People (13) .... (who live) in rural areas and (14) .... (who need) to go to the local supermarket may have to drive to get there.
The cleanest form of transport, (15) .... (which is not included) in the table, is cycling, but this may not be an option for anyone (16) .... (who is elderly), has young children, or has to carry heavy loads over long distances. The message seems to be that we should try to use low carbon transport where the alternative exists. We can also conclude that (17) .... (what will reduce) carbon emissions is likely to be a set of public policies (18) .... (which make) some journeys unnecessary, and (19) .... (which provide) cheap public transport. Any government (20) .... (that can fund and implement) such policies will win the votes of environmentalists.

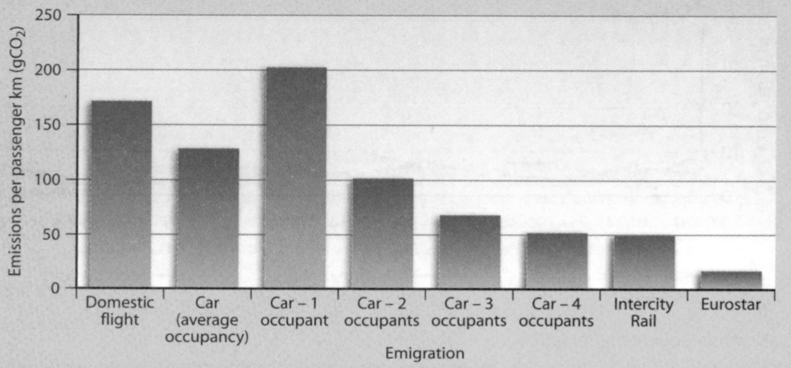

Emissions per passenger km (gCO_2)
250
200
150
100
50
0
Domestic flight
Car (average occupancy)
Car – 1 occupant
Car – 2 occupants
Car – 3 occupants
Car – 4 occupants
Intercity Rail
Eurostar
Emigration

3 Complete the text by writing a phrase (a–r) in each space.

~~a which rather surprisingly~~
b which are designed for
c which can run
d which has many
e which is linked to
f which ticks all the boxes
g that fills most people with
h which are designed to
i which costs
j which is bound to
k which is trying to
l which make charging batteries
m what all these cars
n which all other cars
o which don't contain
p which have
q which looks like
r which predicts that

Electric cars

Electric cars, (1) ....a...... came into existence over 50 years before conventional cars, are often said to be the cars of the future. The European Environment Agency is one of many bodies (2) .... by the middle of the century 25% of all the cars in the world will be electric. For short journeys in the city an electric car is a form of transport (3) .... obvious advantages. In parts of London, (4) .... promote greener forms of transport, electric cars have free parking, and are exempt from the congestion charge (5) .... have to pay to enter the central city area. Government road tax, (6) .... the amount of CO^2 emissions made by the car, is zero for electric cars. In London there are also free power points (7) .... less of a problem. All of these savings for the car owner add up to a set of incentives (8) .... make electric motoring attractive. However, the thought of owning an electric car is not yet a prospect (9) .... enthusiasm. While sales of hybrids, cars (10) .... for short periods on batteries, but (11) .... low-emission petrol or diesel engines, have rocketed, electric cars haven't really taken off. However, this is a situation (12) .... change as fuel costs rise and as more efficient and cheaper models come onto the market. There is an impressive range of cars, from the small, and often odd-looking ones (13) .... taking one person to work and back, to the relatively high-speed sports car (14) .... over £100,000. What the market is waiting for is a car (15) .... the kind of car the average person might want to drive. (16) .... depend on is battery technology, and when the industry can supply low-cost high performance batteries (17) .... dangerous substances, then sales will certainly take off. Although before too long there could just be a vehicle powered by some other source (18) .... : reasonable cost, zero or very low emissions, and high performance. We'll have to wait and see.

31

GRAMMAR

Pronouns and determiners

Pronouns and determiners

Some words can stand alone as pronouns or can be used with a noun as determiners:

Both *looked the same.* (pronoun)

Both *houses looked the same.* (determiner)

Every and *each* + noun

- *Every* and *each* can mean the same, though *each* is often used to mean 'separately' or 'one by one', especially when we are thinking of a definite number:

  Every/Each *time I come here, it seems to be raining.*

  There was a cupboard in ***each*** *corner of the room.* (a definite number)

Each (of), both (of), either, neither

- *Each* refers to one or more things or people separately:

  If two players win, they ***each*** *get a prize/****each of them*** *gets a prize.*

  The winners received €500 ***each****.*

- *Both* refers to one or more things or people together:

  They ***both*** *arrived at the same time.*

  Both (of them) *arrived at the same time.*

  I like ***them both****.*

  I like ***both of them****.*

- *Either (of)* means 'one or the other', when it doesn't matter which one. It uses a singular verb. *Not ... either* is also possible:

  We can use ***either*** *method.* ***Either of them*** *is suitable.*

- *Neither (of)* is the negative form, meaning 'not one nor the other':

  I don't like those methods.

  We ***can't use either****.*

  Neither of them *is suitable.*

Each other, one another, one ... the other

- *Each other* refers to one or more things or people each doing something to the other:

  The two professors accused ***each other*** *of stealing the idea.*

- *One another* has the same meaning. Some speakers prefer to use *each other* for two things or people, and *one another* for more than two:

  Members of the team help ***one another****.*

- *One* and *the other* refer to related things:

  They've got two cats. ***One*** *is white and* ***the other*** *is black.*

Pronouns with *some-*, *any-*, and *no-*

- Formally we refer to the pronoun with *he/him/his*, but *they/them/their* is now usual in informal or spoken English:
  ***Someone/somebody** has left **his/their** wallet on the desk.*

- Impersonal *they/their* is often used instead. In formal writing *he* or *she/his* or *her* is used:
  *Does **everyone** know what **they** are/**he or she** is supposed to be doing?*

- *Someone, something*, etc can be used with an adjective, a comparative adjective or an infinitive:
  *I've got **something important** to tell you.*
  *Have you got **anything smaller**?*
  *He says he's got **nothing to do**.*
  *Is there **anything for us to drink**?*

- This also applies to adverbials *anywhere, somewhere, nowhere*:
  *There's **nowhere** nice to sit.*
  *Do you know **anywhere** cheaper?*

- The determiner *else* can be added to all of these words to mean 'other':
  *I'm in love with **someone else**.*
  *Do you want **anything else**?*

None, none of, one/ones

- *None* means 'not any' or 'not one'. When it is a subject, the verb may be singular or plural, though a singular verb with a plural subject is not considered correct in formal written English:
  ***None of** the experiments **was/were** completely successful.*
  *There**'s none** left.*
  *There **are** none left.*

- We use *one/ones* to avoid repeating a countable noun or person:
  *Are those **the ones** you meant?*
  *Harry was **the one** who helped us most.*

1 Underline the most suitable option in each sentence.

1. There is *nothing/nowhere/neither* to be gained by sending this girl to prison.
2. The police were called when the two neighbours threatened *each other/both/either* with knives.
3. The patient wakes up *either/one/every* morning with stomach pains.
4. The witness pointed at the two defendants and accused them *each other/both/either* of threatening her.
5. The president pointed out that *nothing/neither/none* of the many proposals put before him would deal with the real issues.
6. The director told her that he had been looking for *anyone/someone/everyone* to open a new office in Italy.
7. You are advised to use a different password for *each/each of/each other* website you visit.
8. I am afraid that there is *nowhere/nothing else/neither* we can do to help you at the moment.
9. We think you'll find that Yorkshire really does provide the best of *each/everything/either*!
10. I have replaced the bulbs in *both/either/every* lights, but neither of them works.

2 Complete the second sentence so that it has a similar meaning to the first sentence.

1. The team wins whenever Smith plays.
   Every time Smith plays the team wins .
2. All of the experiments failed.
   None.. .
3. Neither of these books is suitable.
   Both.. .
4. Everyone on the project received a bonus.
   Each.. .
5. The expedition made no discoveries.
   Nothing.. .
6. These two proposals will each be expensive.
   Either.. .
7. This line has an error in it.
   There is something.. .
8. There aren't any seats in this part of the library.
   There's nowhere.. .
9. I have some interesting news for you.
   I have something.. .
10. Do you want more to eat?
    Do you want anything.. ?

3 Complete each short text by writing a suitable pronoun in each space. Add a determiner if necessary.

The Curies

Marie and Pierre Curie were two scientists who married in 1895. They (1) ...both... explored the phenomenon of radioactivity, (2) .... that was barely understood at the time. They assisted one another in their research, and in 1903 they were (3) .... awarded the Nobel Prize. (4) .... Marie and Pierre handled radioactive material with their bare hands. At the time (5) .... of them realized that the radiation they worked with was so dangerous. After Pierre died in an accident in 1906, Marie won a second Nobel Prize in 1911.

Conquering Everest

In May 1953, two men, Tenzing Norgay and Edmund Hillary, conquered Mount Everest, the highest mountain in the world. It was the first time that (6) .... had definitely succeeded in reaching the summit. The two men were part of a team that helped (7) .... to climb the massive, icy mountain but were the only (8) .... who reached the summit.

Road accident

Two people have been injured in a road accident involving two vehicles. (9) .... of the two cars skidded on the icy road forcing (10) .... off the road. (11) .... drivers were trapped in their vehicles but were later released by emergency services, and (12) .... suffered serious injury.

Speed cameras

(13) .... likes being told what to do, especially on the roads. Speed cameras are (14) .... of the ways of encouraging people to drive more responsibly. (15) .... include chicanes and speed humps, also called 'sleeping policemen', (16) .... of which are often used in residential streets to force drivers to slow down. (17) .... of these is as unpopular as speed cameras, however, because (18) .... who is caught by the camera has to pay a fine. (19) .... people argue that it is (20) .... other than a means of raising revenue. It is certainly true that (21) .... time (22) .... is caught, the authority earns more money, which it can use to pay its bills.

4 Write a new sentence with a similar meaning to the first sentence, using the word in bold. Do not change the word given.

1 Is there a place where we can get something to eat?
anywhere
Is there anywhere we can get something to eat?

2 I don't know the answer and you don't know the answer.
us
....

3 The cupboard is empty.
there
....

4 I'll take this one and that one.
them
....

5 Are you all right?
wrong
....

6 We all need someone to love.
needs
....

7 My wallet is nowhere to be found.
find
....

8 We can use this one or that one.
them
....

9 Another person is sitting in my place.
else
....

10 These people are homeless.
live
....

32

GRAMMAR

Prepositional phrases

Prepositions and adverbs

- A preposition always has an object. Some prepositions of place can be used as adverbs (adverb particles) with no object:
  *She ran **across** the road.* (preposition)

- Many prepositions of place can be used as adverbs with no object:
  *The lake is 2 kms **across**.* (adverb)
  Others include: *above, along, around, behind, below, beneath, down, in, inside, near, off, on, opposite, out, outside, round, through, under, underneath, up*

- Many are used in phrases:
  ***behind** the times*
  ***below** zero*
  ***within** a short distance*

Place or position

At, on and *in*, and similar words such as *within, upon* are used with *be* and verbs that describe position, e.g. *sit, stand, live*. They do not describe movement.

- *At* a place, an address, a house, a building, a point on a journey or in a process:
  *It's **at** the entrance/**at** university/**at** 12 Green Street/**at** the cinema/**at** the Grand Hotel/ **at** the beginning/**at** that point.*

- *On* touching something in a particular place:
  *It's **on** the top shelf/**on** the outskirts/**on** the notice board/**on** the west coast*

- *In* a room, container, etc, a city, country direction or area:
  *It's **in** the drawer/**in** New York/**in** Greece/**in** Africa/**in** the district/ **in** the North.*

Movement

With a verb of motion, e.g. *come* and *go*, we use *to, into/onto, out of, towards* and other prepositions or adverbials that involve movement: *along, up/down, through, across*:
*She walked **across** the path and came **to** the side door.*
*He ran **out of** the room and **down** the stairs.*
The following is a list of prepositions of place and movement:

- *Abroad, ahead, ashore* show movement, while *abroad* and *ahead* can describe place or movement. They are adverbs, but *ahead of* + object is a prepositional phrase:
  *Several bodies were washed **ashore** later in the week. (= to the shore)*
  *Many pensioners now live **abroad**.*
  *I'm going **abroad** next week.*
  *It's time for the company to move **ahead**.*
  *Smith is **ahead of** Jones in the race.*

- *Above* and *over* can be used to mean the same thing, especially when something is at a higher level exactly vertically. The opposite is *below*:
  The company started in an office ***over/above*** *a shop.*
  There were strange noises coming from the flat ***below****.*

- *Above* means 'at a higher level' but *over* means 'touching':
  The temperature is 20°C ***above*** *normal.*
  They put a blanket ***over*** *him.*

- *Across, over* have the meaning 'from one side to the other' with a verb of motion:
  She walked ***across/over*** *the road.*

- *Around, round* describes moving in a circle:
  People once believed the Sun went ***around/round*** *the Earth.*

- *Along* describes movement 'in the direction of a line', and can also shown direction in general:
  He walked ***along*** *the top of the wall.*
  She was walking ***along*** *the road.*

- *Alongside* means close to the side. It also means 'together with':
  The road runs ***alongside*** *the canal.*
  Scientists worked ***alongside*** *chefs on the project.*

- *Among* means 'in a number of things':
  Among *the survivors were several children.*

- *Away (from)* describes a movement, the opposite of *towards*:
  Come ***away from*** *the edge! You might fall.*

- *Away* also means you have left home for some time, perhaps to stay somewhere else:
  Helen and Bill are ***away*** *in France.*
  Anna is ***away from*** *school today.*

- *Far away* describes a place:
  I wish I was ***far away*** *from here.*

- *Back* describes a returning movement:
  When will she be ***back****?*
  Come ***back****! I want to talk to you!*

- *Backwards, forwards/forward* describe a direction of movement:
  The car was going ***backwards****.*
  I reached ***forward*** *and took her hand.*

- *Backward* and *forward* are also used as adjectives, e.g. *a* ***forward*** *movement.*

- *Between* means 'being in the middle of two':
  The factory is sited half way ***between*** *London and Dover.*

- *By* and *past* describe something that passes, with verbs of motion:
  We walked ***by*** *the house twice before we recognized it.*
  Time goes ***past*** *very slowly when you are bored.*

- *Over* can mean 'covering an area' or 'above':
  The police put a blanket ***over*** *his head.*
  She jumped ***over*** *the wall.*

- *Out (of)* means 'not at home'. *In* means 'at home':
  The director is ***out/is not in*** *at the moment.*
  She's ***out of*** *town.*

- *Under* can mean 'covered by', but *below* generally means 'at a lower level':
  There's a cat ***under*** *the table.*
  The lake is 100m ***below*** *sea level.*

- *Under* can mean 'less than' and *over* 'more than':
  The total cost of the project was ***over*** *€2 million.*

- *Up* and *down* are used with *road, street,* etc to mean 'along':
  I saw him as I was walking ***up*** *the road.*

Pairs of adverbs

Many adverbs are used in pairs to describe movement:

back *and* ***forth***
backwards *and* ***forwards***
in *and* ***out***
round *and* ***round***
to *and* ***fro***
up *and* ***down***

The figures have been going ***up and down*** *unpredictably*
People were running ***round and round*** *in circles not knowing what to do.*

Phrases

Many prepositions form phrases with nouns. Check meanings with a dictionary:

above *average*
above *the law*
at *rest*
below *average*
in *charge*
in *control*
on *average*
on *the way*
under *construction*
under *pressure*
under *suspicion*

1 Underline the most suitable options in each sentence.

1 The dog ran *opposite/across/at* the road and jumped *over/to/through* a garden wall.
2 According to the story, while Newton was sitting *at/under/below* an apple tree, an apple fell and hit him *on/at/to* the head.
3 Celsius was born *at/to/in* Sweden, and became Professor of Astronomy *at/to/in* the University of Uppsala.
4 Few visitors are now allowed *inside/underneath/alongside* the cave because the paintings *at/in/on* the walls are damaged by their breath.
5 The photo shows plastic debris washed *ashore/around/along* last week *on/at/to* a Pacific island.
6 *In/At/On* average, the Moon orbits *across/away from/around* the Earth at a distance of about 385,000 km.
7 Opportunities for studying *away/abroad/around* are available *on/at/to* a number of European universities.
8 *Inside/Along/Among* the many objects brought *in/at/to* the museum by metal-detectors were these gold coins.
9 It seems that the company has now fallen *off/behind/among* others in the same field, even though when it started out it was *ahead/away/under* of its time.
10 The police officer walked *up and down/in and out/round and round* the street, looking for the man who had jumped *off/past/out* of the car.

2 Complete each sentence (1–10) with one of the endings (a–j).

1 The president said that the opposition was in ....
2 The recently discovered collection of gold and silver artefacts has been put on ....
3 After the agreement signed in 1802 between the two countries, they remained at ....
4 After being taken ill at the end of June, the prime minister did not appear in ....
5 Historians now agree that in fact neither side was directly at ....
6 The king desperately needed money, as the treasury was deeply in ....
7 The heir to the throne, Prince George, was unfortunately not in ....
8 To the commanders, the situation seemed at ....
9 The crisis occurred when the CEO was out of ....
10 The fleet had been trapped in the harbour for weeks, and the crews were out of ....

a public again until the first week of October.
b good health, and seemed unlikely to live for more than a few months.
c peace until their uneasy relationship broke down a year later.
d debt, and parliament was unlikely to grant him any more revenue.
e first sight to hold little danger, but they quickly saw their mistake.
f danger of misleading the public with its plans for reform.
g practice, as no training had been possible.
h fault, and that hostilities could easily have been halted.
i display at the local town hall, before being taken to the museum.
j reach in a secluded country house, and could not easily be contacted.

3 Complete each short text by writing a preposition from the box in each space. Some prepositions are used more than once.

back	far away	in	on	to

Eels

European eels are migratory fish found (1) ....in.......... European countries with coastlines (2) .... the North Atlantic. They spend their adult lives (3) .... freshwater (4) .... rivers such as the Thames, where they remain for up to twenty years before travelling 6,500 kms (5) .... their spawning grounds (6) .... (7) .... the Sargasso Sea. There they die, and the newborn eels then spend as long as three years travelling (8) .... (9) .... fresh water.

at	beneath	beside	down	on	opposite	round	through	to

Guide book directions

Leaving the town, look for the sign (10) .... Albury which can be found (11) .... the end of the village (12) .... the right, (13) .... the filling station. Follow the path (14) .... the railway for 700 metres, and after it passes (15) .... a tunnel (16) .... the motorway, go (17) .... the steps (18) .... the right and follow the path as it circles (19) .... until it comes (20) .... the river bank. There is a notice board with a map (21) .... this point showing the way (22) .... Albury.

alongside	among	in	to	under	within

Eco-towns

New eco-towns are (23) .... construction (24) .... various parts of the country. (25) .... these towns the emphasis will be on providing as many 'green' features as possible, (26) .... which will be: a 'smart' meter (27) .... each house, making it easier to control energy consumption; businesses and schools (28) .... a short distance of every home so everyone can walk or cycle (29) .... work or school; good public transport with timetable information available (30) .... the home; the use of wind and solar power (31) .... conventional energy sources for all homes and businesses; and more green spaces.

4 Write a new sentence with a similar meaning to the first sentence, using the word in bold. Do not change the word given.

1 Generally speaking, women live longer than men.
average
On average, women live longer than men.

2 The new bridge is still being built.
construction
....

3 Tina is the head of the sales department.
charge
....

4 It is suspected that the two men did something wrong.
under
....

5 We are successfully managing the situation.
control
....

6 The president is being forced to consider changing the law.
pressure
....

5 Write a new sentence with a similar meaning to the first sentence, using the preposition in bold. Do not change the word given.

1 The faculty library is located near the office.
within
The faculty library is located within a short distance of the office.

2 We finished the project earlier than scheduled.
ahead
....

3 Government spending cannot be controlled.
out
....

4 For full information, see the bottom of the page.
below
....

5 I am in the middle of the book at the moment.
through
....

6 Most importantly, Koch is remembered for his work on tuberculosis.
above
....

7 Since things are as they are, you'd better leave, and come back next week.
under
....

8 Peter is on a business trip and not at home.
....

33

GRAMMAR

Practice 11

1 Complete the text by writing one suitable preposition in each space.

Homelessness: Trends over time

According to government statistics, the problem of homelessness is being slowly brought (1) ......*under*...... control. Although these figures are not completely (2) .... to date, the table shows that they have changed (3) .... the better. At the beginning of the period (4) .... consideration, over 150,000 households came (5) .... the definition of homeless. (6) .... contrast, ten years later the numbers were well (7) .... this level, at (8) .... 85,000. In 2003, the figures seemed (9) .... danger of rising (10) .... of control, as (11) .... that point they had topped the 200,000 mark. Local authorities have been (12) .... pressure to provide more housing, and their services are much (13) .... demand. However, (14) .... practice they have to prioritize those (15) .... need of housing, which, (16) .... general, means those with special needs or with children, though not all families with children qualify (17) .... the rules. The table shows (18) .... detail how many homeless with 'priority need' have been rehoused during the ten-year period. (19) .... average, only about half of those with children qualify (20) .... this way, so (21) .... addition the table shows numbers of homeless families who have not been rehoused. Note that there is a significant number of homeless who are considered to have lost their accommodation (22) .... purpose. Local authorities are (23) .... no obligation to rehouse this category. The overall figures seem encouraging, but they are (24) .... no means universally accepted as representing the full truth about homelessness.

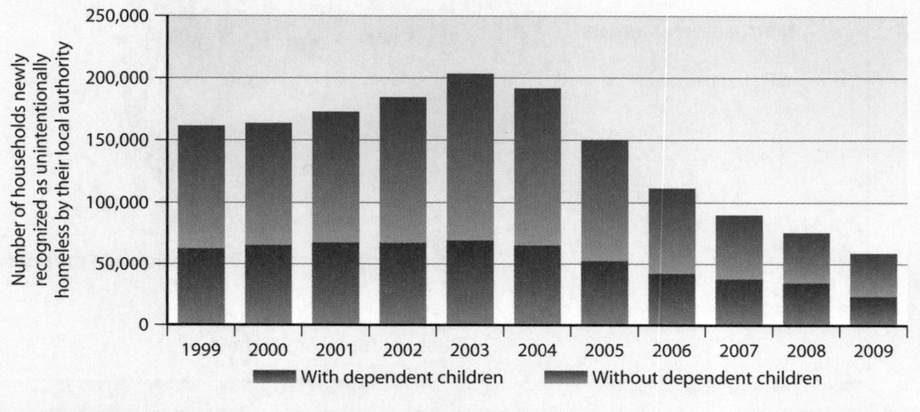

2 Complete the text by writing one suitable word in each space.

Why are people homeless?

(1) ...Anyone...... who has lost their permanent accommodation is classified in the UK as homeless. (2) .... these may be people who have (3) .... to live and are literally sleeping on the street, but (4) .... practice the majority will be people living in temporary accommodation. (5) .... of the bodies concerned with the homeless agree with the government on exact numbers of homeless people, mainly because (6) .... organization has its own way of defining who the homeless are. Leaving this question aside, most are (7) .... agreement about the causes of homelessness. Many people who previous lived (8) .... home with their families, or who were living (9) .... the time being with relatives or friends, end up without a roof (10) .... their heads when they can no longer be helped (11) .... this way. Some people in this category, sometimes known as 'sofa surfers' end up going (12) .... and forth from one house to another, and may not appear (13) .... the statistics at all. Another large group comes (14) .... the heading of 'relationship breakdown'. (15) .... this event, (16) .... or both parties may find themselves with (17) .... to go. Others who may be living, for example, in a flat (18) .... the shop where they work, may find themselves without a home when they are (19) .... of work. Finally there is a small group who have got (20) .... financial difficulties, and cannot pay the rent or the mortgage on their property.

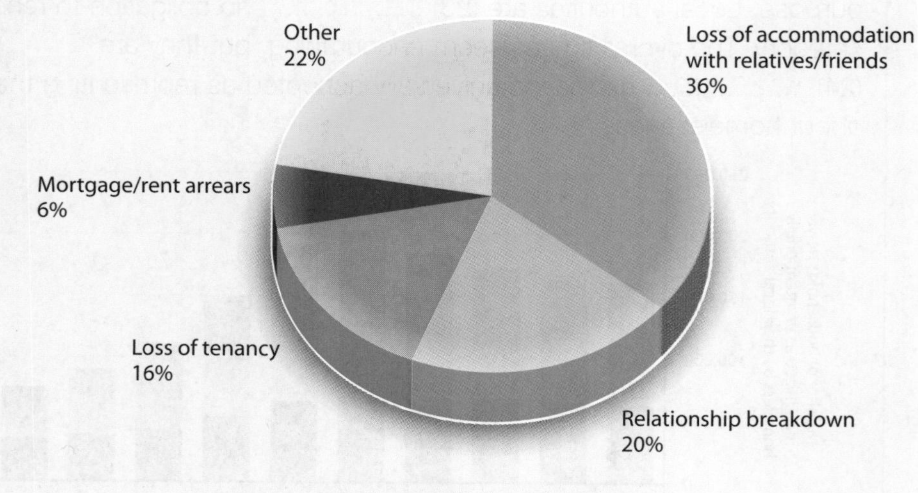

Reasons for homelessness

3 Match the words and phrases in brackets with the words and phrases (a–r) below.

a at present
b whatever they do
c in many cases
d under discussion
e in general
f in common
g be smaller in size
h in charge
i in the first place
j changed for the better
k keep in touch
l with regards to
m on the streets
n for consideration
o in their way
p on hand
q at first hand
r at risk of

Talking to the government

A group of homeless people, some of whom are (1) ...a...... (currently) sleeping (2) .... (rough), have visited a government office to give the minister responsible the opportunity to learn (3) .... (directly by experience) the issues they face. Topics (4) .... (covered) at the meeting included looking at how services for rough sleepers could be (5) .... (improved), and how homelessness could be avoided (6) .... (from the outset). Among the recommendations (7) .... (to be considered) were: that local authorities could provide a helpline for those (8) .... (facing) eviction; that (9) .... (generally) those rehoused people who had experience (10) .... (together) of sleeping rough could be housed close together so they could still (11) .... (talk to each other); that local authorities and government agencies could in general cut down the bureaucratic obstacles that homeless people find (12) .... (stopping them making progress), obstacles which frustrate them (13) .... (at every turn) when they are trying to get off the streets and into accommodation; that hostels for the homeless could (14) .... (contain fewer people), and could be better planned (15) .... (concerning) the needs of individuals; and that there should be help (16) .... (present) in hospitals for homeless people who are (17) .... (often) simply returned to the streets after medical treatment. The minister (18) .... (responsible) assured the visitors that their views would be seriously considered.

34

GRAMMAR

Reporting and hearsay

Report verbs

Academic texts often contain report verbs which present points of view or describe research findings. The following is a list of typical report verbs in context.

*The article **argues that** mobile phones are changing the lifestyles of the younger generation in Bangladesh.*

*A new study **claims that** some medical tests may do more harm than good.*

*Dr Simons **commented that** reports in the press had been exaggerated.*

*The Company **has confirmed that** it is investigating the problem.*

*This fact seems to **demonstrate that** there are limits to possible biological change.*

*The United Nations now **estimates that** over 5,000 civilians have died in the fighting.*

*The doctors **explain that** changes in diet and exercise will help the patients.*

*The team **found that** the planet underwent a steady cooling trend from 1000 AD to about 1880.*

*The report **implies that** because solar panels are increasing in price, the technology is likely to be uneconomic.*

*It should be **noted that** this is not always the case.*

*The author **observes that** despite years of prosperity, most people have become more and more unhappy.*

*The study **points out** that all of these data sets have a similar problem.*

*The report **predicts that** by 2020 newspaper circulations will have fallen by 25%.*

*The study excluded patients with very severe cases, and thus **does not prove that** surgery is best for everyone.*

*A new study **reports that** a Mediterranean diet can lower the risk of Type 2 diabetes.*

*New research **shows that** dirty pigs are healthy pigs.*

*These figures **indicate** that the recovery in some sectors is extremely slow.*

*Brown and Jones (1993) also **stated that** there was no link between the two factors.*

*Latest research **suggests that** there may be some water present after all.*

Hearsay reports

These reports are introduced by a passive form of a report verb, e.g. *say, report, believe, think, consider, know*, either in present simple or past simple form. The report can refer to the present, or past, or a time before the time of reporting:

Present + present

*The patient **is said to be** as well as can be expected.*

Present + past

*The company **is thought to have paid** more than €30 million.*

Past + present

*The government **was said to be** undecided.*

Past + past

*Smith **was believed to have died** before reaching the top.*

Present + continuous

*The elephants **are said to be increasing** in number.*

Past + present/past continuous infinitive

*The company **was reported to be/have been considering** the offer.*

Present + present passive infinitive

*These diseases which **are known to be caused** by poor hygiene.*

Present + past passive infinitive

*The plans **are said to have been destroyed**.*

➜ SEE ALSO
Grammar 5: Past perfect, *used to*
Grammar 10: Direct and indirect questions

1 Underline the most suitable verb in each sentence.

1 The author *estimates/predicts/claims* that previous research in this area has been flawed.
2 The report makes no definite claims, but *confirms/implies/shows* that government interference may have played a role in the decision of the court.
3 After a careful examination of the data, the team *found/pointed out/suggested* that there was no reason to remove this medication from the market.
4 The university now *finds/argues/estimates* that there will be around 250 fewer places for new students in the coming academic year.
5 The IMF now *predicts/comments/demonstrates* that the economy will grow by 1.2% in the next year.
6 Contemporary research seems to *state/demonstrate/observe* that this account of the history of the Viking invasions is misleading.
7 The report *explains/predicts/estimates* that the scheme is intended as an interim measure.
8 Despite repeated denials, the company has now *shown/confirmed/argued* that it was responsible for the pollution of the river.
9 The findings *suggest/comment/state* that the brain does remain adaptable after the end of childhood.
10 A spokesperson *demonstrated/commented/showed* that the company believed it had the best interest of its customers at heart.

2 Complete each sentence with a form of a verb from the box. More than once answer may be possible.

~~predict~~	claim	confirm	estimate
point out	prove	suggest	imply

1 The report ...predicts... that, without intervention by health authorities and governments, smoking in African countries is set to increase by up to 100% within the next decade.
2 Although the committee tactfully avoids the use of the word 'faked', their report .... that some of the data used may not have been entirely reliable.
3 The authors also .... that in fact some sections of the article in question have been copied without acknowledgement from *Wilson and Vincent 2004*.
4 The study .... that by adopting these measures, the government would save around €100 million over a ten-year period
5 The authors .... that the sword is of Byzantine origin, but produce very little evidence to support this view.
6 The evidence put forward in this study, showing that not everyone will benefit from exercise, ... the views of earlier research in this field.
7 Dr Roberts also .... that the link between the two conditions is not as straightforward as was previously supposed.
8 The author .... conclusively that Sickert could not have been Jack the Ripper, as he was absent in France at the time of the murders.

3 Complete the second sentence so that it has a similar meaning to the first sentence.

1 People once believed that the Sun circled round the Earth.
The Sun...was once believed to circle round the Earth .
2 People think that heavy traffic caused the subsidence.
The subsidence.. .
3 People know that more than half a million people are at risk.
More than.. .
4 People say that the situation is growing worse all the time.
The situation.. .
5 People reported that the government had offered financial assistance.
The government.. .
6 People consider that this equipment to be the best available.
This equipment.. .
7 People say that the statue was found in the 18th century.
The statue.. .
8 People believe that the spacecraft is experiencing communication problems.
The spacecraft.. .
9 People think that this bird became extinct at the end of the 19th century.
This bird.. .
10 People say that the company is suffering from lack of investment.
The company.. .

4 Write a new sentence with a similar meaning to the first sentence, using the word in bold. Do not change the word given.

1 According to Professor Scott, the effects of global warming have been greatly exaggerated – or so the argument goes.
argue
Professor Scott argues that the effects of global warming have been greatly exaggerated.

2 The Institute has announced that it is indeed true that Professor Dawking has resigned.
confirm
....

3 The scientists went into detail, saying that the disease is not transmitted by human contact.
explain
....

4 The report says that it is true that this kind of medication has little beneficial effect.
claim
....

5 The UN agency thinks that there are roughly two million people affected by the drought.
estimate
....

35

GRAMMAR

Verbs followed by *-ing* or infinitive

Certain verbs may be followed by either the *-ing* form or *to*-infinitive. This unit does not include verbs that are only followed by *to*-infinitive, or only followed by *-ing*. Always check with a dictionary.

Verbs followed by *-ing* + object

- **Admit, avoid, delay, *deny, dislike, enjoy, escape, face, fancy, feel like, finish, can't help, involve, keep, *mention, mind, miss, practise, risk, spend/waste* (*time*)

  *To do otherwise would **risk harming** the patient.*

- Verbs marked * can also be followed by a *that* clause:

  *He **admitted stealing** the car/**that he had stolen** the car.*

- The *-ing* form can be preceded by a possessive:

  *I **dislike your making** such a fuss about it.*

Verbs followed by *-ing* or *to*-infinitive with change of meaning

- *Forget, remember*

  Forget/remember to do describes an obligation:

  *Can you **remember to turn** off the lights?*

  *Don't **forget to buy** your ticket!* (present time, future event)

  Forget/remember doing describes a past event:

  *The older inhabitants **remember hearing** about the outbreak of the war.* (present time, past event)

- *Go on, continue*

  Go on/continue doing describe a continuing action:

  *The researchers **went on collecting** data for a week.*

  Go on/continue to do describe how things continued in the future:

  *That small girl **went on to become** a world famous scientist.*

  Go on/continue to do also describe what someone says later in a speech:

  *The Prime Minister began by describing what measures had already been taken, and **went on to outline** new proposals.*

- *Mean*

  *If we agree to the offer, **it means selling** immediately.* (it involves)

  *I **meant to post** these letters, but I forgot.* (I intended to)

- *Regret*

  Regret doing describes being sorry for a past action:

  *Alan **regretted not paying/not having paid** more attention in his maths lessons.*

  Regret to do describes a person's feelings when something happens:

  *We **regret to tell you** that the post has been given to another candidate.*

- *Stop*

  Stop doing describes stopping an action:

  *The government **stopped giving** grants to students some years ago.* (it no longer happens)

  Stop to do describes stopping one action in order to do another:

  *We **stopped** the experiment for ten minutes **to check** the equipment.* (it started happening)

- *Try*

  Try to do describes an attempt:

  *The engineers **tried to rebuild** the bridge, but failed.*

  Try doing describes an experience, or an experiment:

  *Have you **tried changing** the batteries? That might work.*

  *If you feel faint, **try putting** your head between your knees.*

Verbs followed by *-ing* or *to*-infinitive with no change of meaning

- *Can't bear, love, like, hate, prefer*

  *I **like working** in the library.*

  *I **love to watch** films on my laptop.*

  With an object + *to*-infinitive, they describe a particular way of doing something:

  *My boss **prefers me to dress** formally at the office.*

- *Suggest*

  ***I suggest we talk** about this matter on another occasion.*

  *In that case, **I suggest setting** a date for a meeting.*

  *I **suggest that we should set** another date for a meeting.* (formal)

Verbs followed by *to*-infinitive or *that* clause

- *Agree, arrange, decide, demand, expect, hope, learn, plan, pretend, promise, swear, threaten, wish*

  These are normally followed by *to*-infinitive or *that* clause with no change of meaning:

  *We **agreed to meet** again.*

  *We **agreed that we would meet** again.*

- *Appear, happen, seem*

  These are followed by *to*-infinitive or *it* + *that* clause with no change of meaning:

  *This **appears to be** the place.*

  *It **appears that this is** the place.*

Verbs followed by an object and *to*-infinitive

- *Assist, advise, beg, command, dare, employ, instruct, enable, encourage, invite, order, persuade, recommend, select, send, *teach, *tell, train, urge, *warn*
  *The nurse **assisted the old man to climb** the stairs.*

- Verbs marked * can also be followed by a *that* clause:
  *The police officer **warned Brian not to touch** anything.*
  *The lawyer **warned the accused that he would probably go to prison**.*

Verbs followed by infinitive without *to*

- *Help* is followed by an object + infinitive with or without *to*:
  *The doctor **helped the patient (to) breathe** more easily.*

- *Make* and *let* are followed by an object + infinitive without *to* in active forms:
  *The company **made them work** on a public holiday.*
  *The authorities **wouldn't let** the refugees come into the country.*

- In the passive, *make* and *help* are followed by *to*-infinitive (when *make* means 'force'):
  *They **were made to work** on a public holiday.*
  *He **was helped to** set up a small business.*

- Passive *be allowed* is usually preferred to passive *be let*:
  *I **wasn't allowed to stay up** when I was a child.*

Other structures

Some verbs may be followed by *-ing* or a different form with little difference in meaning.

- *Consider doing*, and *be considered to be*:
  *He **considered running** the experiment again.* (he thought about doing it)
  *He **considered that he might be** wrong.* (he thought of the possibility)
  *He **is considered to be** the best surgeon in the country.* (an opinion)

- *Imagine* (+ object) *doing, imagine that* and *imagine that something will/would/might be*:
  *He couldn't **imagine (them) making** the same mistake twice.*
  *We **didn't imagine that** we would discover the answer.*
  *They **imagined (that) walking on the Moon would be** a lot easier.*

- *Need doing, need to be done, need someone to do something*:
  *The results **need checking**.*
  *These results **need to be checked**.*
  *I **need you to check** the results.*

1 <u>Underline</u> the most suitable verb in each sentence.

1 Holding a referendum on the issue will *<u>involve</u>/plan/employ* spending some £80 million.
2 The lab assistant *enabled/missed/meant* to check the progress of the experiment but forgot.
3 The company *faces/expects/tries* to take delivery of the new equipment next month.
4 In the end, the manager *persuaded/avoided/stopped* the strikers to return to work.
5 The government is *mentioning/promising/encouraging* small businesses to apply for financial assistance.
6 I can't *help/imagine/train* this project taking as long as you suggest.
7 He keeps *meaning/complaining/demanding* that nobody takes his ideas seriously.
8 We *stop/regret/forgot* to announce that the 5.15 to Leeds has been cancelled.
9 Unfortunately the last person to leave *avoided/missed/forgot* to lock the door.
10 After questioning him, the officers *stopped/let/commanded* him go.

2 Complete the text by writing an infinitive form or an -*ing* form of the verb in brackets in each space.

Legal problems

A solicitor who admitted (1) ...*misleading*... (mislead) clients who were trying (2) .... (claim) compensation has been fined by the Law Society. Charles Dennis admitted (3) .... (give) inaccurate information which encouraged clients (4) .... (believe) that their claims would be trouble-free. Mr Dennis said that he now regretted (5) .... (not check) the information which had been put together by a colleague.

Astronaut training

Astronauts are expected (6) .... (deal with) isolation and other forms of stress, but being in space also involves (7) .... (get on with) others in cramped conditions. As space flights grow longer and crews become multi-national, they are more likely to spend time simply (8) .... (live) together. Now NASA is training astronauts (9) .... (cooperate) with other crew members. Trainee astronauts practise (10) .... (survive) in wilderness conditions, which encourages them (11) .... (respect) personality differences, and helps them (12) .... (develop) interpersonal and leadership skills.

3 Write a new sentence with a similar meaning to the first sentence and containing the words in bold. There may be more than one answer.

1 Why don't we run the experiment again?
suggest
I suggest running/that we run/that we should run the experiment again.

2 I hope you are happy to work late tonight.
mind
....

3 The rain continued to fall for twenty four hours.
went
....

4 James was sorry that he had not kept another copy of the data.
regretted
....

5 Helen is taking flying lessons.
learning
....

6 They asked him if he'd like to send in an application.
invited
....

7 The results must be checked twice.
need
....

4 Write a new sentence with a similar meaning to the first sentence, using the word in bold. Do not change the word given.

1 I think this is the solution.
appear
This appears to be the solution.

2 The defendant had to pay £500 costs.
make
....

3 I happened to notice that the other rooms were empty.
help
....

4 We would rather that people did not use plastic bags.
prefer
....

5 They made an arrangement that they would lend the company the money.
arrange
....

6 The company discovered what their customers wanted by using a team of researchers.
employed
....

36

GRAMMAR

Practice 12

1 Complete the text by writing a verb from the box in each space.

~~want~~	advised	appears	argue	arrange
avoid	considered	decide	encouraging	estimated
expected	help	involve	needs	prefer
risks	shows	suggests	thought	waiting

Medical tourism

Many people in the UK, who do not (1) ...want... to waste time (2) .... for an operation in an NHS* hospital, and who (3) .... not to pay the high prices for private surgery in the UK, (4) .... to travel abroad for expensive medical procedures. Research (5) .... that this is becoming an increasingly popular way of having medical treatment, with more than 50,000 people travelling abroad from the UK in 2007. It has been (6) .... that the cost of medical tourism is worth around £161 million, and this is (7) .... to rise year on year. Patients who feel that their treatment (8) .... to take place sooner rather than later can (9) .... to visit a hospital in another country through private companies which (10) .... them to choose a suitable package abroad.

Country	Price	Saving %	Travel and hotel 7 nights	Package saving %
Malaysia	£2205	72%	£1000	60%
Bulgaria	£2000	87%	£475	69%
France	£5689	29%	£480	23%
Hungary	£4450	44%	£380	40%
Tunisia	£3000	63%	£505	56%
India	£3547	56%	£560	49%
Spain	£5695	29%	£485	23%

Hip replacement UK price £8000 (2007 prices Information: Treatment Abroad)

The table (11) .... that costs vary considerably from place to place. Travelling a long distance, to Malaysia for example, may (12) .... spending more on travel and accommodation costs, but the patient will (13) .... paying a high price for the operation itself. Nearly 75% of treatments abroad are (14) .... to be dental and cosmetic procedures. Anyone who needs complex dental treatment in the UK (15) .... having to pay out a great deal, and cheaper treatment in Europe or further afield has become popular. The increasing popularity of cosmetic procedures (16) .... to have come about as the result of changing attitudes. They are now (17) .... to be more acceptable, although some commentators (18) .... that advertising has played a role in (19) .... people to feel uncomfortable with their appearance. Younger people are (20) .... not to have such treatments before consultation with a doctor.

*NHS = UK National Health Service

2 Complete the text by putting the verbs in brackets into an *–ing* form or an infinitive.

Having a hip replacement in France

Jane Taylor, an active 70-year old who always enjoyed (1) ....walking.... (walk), had her hip replacement done in France. In the UK she faced (2) .... (have) to wait nine eight months for her operation. 'I finally stopped (3) .... (worry) about the cost of private treatment and opted for an operation abroad. I had always hoped (4) .... (have) it done at home on the NHS, but my doctor explained that there was a long waiting list, and I wasn't an urgent case. Besides, a lot of people I knew who went into the local hospital seemed (5) .... (pick up) infections, so I decided (6) .... (have) it done privately. My doctor warned me (7) .... (make sure) I chose a reputable company, and I started (8) .... (do) some research, which mainly involved (9) .... (surf) the Net. I couldn't make up my mind, but then a friend suggested (10) .... (get) in touch with FranceMedical because they were a top-rated organization. I read through their prospectus, and then arranged (11) .... (go) to France for tests. I remember (12) .... (be) so surprised when I was greeted at the airport by one of their representatives, who was holding a bunch of flowers! I stayed in Toulouse for two nights and I really didn't expect (13) .... (enjoy) it so much. Everything was so well organized and they treated me so well. Two weeks later I went back to France for the operation, and follow-up physiotherapy. I couldn't imagine the hospital staff (14) .... (be) any better, and the operation went smoothly. I was well looked after there, and then went to a rehabilitation clinic where I spent three weeks (15) .... (have) physiotherapy. I was taught (16) .... (walk and balance) correctly, and given an exercise routine. In the end I couldn't help (17) .... (wonder) how the company did it all at the price! Ten months later I am free from pain and have just been on a walking holiday in Italy. I would recommend treatment abroad without hesitation. I only regret (18) .... (not take) control of my own treatment much earlier.'

37

GRAMMAR

Organizing text 1

This unit and Grammar 38 and 39 include words and phrases which writers use to organize text. Not all their uses are given here, and many can be used in other ways.

Adding a point

- *Also* is used in formal speech and writing. It is not normally used as a connector at the beginning of a sentence:
  Eating too much sugar leads to overweight, and ***also*** *damages the teeth.*
- *As well as* is followed by a noun or *-ing*:
  Eating too much sugar leads to overweight, ***as well as damaging*** *the teeth.*
- *As well as this* can be used as a connector, referring to a previous sentence:
  Eating too much sugar leads to overweight, and also damages the teeth. ***As well as this****, it has been linked with increased incidence of Type 2 diabetes.*
- *In addition* is a connector. *In addition to* begins a phrase adding to a clause:
  Eating too much sugar leads to overweight, and also damages the teeth. ***In addition****, it has been linked with increased incidence of Type 2 diabetes.*
  In addition to *strengthening your heart, exercise improves your immune system.*
- *Moreover, furthermore* and *what is more* are more formal connectors and emphasize that there is an additional point to be made:
  Eating too much sugar leads to overweight, and also damages the teeth, and ***what is more****, it has been linked with increased incidence of Type 2 diabetes.*
- *Above all* is a connector which adds a point, and stresses it is the most important one:
  Eating too much sugar leads to overweight, and also damages the teeth. ***Above all****, it has been linked with increased incidence of Type 2 diabetes.*
- *Besides* is a connector with a similar meaning to *anyway* or *in any case*:
  It's too late to go to the cinema, and, ***besides****, there aren't any good films on.*

Contrast or concession

- *However* can be used as a connector at the beginning or end of the sentence. Note that there is always punctuation on both sides of it, generally a full stop or comma:
  Recycling is increasing. ***However,*** *there is still a waste disposal problem.*
  Recycling is increasing. There is still a waste disposal problem, ***however.***
- *Yet* can be used at the beginning of the contrast clause:
  Recycling is increasing, ***yet*** *there is still a waste disposal problem.*

- Compare the use of *although*:
  *Recycling is increasing, **although** there is still a waste disposal problem.*
  ***Although** recycling is increasing, there is still a waste disposal problem.*

- *Despite (this)* contrasts a previous point with one coming after it. Note that *despite* is followed by a noun or *-ing* form of the verb:
  ***Despite** increased **recycling**, there is still a waste disposal problem.*
  ***Despite the increase** in recycling, there is still a waste disposal problem.*

- *In spite of* (+ noun) is used in a similar way:
  ***In spite of** increased **recycling**, there is still a waste disposal problem.*
  ***In spite of the fact** that recycling has increased ...*

- *Nevertheless* and the more formal *nonetheless* are more formal connectors referring back to the previous point, and can also come at the end of the sentence. *But* can come first:
  *Recycling is increasing. **Nevertheless/Nonetheless**, there is still a waste disposal problem.*
  *There is still a waste disposal problem, **nevertheless/nonetheless**.*
  *Recycling is increasing, **but nevertheless/nonetheless**, there is still ...*

Degree

- *To some extent* and *to a certain extent* are ways of saying 'partly'. They can come at the beginning, in the middle or at the end of a sentence. Note that this changes the meaning:
  ***To some extent**, experts believe that this is true.* (not all experts believe this)
  *Experts believe **to some extent** that this is true.* (they do not completely believe it)
  *Experts believe that this is true **to some extent**.* (it is partly true)

- *In some respects* and *In some ways* are connectors limiting what comes before or after:
  *Many economists argue that the crisis was caused by government inaction. **In some respects**, this is true.*

- *More or less* is an adverbial expression with the same meaning and comes before an adjective, or alone at the end of a sentence:
  *Most experts believe that this is true more or less/that this is **more or less** true.*

Comparing and contrasting

- *On the one hand ... (but/while) on the other hand* introduces contrasting points:
  ***On the one hand,** raising taxes increases government revenue, **but on the other hand** it may take away incentives for some earners.*
  We can use *on the other hand* to introduce a contrasting paragraph.

- *On the contrary* points out that something is true, but the opposite of a previous point:
  *Widespread use of pesticides did not eradicate the disease. **On the contrary,** in some areas, the incidence of the disease actually increased.*

- *Compared to, in comparison to/with* are used in introductory or closing phrases:
  In comparison to/Compared with/to *last year, there has been improvement.*
  There has been improvement ***in comparison to/compared with/to*** *last year.*

- *In the same way* introduces a second point which is said to be similar to the first:
  Wave power generators use the movement of the waves to produce electricity. ***In the same way****, tidal generators use the back and forward motion of the tides.*

- *(But) at least* shows that there is an advantage, despite a disadvantage just mentioned.
  Electric cars cannot travel long distances, ***but at least*** *they are pollution free.*

Exceptions and alternatives

- *Except (for)* and *apart from* can mean the same:
  Nobody was hurt, ***except for*** *one passenger who suffered minor injuries.*
  Nobody was hurt, ***apart from*** *one passenger who suffered minor injuries.*

- *Apart from* can also mean in addition to/as well as:
  Apart from *providing accommodation, the Society also offers free meals.*

- *Instead (of)* means that one thing replaces another:
  They decided not to fly, but to go by train ***instead.***
  Instead of flying*, they decided to go by train.*

- *Alternatively* is a more formal way of starting a sentence meaning *or*:
  We could fly. ***Instead/Alternatively****, we could go by train.*
  We could fly, or ***alternatively****, we could go by train/or we could go by train* ***instead****.*

→ SEE ALSO
Grammar 38: Organizing text 2
Grammar 39: Organizing text 3

1 Underline the most suitable option in each sentence.

1 *Despite/Although/Apart from* every effort to keep costs down, we have now found it necessary to increase our prices.
2 From the point of view of medical research, this project has been very successful and resulted in several publications and, *on the other hand/ furthermore/however*, it has inspired other researchers in the field.
3 While this is true *nevertheless/on the contrary/to some extent*, in fact the underlying causes of the unrest are more complex.
4 They decided not to use mains electricity, but to use solar panels and a wind turbine *nevertheless/on the other hand/instead.*
5 The magazine publishes prose and poetry by up-and-coming young writers, *as well as/what is more/despite* providing a platform for established writers.
6 *As well as/In spite of/Except for* increased competition, the company was able to post a €2 million profit in 2010.
7 This argument runs counter to the central proposition, but *in the same way/on the contrary/nevertheless* there is some evidence in its favour.
8 Everything in the text was accurate, *apart from/instead of/despite* one small error.
9 The economy is considered to be a part of national security and, *in the same way/ nevertheless/besides*, we should view the environment as a vital national interest.
10 The table shows that in 1932 Britain's share of this trade was 48% *on the other hand/compared with/instead of* Japan's 50%.

2 Complete the text by writing one suitable word in each space.

The world of the future

Over the past twenty years the world has been turned upside down, (1) ....more....... or less, by advances in communications. (2) .... some of us might not yet realize it, computers, the internet and mobile phone technology have in some (3) .... changed society. In (4) .... with the old world that existed up to the end of the 1980s, everything we do is faster, more complex and, to some (5) .... , out of our control. On the other (6) .... , the high-tech streamlined world we have created gives us more opportunities to enjoy ourselves, to learn and to draw closer to others. It is true that we spend more time on our own gazing at screens or talking into our hands, and (7) .... we can communicate easily with people wherever we are. (8) .... from these ways in which the electronic world draws us closer together, there are also the ways in which our minds have become extended by media. We could argue that all these technical advances make us less human. On the (9) .... , they make us more human than ever before, because we can now communicate easily and instantly with people all over the world. So (10) .... of looking back to a lost pre-electronic world, we would do better to look to the future, and consider the possibilities of a joined-up world.

3 Write a new sentence with a similar meaning to the first sentence, using the word in bold.

1 These chemicals can cause long-term damage to the environment and harm those who come into contact with them.
well
These chemicals can cause long-term damage to the environment as well as harming those who come into contact with them.

2 The victimization of this ethnic group is increasing and, in addition, this is being generally ignored by the media.
more
....

3 Fluids are a subset of the different kinds of matter and include liquids, gases, plasmas and, in part, plastic solids.
extent
....

4 The historic centre of the centre is still there approximately as it was in the 17th century.
more
....

5 Road communications in the area are extremely good, but rail services, in contrast, are not adequate.
hand
....

6 Although some Members of Parliament denounced the law as a flagrant violation of human rights, the government continued to enforce it.
nevertheless
....

7 Although he owned slaves himself, Jefferson always spoke out against slavery.
spite
....

8 The city suffers from terrible traffic congestion, but on the other hand there is an efficient metro system.
least
....

9 In general this camera has a very satisfactory design, though there is one small detail which is not satisfactory.
apart
....

10 Wages in the country this year are 5% higher than last year.
compared
....

4 Complete the text by writing a word from the box in each space. More than one answer may be possible.

~~although~~	also	above all	as well as
at least	despite	in some respects	in spite of
instead of	on the contrary	on the other hand	to some extent

The problem of obesity

(1) ...Although... health services in western countries have greatly improved the health of populations over the past century, the problem of obesity seems to be getting worse. (2) .... this problem is an integral part of modern life. (3) .... making it possible for people to eat more, a prosperous mechanized society means that most people take less exercise. (4) .... health campaigns encouraging people to eat fruit and vegetables, there seems little chance of a change in attitude. (5) .... , the situation may even be getting worse. (6) .... walking to work or to do our shopping, we spend our time sitting in cars, and (7) .... government health warnings, we eat more and more so-called 'junk' food and drink more and more high-calorie drinks. (8) .... , we can blame obesity problems on pressurized marketing which glamorizes certain foods and drinks, but, (9) .... , individuals themselves must learn to be responsible for their own health. It is that word 'learn' which is important, (10) .... For if we were better informed about the risks involved in excessive consumption of food and fizzy drinks and alcohol, we might (11) .... be able to help ourselves. This is why the problem of obesity is (12) .... a problem of education.

5 Write a new sentence with a similar meaning to the first sentence.

1 The interest on the account is not high, but at least it is tax-free.
Although.. .

2 The government itself was partly responsible for the crisis.
In some.. .

3 The book provides the reader with a general outline. It also includes some controversial material.
As well as.. .

4 Weather conditions were good, but the temperature was unusually low.
Except for.. .

5 You must send your CV, and also send a covering letter..
In addition to.. .

GRAMMAR

Organizing text 2

See Grammar 37 and 39 for other text organizers.

Sequences

- Writers often signal that they are going to make a list of points:
  ***There are a number of ways** in which this can be done.*
  ***There are several ways** of looking at this matter.*

- Points in a sequence are often numbered:
  ***First of all**, there is the issue of cost.*
  ***Secondly**, ...*
  ***Next** ...*
  ***Finally** ...*

- Words such as *point, issue, problem, advantage,* etc can also be numbered:
  *The **first problem** facing the government is ...*

- *In conclusion* and *finally* are used to close an argument:
  ***In conclusion,** we could say that ...*

Summarizing and explaining

- *To sum up* introduces a summarizing comment at the end of an argument:
  ***To sum up**, it seems clear that ...*

- *And so forth* and *and so on* generalize about points we do not mention by name:
  *Costs are affected by transport, rent, electricity charges, **and so forth.***

- *Etc* is an abbreviation from Latin ***et cetera*** meaning 'and the rest' and is used in lists of items to indicate that others of the same type are included:
  *We still have to discuss costs, schedule, **etc**.*

- *So* can introduce a question introducing solutions to issues raised, or a summary of problems:
  ***So**, where does the government go from here?*
  ***So**, in the end there is nothing the government can do.*

- *Thus* is a formal way of saying *therefore* and can explain the results what comes before:
  *No fingerprints were found. **Thus** it was impossible to identify the culprit.*

Making assertions

- Viewpoints can be made stronger with *completely, totally, simply really, quite*, etc:
  The whole plan was ***completely/totally/quite/really*** *ridiculous.*

- *Utterly* tends to be used with negative adjectives. *Simply* can be used with positive or negative adjectives:
  This is ***simply*** *wonderful!*
  It is ***simply/utterly*** *wrong to argue this.*

- *Utter* tends to be used with negative nouns. *Sheer* can be used with positive or negative nouns, and emphasizes the size or amount:
  This is ***utter nonsense!***
  It was ***sheer madness*** *to buy so many shares!*

- *Merely* is a stronger way of saying *only/just* to make what follows seem unimportant:
  The Earth is ***merely*** *a tiny planet in a very large universe.*

- *Mere* is used before nouns with the same meaning:
  The sun is a ***mere*** *speck in the universe.*

- *Literally* emphasizes that what has been said is not an exaggeration but is really true:
  There are ***literally*** *hundreds of people sleeping on the street.*

Giving examples

- *For example, examples include* and *to take an example* introduce examples:
  Some countries are already suffering from the effects of global warming. ***For example,*** *some Pacific islands are in danger of disappearing.*
  Some Pacific islands, ***for example,*** *are ...*
  Examples include *some Pacific islands, which are ...*
  To take an example, *some Pacific islands are ...*

- *E.g.* means 'for example' and is an abbreviation from Latin *exempli gratia*:
  Some countries in Europe ***e.g.*** *the UK, France, and Italy, have introduced strict new laws.*

- *Such as* introduces an example:
  Some countries in Europe ***such as*** *the UK, France, and Italy, have introduced strict new laws.*

- *As far as* (subject) *(be) concerned* connects the topic to a specific example:
  As far as Europe is concerned, *some countries have introduced strict new laws, but in Asia ...*

- *Namely* is a way of making a more specific reference after a general one:
  Some areas, ***namely*** *the mountains in the south, and the coastal plain, have no problems with drought.*

Making clear

- *In other words* and *to put it another way* makes a point clearer by repeating it in a different way.
  I think you should go out more with friends, or perhaps take a part-time job.
  ***In other words**, make more of an effort to be sociable.*
  ***To put it another way**, I think you should try to be more sociable.*

- *That is to say* and *i.e.* explain exactly what you mean. *i.e.* means 'that is' and is an abbreviation from Latin ***id est***:
  *A number of others are usually referred to as 'ballroom dances', **i.e./that is to say** the waltz, foxtrot, quickstep, and so on.*

- *To be precise* makes a point more exact:
  *It was extremely hot, over 200° **to be precise.***

- *In particular* means the same as *especially*, and makes one point more specific:
  *I enjoyed the second book **in particular**.*

Making statements less direct

- *In a way*, *in some ways*, *in this respect* and *in some respects* give one point of view or side of an opinion:
  ***In a way,** the ending of the film is not completely unexpected.*
  ***In this respect,** the operation was a success.*

- *A kind of*, *a sort* of describe a type of something:
  *An okapi is **a kind of** small giraffe.*

Comment and viewpoint

- Comment adverbs show the attitude of the writer:
  *It was **obviously** a problem.*
  ***Unusually**, plenty of money was available.*
  ***Interestingly**, the Minister would not comment on this.*

- Some sentence adverbs that indicate how we should understand what follows:
  ***Apparently/supposedly**, the government knew nothing of this.*
  ***Generally**, this is not a problem. **Increasingly,** this is becoming the norm.*

- Viewpoint adverbs also tell us from what point of view the speaker is talking:
  ***Environmentally**, this was a disaster.* (from an environmental point of view ...)
  ***Logically**, this can't be correct.*
  Others are *financially*, *politically*, *technically* (which also means 'strictly speaking').

➜ SEE ALSO
Grammar 37: Organizing text 1
Grammar 39: Organizing text 3

1 Underline the most suitable option in each sentence.

1 That brings me to the end of my presentation, and *next*/*in conclusion*/*secondly* I would like to summarize my main points.
2 Farmers here plant a number of different crops in the same field. *To sum up*/*Such as*/*For example*, maize and millet are planted with black-eyed peas and pumpkins.
3 Some people argue that recycling consumes more energy than it saves, *and thus*/*and so forth*/*and finally* is not worth the effort.
4 Does homeopathic medicine really work, or does it *utterly*/*literally*/*merely* function as a placebo?
5 Radioactive substances in ground water, *such as*/*in other words*/*first of all* radium, uranium and thorium, occur naturally.
6 Whether you agree with this argument or not, in the end it is *simply*/*to sum up*/*for example* a matter of common sense.
7 *For example Africa*/*As far as Africa is concerned*/*First of all Africa*, the Cold War resembled colonialism in many ways
8 *Literally*/*Logically*/*Namely*, the place where most money can be saved is the place where most money is spent, and that is in public services.
9 The company has been involved with broadcast ratings, *that is to say*/*in a way*/*for example*, the measurement of audience behaviour, for more than twenty years.
10 The government acknowledged that some groups, *to put it another way*/*namely*/*and so forth* single parents, people with disabilities, and people over the age of 80, would need extra help.

2 Complete the text by writing one suitable word in each space.

Do UFOs really exist, or are eye-witness reports (1) ....utter........ nonsense? The (2) .... number of people seeing strange objects in the sky might suggest that some of them have seen the real thing, but there are a (3) .... of simpler explanations. First of (4) .... , there are sightings which on investigation turn out to be mistaken. (5) .... of these include misinterpretations of weather phenomena, (6) .... as clouds catching the sunlight at sunset, and sightings of aircraft or meteorological balloons. Many descriptions of strange flying machines can be explained (7) .... as unfamiliar aircraft or high-flying airliners. In other (8) .... , many sightings turn out to be optical illusions of various kinds. (9) .... , some reports of UFOs are made by unreliable witnesses, or to (10) .... it another way, people who are suffering from delusions, or who are being deliberately misleading. (11) .... , the shape of the flying craft UFO spotters describe tends to reflect current trends in technology and in films. (12) .... in the 1950s, (13) .... example, the idea of round vertical-take-off planes was much discussed, and (14) .... UFOs tended to be saucer-shaped. More recent UFOs are usually described as triangular in shape, that is to (15) .... the same shape as US Stealth bombers and as the alien craft in recent science fiction films such (16) .... 'Independence Day'.

3 Write a new sentence with a similar meaning to the first sentence, beginning with a word from the box.

~~obviously~~	generally	financially	politically	supposedly	unusually

1 The implications must be considered, as is quite clearly the case, not only in respect of the management but also of the staff.
Obviously, the implications must be considered, as is quite clearly the case, not only in respect of the management but also of the staff.

2 The story is told not as one might expect, but only from the point of view of a ten-year-old child, who cannot fully understand what is happening.

....

3 The directors of the company, we are led to believe, knew nothing of the true financial situation.

....

4 The European Union cannot afford, from a political point of view, to allow the pressure on the Euro to divide the Union into two camps.

....

5 There is a huge disparity between the public sector and the private sector as far as money is concerned.

....

6 The results of these experiments more or less match our predictions.

....

4 Write a new sentence with a similar meaning to the first sentence, using the word in bold.

1 Some sectors of the economy, e.g. manufacturing and heavy industry, have suffered most.
such
Some sectors of the economy, such as manufacturing and heavy industry, have suffered most.

2 Several new measures will be introduced.
number

....

3 The site will also provide pitches for football, rugby, hockey, etc.
forth

....

4 People really were jumping up and down with joy.
literally

....

5 The project finished on time, and from this point of view it was satisfactory.
respect

....

6 Birds of this species tend not to migrate as such.
generally

....

5 Complete the text by writing a word or phrase from the box in each space.

~~such as~~	environmentally	finally	first of all
in conclusion	in other words	secondly	thus
in this respect	simply wrong	to put it another way	
that is to say	in a way	as far as the developing world is concerned	

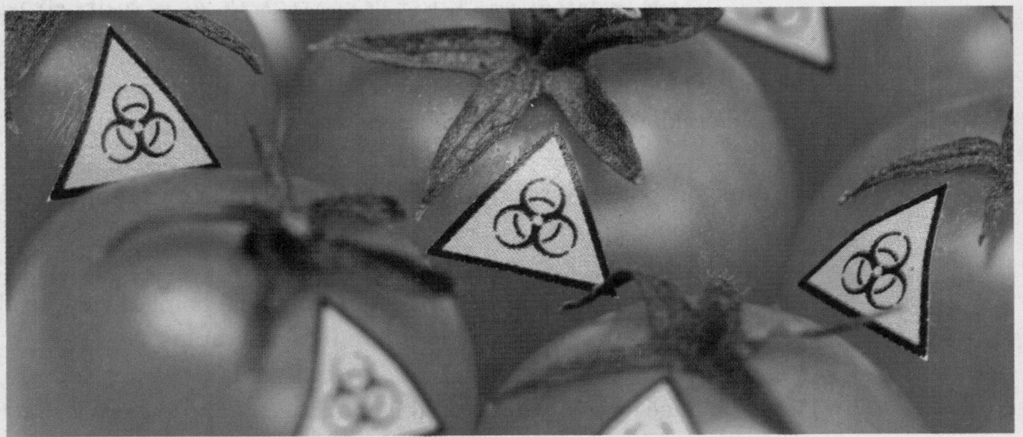

Those who support the use of genetically modified (GM) crops point out that thousands of crops, (1) ....such as.... cereals and fruit, and most farm animals, have been developed by human intervention, and that, (2) .... , GM is part of a long agricultural tradition. They go on to argue that (3) .... , GM crops offer the only solution to the demand for food. Apart from those critics who feel that the idea of genetically modified food is (4) .... , scientists and others make a number of objections to GM. (5) .... , there is the safety issue. Are GM foods safe? The answer to this question seems to depend on which camp you belong to. (6) .... , those who are worried about GM often cite test results which seem to show that GM cereal crops, for example, may cause liver, kidney and heart damage, while their opponents, (7) .... the large companies which develop GM crops, quote other research which proves that GM foods are safe. (8) .... , there are concerns that GM crops will cross-breed with other plants and spread out of control through the environment. (9) .... , will GM crops alter or destroy the natural biodiversity in the environment? (10) .... , they could be a disaster. However, so far, this does not seem to have happened. (11) .... , opponents argue that GM crops are economically damaging. Farmers who use GM crops buy the seeds from large companies which own the 'copyright' of the seeds. (12) .... the farmers are not allowed to save seed to plant the following year and (13) .... , although crop yields may be higher, the crops cost more to plant. So, (14) .... , what can we say about GM foods? Only that they are here to stay, despite the doubts of many people.

39

GRAMMAR

Organizing text 3

See Grammar 37 and 38 for other text organizers.

Reference words: pronouns

- Pronouns such as *this, that, these, those* and *it* can refer backwards in the text:
  There is also a metro system. ***This*** *is the fastest way of reaching the city centre.*
  this = (the metro system)
  There are several car parks in the centre. One of ***these*** *is close to the station.*
  these = (car parks)

- The reference may be to an idea rather than to a single word:
  More people are using public transport, and it is hoped that ***this*** *will continue.*

- In some cases, either *it* or *this* are possible:
  Using cycles for commuting is becoming popular, and in urban areas ***it/this*** *can be faster than public transport.*

- *This* and *that* can also refer forwards:
  This *was what occurred the next time they ran the test. First of all, there were no allergic reactions to the new drug. Then ...*

- Many uses of *it* do not have a precise reference as *it* is also used as a 'dummy' subject with *be* and verbs describing weather:
  It's *comfortable here by the pool.*
  It's *a long way to Hamburg.*
  It *seems to be getting darker.*
  It's *beginning to snow.*
  It *has stopped raining.*

Reference words: *the former, the latter*

The former refers formally to the first of two things mentioned in the text. *The latter* refers to the second item mentioned:

People without insurance are approximately two and one-half times as likely as those with insurance to be unable to obtain care. In the 1994 survey 34 per cent of ***the former*** (the uninsured), *compared with 14 per cent of* ***the latter*** (the insured), *reported they were unable to obtain adequate medical services.*

Emphasis: *It* clauses

Clauses introduced by *It is/was* put emphasis on what follows.

- Infinitive + *that* clause:
  It was *to avoid a complete financial meltdown* ***that*** *this action was taken.* (This action was taken to avoid a complete financial meltdown.)

- Noun phrase (including *-ing*) + *that/which/who* clause:

  It's *getting the results in on time* ***that/which*** *matters most.* (What matters most is getting the results in on time.)
  It was *Newton who finally came up with the answer.* (Newton was the one who finally came up with the answer.)

- *When, how, what, because* clause + *that* clause:

  It was *when he saw what had happened to the slide* ***that*** *Fleming became excited.* (When Fleming saw what had happened to the slide he became excited.)

Emphasis: *What* clauses

These clauses also put more emphasis on what follows.

- *What* + verb + object

  In these sentences the *what* clause can be put at the beginning or the end of the sentence:

  What concerned them *was the rate of the infection.*
  The rate of the infection was ***what concerned them****.*

- *What* + verb phrase + *is/was* + noun phrase

  What surprised *the scientists* ***was*** *the way the gas reacted* (The way the gas reacted surprised the scientists.)
  What nobody has explained is *the reason for this.*

- A *what* clause of this kind can be preceded by *This is*, referring back to the topic:

  All results were negative. ***This is what puzzled everyone*** *at first.*

Emphasis: negatives

- *Not at all, not in the least/the slightest, not the least/slightest bit*:

  Such reactions are ***not at all*** *unusual.*
  Smith was ***not in the least*** *deterred by this setback.*
  The witness was ***not in the slightest degree*** *affected while she gave evidence.*

- *No* + noun and *none* can be emphasized by *no ... whatsoever, none at all* or *none whatsoever*:

  There is ***no money whatsoever*** *available for research at the moment.*

Emphasis: *very, all*

- We can use *very (much)* to add emphasis:

  Her work was ***very much*** *admired in Impressionist circles.*

- We can also use *very* to mean *the exact*:

  The researchers discovered that this gene shows ***the very same*** *changes.*
  The ***very act of talking*** *about traumatic events is a way for a child to start on the road to recovery.*

- We can put *all* (meaning 'the only thing') at the beginning of a clause for emphasis:

  All *we can sure of is that this will not be the last time it happens.*

Inversion

This gives emphasis by using the question form of the verb after an adverbial with a negative or restrictive meaning comes at the beginning of the sentence. These structures are normally only used in formal speech and writing. Note that all of these adverbials can be used without inversion if they come in the normal position.

The government ***has never had*** *a better opportunity.* (normal position)
Never has *the government* ***had*** *a better opportunity.*

Such an infection ***rarely proves*** *fatal.*
Rarely does *such an infection* ***prove*** *fatal.*

A scientific discovery ***has seldom had*** *such an impact.*
Seldom has *a scientific discovery* ***had*** *such an impact.*

The war had ***no sooner begun*** *than the army found itself in difficulties.*
Hardly/Scarcely had *the meeting* ***begun*** *when there was an interruption.*

These creatures ***will only be able*** *to survive in exactly the right conditions.*
Only *in exactly the right conditions* ***will*** *these creatures* ***be able*** *to survive.*

These substances ***should under no circumstances be mixed*** *together.*
Under no circumstances should *these substances* ***be mixed*** *together.*

Such activities ***were not only*** *legal, but (they) were also common practice.*
Not only were *such activities legal, but they were also common practice.*

The suspects ***little realized*** *that all their calls were being recorded.*
Little did *the suspects* ***realize*** *that all their calls were being recorded.*

Such a crisis had ***not occurred since*** *the end of the 19th century.*
Not since *the end of the 19th century* ***had*** *such a crisis* ***occurred****.*

The complete truth about this event ***did not emerge*** *until the war was over.*
Not *until the war was over* ***did*** *the complete truth about this event* ***emerge****.*

→ **SEE ALSO**
Grammar 37: Organizing text 1
Grammar 38: Organizing text 2

1 Underline the most suitable option in each sentence.

1 From the *very/former/only* moment the inscription was uncovered, Richards realized that it was something special.
2 As soon as I switched on the monitor, I could see that *this/it/what* wasn't working properly.
3 Temperatures as high as 140°C are *none whatsoever/not whatsoever/not at all* unusual.
4 *Never/Not only/No sooner* had he taken up his new position, than his boss fell ill.
5 Marie and Pierre Curie both won the Nobel Prize, *the former/this/the latter* adding a prize for Chemistry to her earlier prize for Physics.
6 This model *is very much/is very/is the slightest* recommended for anyone looking for a high-quality low-price camera.
7 *Rarely/What/It* worried the doctor most was the patient's slow rate of breathing.
8 The blinds were down in all three rooms and *this/these/it* was very dark inside.
9 When Henderson was what had happened, he was *none whatsoever/not in the least/what* surprised.
10 It was only when they checked the results a second time *did they realize/that they realized/realized they* something strange had happened.

2 Complete the text by writing a phrase (a–o) in each space.

a ~~what interested~~	f it is	k the very process of
b it all seemed	g it meant	l this turned out to be
c it hadn't been	h it was when	m this was something
d it's having	i no problems whatsoever	n what I was interested in
e it wasn't until	j what pleases me	o didn't find it at all

Studying abroad

(1) .a.. me in studying abroad was my awareness that I'd never lived in a foreign country, and that (2) ..... I needed to do. (3) ..... I started thinking about a future career that I decided I'd like to learn German. Of course, (4) ..... being away from friends and family, but Berlin isn't so far away, and I (5) ..... a problem. (6) ..... was some kind of business studies course combined with learning German, and (7) ..... quite easy to arrange. (8) ..... signing up on my courses and finding somewhere to stay was good practice for my German. Up that that point (9) ..... very good, I have to admit, but I soon learned a lot. (10) ..... I'd been there a few months, however, that I began to feel at home. (11) ..... just like home, and I really had (12) ..... . Of course, I suppose (13) ..... a fairly easy country to live in, but (14) ..... the experience of being in a foreign country which is important. (15) ..... most about the time I spent there is that now I feel more confident, more able to get on with people.

3 Write a new sentence with a similar meaning to the first sentence and beginning with an adverbial.

1 There has rarely been such appreciation and enthusiasm for a conference of this kind.
Rarely has there been such appreciation and enthusiasm for a conference of this kind.

2 Such a complex topic has seldom been presented with such insight.
...

3 This regulation applies to non-residents only in certain circumstances.
...

4 The research project will not make any contribution to the development programme until there has been time to collect and evaluate all the data.
...

5 Personal details will not be made available to commercial organizations or unauthorized members of the public under any circumstances.
...

6 The pace of technological advance has never been greater than it is at present.
...

4 Complete the text by writing one suitable word in each space.

Measurements in the middle ages

(1) ...What... may surprise us is that during the construction of Chartres Cathedral, the various builders supervising the work all used different units of measurement, and (2) .... seems to have been not at (3) .... unusual. Occasionally a builder may have used several measures, but (4) .... in no way means that measures were used at random. The (5) .... fact that these measures always had a clear proportional relationship to one another is significant. The master builder Scarlet, for example, used two measures, the Roman Foot and the *Ped Manualis*, the (6) .... measuring 294.4 mm and the (7) .... 353.3 mm, making a ratio of 5:6. (8) .... this tells us about the way the masons worked is instructive. (9) .... seems that each mason planned his buildings using his own measure, and (10) .... caused no practical difficulties. One mason was not in the (11) .... concerned to share another's measures, and there is no sense (12) .... that a common measure was either necessary or desirable. Seldom (13) .... any of the masons use the 'official' royal measures, and (14) .... seems more likely is that they employed the units of their city, their stone quarry, or their lord. (15) .... was only much later, in the 1790s, that standardized metric measures were introduced in France, and only gradually (16) .... these accepted in other parts of first Europe and then the rest of the world.

40

GRAMMAR

Practice 13

1 Complete the text by writing one word in each space.

If you're interested in things electrical, then a degree in electronic or electrical engineering (EEE) may be for you. (1) Increasingly... , (2) .... makes a degree in EEE attractive are the prospects of employment at the end of (3) .... In 2009, a majority of graduates, two thirds of (4) .... to be (5) .... , went straight into employment, with another 15% continuing to study, with some of (6) .... working at the same time. Only about 10% remained unemployed, though this situation will probably change (7) .... some extent in future years because of the economic crisis. (8) .... , employment prospects remain good. Fortunately, a degree in EEE leads to a (9) .... of career options. In 2009, as (10) .... as taking jobs in engineering, which accounts for around a third of all graduates, over 20% found jobs in IT. (11) .... , EEE graduates also found work in other sectors, (12) .... as retail, catering or management. Other types of employment included the arts, design, culture and sports, (13) .... the business and financial sectors. (14) .... makes EEE a particularly attractive course of study is that (15) .... develops a number of practical skills, in (16) .... problem solving, teamwork, project and time management, and the ability to turn a concept into reality. In other (17) .... , EEE graduates can expect to be valued for how they work, as much as for what they know. As (18) .... as business and commercial organizations are concerned, (19) .... is what they are looking for. (20) .... to some other graduates, EEE graduates stand out when it comes to numeracy, team working, analytical and project management skills.

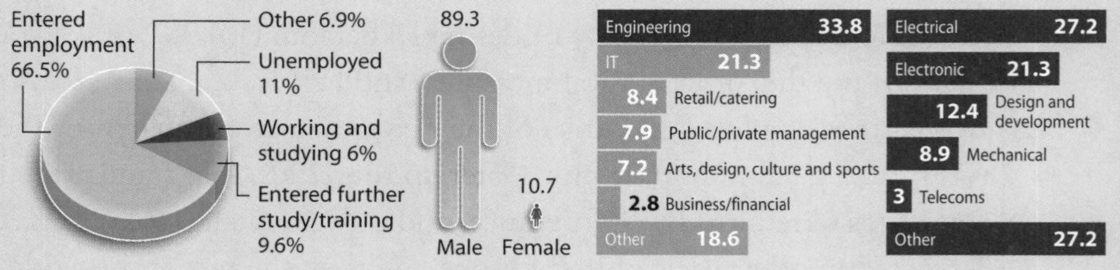

Entered employment 66.5%
Other 6.9%
Unemployed 11%
Working and studying 6%
Entered further study/training 9.6%

89.3 Male
10.7 Female

Engineering	33.8
IT	21.3
Retail/catering	8.4
Public/private management	7.9
Arts, design, culture and sports	7.2
Business/financial	2.8
Other	18.6

Electrical	27.2
Electronic	21.3
Design and development	12.4
Mechanical	8.9
Telecoms	3
Other	27.2

3 Match the sentence beginnings (1–10) with their endings (a–j) to form a continuous text.

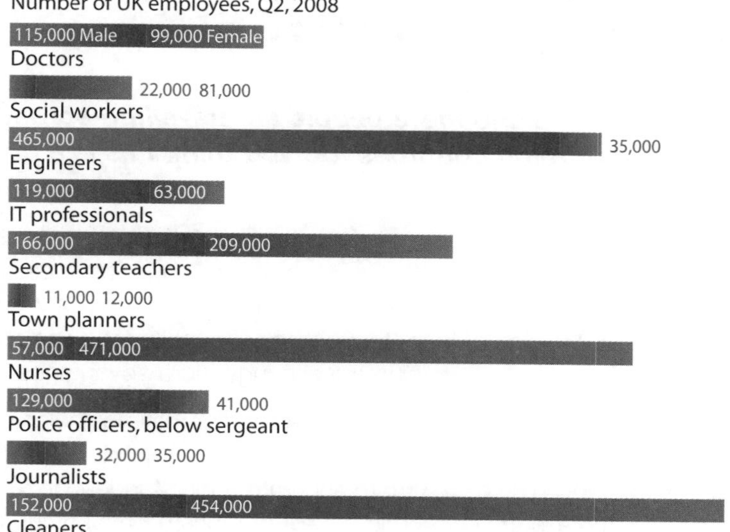

1 To some extent ....a....
2 For example, ...
3 This ....
4 In other words, ...
5 Besides ....
6 In contrast, ...
7 Apart from ....
8 In some ways, ...
9 Thus ....
10 What ....

a the figures shown here are unsurprising.
b 46% of doctors are women, and it is predicted that by 2013 they will make up the majority of GPs, and by 2017, hospital doctors.
c these figures also seem to show, therefore, is that we are still far from any equality of the sexes in many sectors of employment.
d probably reflects the fact that cleaning has been traditionally a 'woman's job', relatively unskilled and low-paid.
e this reflects the traditional assumption that women are attracted to the 'caring' professions.
f the fact that there are nearly three times as many female cleaners as male cleaners seems entirely predictable.
g engineering and IT remain predominantly male professions.
h many women end up as cleaners because employers prefer to pay women less than men.
i this economic explanation, there is a further sexist element: cleaning is regarded as women's work.
j the large number of women doctors, the figures also show a majority of women secondary teachers and social workers.

1

VOCABULARY

Travel and tourism

Nowadays more and more people are travelling abroad to spend their holidays in foreign countries. Do you think this is a positive or negative development?

Last year, there were millions of international tourist arrivals across the globe. Whether they were students on their (1) ...C..... years looking for overseas adventure, stressed-out workers hoping to (2) .... away for a weekend, or retirees wishing to relax in an exotic location – clearly none of them thought they could find the same experience at home. The question is (3) .... foreign travel brings more advantages or disadvantages.

An obvious positive point is that going abroad sometimes helps people to expand their knowledge of the world. If they are (4) .... -minded, they can learn about new cultures and hopefully gain a more accurate understanding about their (5) .... of life. In addition, there is the economic benefit of tourism to countries which have few other resources. It can provide an income to many people within the industry.

Having said this, some people simply go to a foreign (6) .... surrounded by high walls and therefore learn little about their holiday (7) .... Another issue is that (8) .... of tourists often spoil the 'unspoilt' places they visit. The most recent example of this is Antarctica, where last year cruise ships took thousands of visitors to view the disappearing icebergs and wildlife. Vegetation, nesting penguins and resting walrus are vulnerable when humans (9) ....

Certainly a trip to a foreign country is attractive, but it may be worth (10) .... one's own country first. By doing so, (11) .... travellers can support their own economy, cut down on fuel use and find out about their own national (12) ....

1 Choose the answer (A, B, C or D) that best fits each space.

	A	B	C	D
1	**A** break	**B** space	**C** gap	**D** pause
2	**A** get	**B** deal	**C** organize	**D** escape
3	**A** which	**B** how	**C** although	**D** whether
4	**A** open	**B** wide	**C** large	**D** free
5	**A** form	**B** means	**C** way	**D** belief
6	**A** reserve	**B** sanctuary	**C** resort	**D** shelter
7	**A** departure	**B** direction	**C** destination	**D** situation
8	**A** hordes	**B** sets	**C** series	**D** crews
9	**A** influence	**B** impact	**C** enter	**D** intrude
10	**A** trekking	**B** tracking	**C** exploring	**D** locating
11	**A** domestic	**B** internal	**C** border	**D** insular
12	**A** background	**B** upbringing	**C** heritage	**D** formation

2 **Complete the dialogues by writing an appropriate word from the box in each space.**

Booking hotel rooms for a family

~~available~~	double	charge	twin	access
unit	facilities	reservation	contact	ensuite

Caller:	Hi, I was wondering if you have anything (1) ..available.. for June 30th? We're looking for two rooms, one with a (2) .... bed, the other should be a (3) .... room – I mean something with two single beds for the children.
Receptionist:	Let's see. Yes, we have a family (4) .... , and that comes with an (5) .... bathroom and some basic cooking (6) ....
Caller:	Great. Um, how about (7) .... to the Internet?
Receptionist:	You can connect from your room. There's a small (8) .... , $5 per 30 minutes.
Caller:	OK, well I'd like to make a (9) .... , please. My name's Jack Raymond.
Receptionist:	OK Mr Raymond, can I have a (10) .... phone number, please?

Booking a room for a large business meeting

reception	whiteboard	participants	screen	book	suite
conference	maximum	refreshments	equipment	arrangements	

Caller:	Good morning. I'd like to (11) .... a room in your hotel for a business (12) .... we're having on the 2nd of October, if that's possible.
Receptionist:	Well, I'm afraid the largest (13) .... we have is already being used for a wedding (14) .... , but the Cambridge room is also fairly large. How many (15) .... would attend?
Caller:	It would be a (16) .... of twelve.
Receptionist:	That would work. Were you also wanting to hire any (17) .... to help with the meeting?
Caller:	I'll be giving a presentation so I guess a (18) .... will be necessary.
Receptionist:	Right. I'll make the (19) .... for that to be brought along. Anything else you need?
Caller:	Possibly a (20) .... and pens. Hopefully we'll be brainstorming some good ideas.
Receptionist:	Now, how about (21) .... ? We usually serve coffee at 10am and then ...

Making enquiries about local tourism

wildlife	trip	harbour	playground	library	canoe
exhibition	activities	cruise	guide	museum	sunscreen

Caller: Hi, we're planning our (22) .... for the school holidays and I think we'll be staying in Westport for a few days. Could you tell me what local (23) .... there are?

Receptionist: Certainly. Em, hiring a (24) .... or kayak is very popular. You can hire your own, or a (25) .... can take you out on the river and show you around, all the way to the (26) .... where you'll see all the fishing boats come in. On the river you'll see lots of local (27) .... – native birds, fish, dragonflies, that sort of thing. Or, you could go on a (28) .... around some of the local islands – that's very relaxing as you don't have to do anything! Just take lots of (29) .... and plenty of bottled water.

Caller: That all sounds great. What's in the town itself? Do you have an outdoor (30) .... for kids?

Receptionist: Yes we do. Your children might also be interested in our small (31) .... – it has a fascinating (32) .... of photos and household objects that show how the first people here used to live. We've also got a good (33) .... with a large children's section, too, if they enjoy reading.

3 Complete each sentence with a form of the word in CAPITALS.

1 As a significant ..tourist..... attraction, the old city must be preserved. TOUR
2 I'm afraid I'm calling to make a .... about my room. COMPLAIN
3 The main problem was that the .... was delayed for hours. FLY
4 Will there be any .... events happening at that time? CULTURE
5 I'd recommend that you get .... before you leave. INSURE
6 Do you have any special .... regarding food? REQUIRE
7 For many people, a holiday is simply not .... AFFORD
8 .... of the coastline can take many days. EXPLORE
9 Beijing is a destination which is gaining .... with foreign visitors. POPULAR
10 There will be a one-hour .... of traditional dance. PERFORM
11 One benefit of tourism is that it can be .... beneficial to a number of local business. ECONOMY
12 The construction of so many hotels has had an .... impact on the local ecosystem. INVADE

2

VOCABULARY

The natural world

1 Choose the answer (A, B, C or D) that best fits each space.

The wildlife of the Juan Fernández Archipelago remained undisturbed until the arrival of European settlers, who (1) .... their animals to the islands. Amongst these were goats and cows to be (2) .... for meat and milk, but also rats and mice which had jumped ship. Cats later brought over to kill these pests also quickly escaped into the (3) .... Little did the settlers understand the impact this would have on local species. The rabbits they'd brought over too, could not be held in (4) .... for long, and their numbers rapidly expanded. But it was not just fauna that arrived but also (5) .... Plants such as the blackberry bramble flourished in the tropical climate and spread throughout the (6) .... forest.

In the past, the islands' birds had no natural (7) .... Many therefore evolved to lay their eggs in ground nests. This habit now makes them incredibly (8) .... as rats and mice destroy their eggs and cats devour the newly hatched chicks. Meanwhile grazing goats, rabbits and cows have (9) .... once fertile valleys into wasteland. One now rare tree species is known as the Luma, in which firecrown hummingbirds (10) .... Today the Luma is being covered over by spiky blackberry brambles, the hummingbird's natural (11) .... is disappearing and the fear is that they will soon (12) .... Conservationists from Chile and around the world are uniting to show the urgent need for (13) .... of these islands' original and unique species. They know the best way to do this is to (14) .... the plants and animals that are (15) .... species.

	A	B	C	D
1	**A** entered	**B** introduced	**C** accessed	**D** provided
2	**A** bred	**B** populated	**C** multiplied	**D** cultivated
3	**A** landscape	**B** scenery	**C** surroundings	**D** wild
4	**A** custody	**B** captivity	**C** territory	**D** vicinity
5	**A** crops	**B** weeds	**C** flora	**D** vegetation
6	**A** native	**B** domestic	**C** endemic	**D** authentic
7	**A** opponents	**B** predators	**C** prey	**D** challengers
8	**A** susceptible	**B** risky	**C** incapable	**D** vulnerable
9	**A** adapted	**B** altered	**C** turned	**D** made
10	**A** nest	**B** construct	**C** collect	**D** house
11	**A** interior	**B** boundary	**C** habitat	**D** place
12	**A** wipe out	**B** extinguish	**C** expire	**D** die out
13	**A** continuation	**B** maintenance	**C** duration	**D** preservation
14	**A** eradicate	**B** abolish	**C** ban	**D** demolish
15	**A** strange	**B** abnormal	**C** alien	**D** extra

2 Underline the correct word in the statements about the text in exercise 1. Then decide if they are true (T), false (F) or not given (NG) according to the text.

1 The first animals that *resided/located/inhabited* the archipelago were brought by Europeans. ..NG....
2 The settlers failed to realize the long term ecological *decay/damage/injury* that their cats would cause. ....
3 Rabbit *populations/groups/societies* were unable to increase in the archipelago. ....
4 Many endemic bird species became flightless in the *course/progress/direction* of evolution. ....
5 The solution to the archipelago's environmental problems is to wipe out *tresspassing/invasive/attacking* species. ....

3 Complete each definition of an animal with a word from the box.

~~mammals~~	hybrids	organisms	reptiles
invertebrates	marsupials	primates	amphibians

1 Mammals are animals that have live young, not eggs, which drink their mother's milk.
2 Frogs and turtles are .... , because they can live both on land and in water.
3 Monkeys and apes are .... , a group which also includes humans.
4 95% of animals have no skeleton, and are referred to as ....
5 .... are animals or plants which have been produced from two different types of animal or plant.
6 Koalas and kangaroos are .... : animals whose babies live in a pouch in the mother's skin on the outside of her stomach until they are fully developed.
7 .... are living things; ranging from single-celled life forms to something with billions of cells, like a human being.
8 .... are usually cold-blooded, are covered in scales and generally lay eggs.

4 Replace the phrases in *italics* with a more academic phrase from the box.

~~is indigenous to~~	is nocturnal	is carnivorous	is asexual	is dominant
is feral	is submissive	is tame	is invasive	is venomous

1 The panda is a member of the bear family and *originally came from* China. is indigenous to
2 When it licks its owner's face, a dog is showing that it *knows it is less powerful.* ....
3 As this bat *sleeps during the day and is active at night*, it may only be seen after dark. ....
4 The rabbits which now inhabit Australia are a species which *came from other countries, spread quickly and is harmful to the local ecosystem.* ....
5 A cat which turns *into a wild animal again* will prey on native birds. ....

6 Although a chimpanzee can be trained to perform specific tasks, it is debatable whether it *is completely comfortable and calm with humans.* ....
7 Look at the teeth of this animal and you can clearly see it *eats the flesh of other animals.* ....
8 The lion which *is the strongest and most powerful* will be first to feed on the antelope. ....
9 The brown snake *produces a poison* and its bite can kill a person. ....
10 The jellyfish is an organism which *is capable of reproducing by itself.* ....

5 Complete the text by writing a word from the box in each space.

~~creatures~~	giants	feathers	young	characteristics
fossils	packs	skeletons	scales	migrations

Dinosaur discovery
Until relatively recently, most textbook and museum illustrations of dinosaurs showed them as dull, green-brown lizard-like (1) creatures which were covered head to foot in (2) .... Such images arose because researchers had to rely on prehistoric (3) .... that were often incomplete. It had been rare to find complete (4) .... , and the bones of these tended to come from the (5) .... and not the smaller types. However, the recent discovery of over twenty new very well preserved dinosaurs in China has shed new light on their (6) .... and probable behaviour. There appears to be evidence of annual (7) .... amongst some dinosaurs and of some larger carnivores hunting in (8) .... One parrot-beaked dinosaur, psittacosaurus, was discovered incubating a nest of over thirty (9) .... Perhaps most intriguing of all has been the discovery of dinosaurs covered in something like (10) .... This has convinced many palaeontologists that dinosaurs are indeed the ancestors of modern birds.

6 Complete each sentence with a form of the word in CAPITALS. Use a gerund or a noun ending in *-ion* or *-ance*. A prefix may also be needed.

The (1) dumping of phosphates and fertilizers into rivers speeds up the	DUMP
growth of algae. These plants then take over the rivers, and in the process	
of (2) .... they begin to use up the oxygen in the water. As a result,	RESPIRE
local aquatic life often dies from (3) .... , and we may soon see	SUFFOCATE
the (4) .... of many native fish from our waterways.	APPEAR
The illegal (5) .... of trees to supply foreign buyers with timber	LOG
products quickly leads to (6) .... In turn, this soon causes the	FOREST
(7) .... of topsoil. Without topsoil, as soon as heavy rain arrives,	ERODE
(8) .... is likely to occur as a result.	FLOOD
Herbicides have long been used for the (9) .... of disease in	ERADICATE
crops. However, genetic engineering experiments have led to the	
successful (10) .... of certain plant genes. Therefore, the	MODIFY
(11) .... of crops such as corn and wheat which have a	CULTIVATE
stronger (12) .... to disease is now possible.	RESIST

3

VOCABULARY

Geography and geology

1 Choose the answer (A, B, C or D) that best fits each space.

What is the world's largest desert? I'm sure the first that (1) ....D.... to mind is the legendary Sahara – but that's 3rd. It's actually the desert on the Antarctic (2) .... , measuring just under 14,000,000 kms^2, closely followed by the Arctic desert. Most people living away from deserts associate this kind of (3) .... with sand, but only 10% of deserts are actually made up of sand (4) ....
The term 'desert' in fact describes a (5) .... which receives almost no (6) .... , meaning rainfall, snow, ice or hail. The term can also apply to regions where there is greater evaporation of (7) .... than rainfall. In other words, more water is absorbed back into the (8) .... than stays on or within the ground. So, in (9) .... deserts, you're mainly talking about ice sheets and a little rock, not sand, of course. The surface of many other deserts is comprised of loose rock where the finer particles of dust and sand have been (10) .... away.
It may surprise you to know that deserts exist all over the (11) .... , from the Kalahari in Africa to the Great Victoria in Australia and so on, and that they (12) .... just over a fifth of the earth's land area. The world's largest hot desert, the Sahara, actually (13) .... temperatures of 122°F. Other arid deserts may not be so hot but in common with the Sahara, they (14) .... considerably at night.
An issue that is worrying geologists, governments and the people that live on the (15) .... of deserts, is the way they are spreading. You might think that the reason for this is (16) .... – but lack of rain is not the cause.

1	**A** jumps	**B** leaps	**C** rises	**D** springs
2	**A** country	**B** continent	**C** territory	**D** pole
3	**A** terrain	**B** plain	**C** horizon	**D** nature
4	**A** hills	**B** dunes	**C** piles	**D** slopes
5	**A** base	**B** landscape	**C** ground	**D** soil
6	**A** wildlife	**B** agriculture	**C** precipitation	**D** alteration
7	**A** moisture	**B** drops	**C** dampness	**D** drizzle
8	**A** setting	**B** atmosphere	**C** environment	**D** surroundings
9	**A** extreme	**B** Mediterranean	**C** typical	**D** polar
10	**A** left	**B** disappeared	**C** blown	**D** removed
11	**A** globe	**B** sphere	**C** atlas	**D** orb
12	**A** contain	**B** expand	**C** cover	**D** cross
13	**A** obtains	**B** reaches	**C** stretches	**D** raises
14	**A** cool	**B** fall	**C** freeze	**D** decrease
15	**A** sections	**B** edges	**C** outlines	**D** sides
16	**A** storms	**B** climate	**C** heat	**D** drought

2 Complete the dialogues by writing a word from the box in each space.

~~volcanoes~~	waves	destruction	stress
tremors	construction	magnitude	

James: So how about Italy? Do you have earthquakes?
Agostino: Yes, because we have a few active (1) volcanoes , but mostly the quakes are minor so we just get small (2) .... you hardly notice.
James: And major earthquakes?
Agostino: Well, it's possible to have a (3) .... 7 or 8 earthquake, yes.
James: Caused by seismic (4) .... that come up to the surface?
Agostino: That's right. They can lead to the (5) .... of whole villages.
James: So when engineers are planning the (6) .... of new buildings, do they have to take potential quakes into account?
Agostino: Yes, definitely. The building has to sway, rather than break, under the (7) .... of a quake.

path	climate	factors	bank	dams	statistics	countryside	tsunamis

Erika: I've been looking at the (8) .... for flooding last year.
Sylvia: OK. We'll need to look at (9) .... causing the problem, like coastal flooding caused by (10) .... or when (11) .... suddenly burst and flood into valleys. That can cause tremendous damage.
Erika: Mm. I suppose a more common cause is when the rising water in rivers overflows and goes right over the river (12) .... and into fields.
Sylvia: Yes, that's in the (13) .... , but urban areas can suffer, too. Quite a few towns in my country were affected by flash floods last year.
Erika: What do you mean?
Sylvia: Well, the rain was torrential and the water came down the hills really fast and washed away everything in its (14) .... It was terrible, actually.
Erika: I'm sure it's all down to (15) .... change!

speeds	warnings	typhoon	forecasts	eye	equator	hemisphere

Stephan: I know what a cyclone is, but what's the difference between a hurricane and a (16) ....? and a cyclone?
Kelly: It depends where they end up, but all of them originate in tropical regions around the (17) .... , because they need warm air to start off.
Stephan: OK. In my notes I wrote that if the wind (18) .... are 39–73 mph, it's classified as a storm, and if it's over 74 mph it's a hurricane. Also, the hurricane season in the northern (19) .... goes from June 1st to November 30th, and in the southern, from January to March. Oh yes, and that the (20) .... of the hurricane, the area in the centre, is actually calm.
Kelly: Great! Another thing to look at is the accuracy of hurricane (21) .... I mean, when scientists are right, at least they can release public (22) ....

3 Complete the definitions of substances by writing a word from the box in each space.

~~timber~~	crude oil	mud	iron	bamboo
clay	diamonds	minerals	calcium	coal

1 ..Timber..... is produced from forests and is used mainly for construction and fire.
2 .... are gemstones formed thousands of feet under the earth's surface.
3 .... is earth that becomes soft and wet after rain.
4 .... is a kind of wet soil, often grey or orange, that hardens when baked.
5 .... is a hard, heavy metal used for making steel.
6 .... are solid substances in crystal form, for example salt or quartz.
7 .... is a liquid found under the ground or sea, and is often used as a fuel.
8 .... is found in some types of rock but also in bones and teeth.
9 .... is a hard black substance found underground that is used as fuel.
10 .... is a plant with thick, light-brown stems, found originally in Asia, and often used for furniture and fencing.

4 Complete the descriptions of jobs by writing a word from the box in each space.

~~mineralogist~~	seismologist	geologist	climatologist	geographer
volcanologist	glaciologist	cartographer	oceanographer	

1 Someone studying minerals is a mineralogist.
2 Someone studying and making maps is a ....
3 Someone studying the earth's structure and its changes over time is a ....
4 Someone studying weather patterns over long periods of time is a ....
5 Someone studying volcanoes, their history and current activity is a ....
6 Someone studying the behaviour of ice, often in polar regions is a ....
7 Someone who collects data about the sea floor is a ....
8 Someone studying earthquakes and related effects such as tsunamis is a ....
9 Someone studying the earth, its lands, features and inhabitants is a ....

5 Underline the correct word in each sentence.

1 Few visitors could survive on the arctic *tundra/savannah* with its lack of vegetation.
2 A volcano is basically a *vent/tunnel* for the magma to travel through.
3 The earth's surface is made up of fourteen enormous *shelves/plates*.
4 The chances of being struck by *thunder/lightning* during a storm are minimal.
5 An avalanche can occur when the *levels/layers* of built-up snow are unstable.
6 Lines of *longitude/latitude* are the horizontal lines running across a map.
7 The sea *bed/ground* has yet to be fully explored by scientists.
8 Last year the glacier *retreated/withdrew* further than ever before.

6 Underline the most suitable options to complete the text.

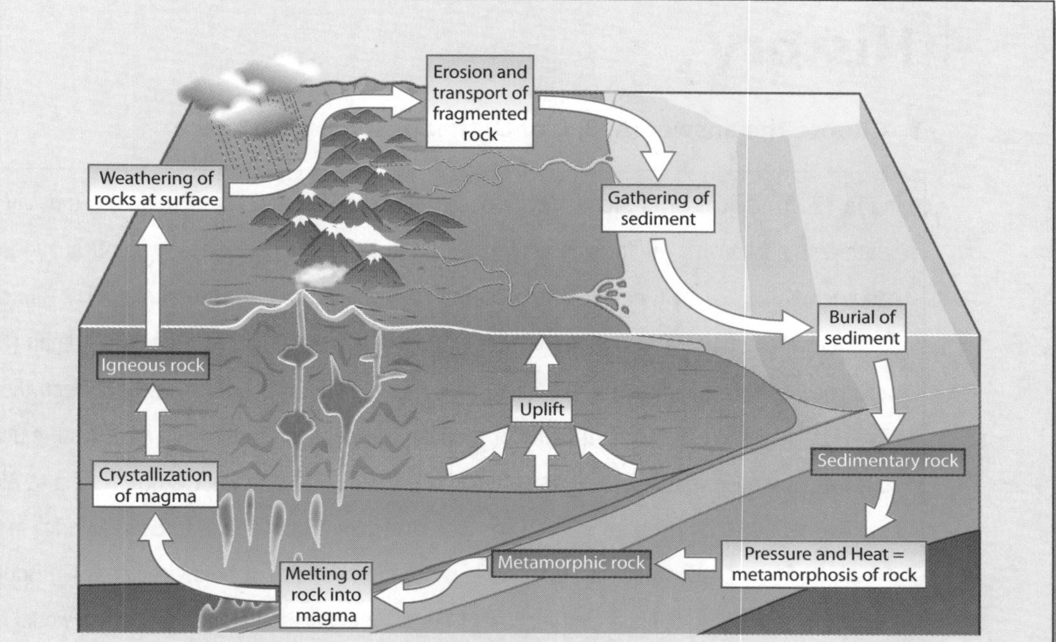

The rock cycle

The rocks of our planet are (1) *classified/referred/divided* as three types: igneous, sedimentary and metamorphic. Over time, each type of rock may be (2) *revitalized/recycled/rebuilt* into another type through different processes. Igneous rock is the rock type which (3) *takes/makes/comes* up most of the earth's outer crust, and is divided into plutonic and volcanic rocks. Volcanic rocks are formed when magma (4) *rises/raises/increases* to the earth's surface and (5) *fires/leaks/pours* out from a volcano. At this stage, it is known as 'lava'. When it (6) *congeals/solidifies/sets*, it becomes volcanic rock. After a volcanic eruption, lava cools down rapidly and the rocks it forms sometimes look like dark glass. However, some magma remains (7) *trapped/surrounded/enveloped* in subterranean passages and chambers. It becomes hard as it (8) *crystallizes/petrifies/adapts.* A typical example of these plutonic rocks is granite.

Both types of igneous rock on the surface are gradually (9) *weathered/broken/smashed* – in other words, they are eroded by rivers, wind, frost, waves and glaciers. The eroded rock splits into small fragments and becomes sediment, along with the tiny bones and shells of living organisms. This (10) *moves/appears/ends* up in lakes, seas, oceans and other natural basins when it is (11) *transported/undertaken/diverted* by the wind, water and ice flow. The sediment in the basins can be thousands of feet deep so the water in the lower layers is (12) *flooded/squeezed/washed* out and new minerals are formed. At this stage, loose sediment becomes sedimentary rock. However, both igneous rock and sedimentary rock can also (13) *undertake/undergo/underlie* dramatic change through the underground forces of extreme heat or pressure and can become metamorphic rock. If forced down deep enough, any type of rock can even (14) *burn/melt/mould* into magma again and eventually cool into igneous rock. In turn, all three types of rock can undergo weathering, erosion and sedimentation to (15) *reappear/revert/remain* to sedimentary rock. The 18th century geologist and discoverer of the rock cycle, James Hutton, said this about it; 'no vestige of a beginning, and no prospect of an end' – a perfect description indeed.

4

VOCABULARY

History

1 Choose the answer (A, B, C or D) that best fits each space.

In the 1930s, a number of stone spear points were discovered in (1) ..D... across the American Southwest, particularly at Clovis, New Mexico. The fact that they were nearly identical suggested they had been (2) .... by a people with a shared cultural (3) .... The simple (4) .... discovered at Clovis were estimated to be approximately 11,000 years old, and as no earlier human (5) .... were known, the commonly held (6) .... was that the 'Clovis people' must have been the first to (7) .... foot there. Towards the end of the last ice age, sea levels would have been much lower, so it was proposed that Asian migrants must have (8) .... from what is now Russia to Alaska by a land bridge, and then used an ice-free corridor stretching from Canada to Latin America in the (9) .... of their migration. In 1997, however, the (10) .... of huts, fireplaces and tools were found in Monte Verde in Chile, and further (11) .... unearthed stone tools which would have been used by a hunting-and- (12) .... people. Radiocarbon dating analyses established that human (13) .... first occurred around 12,500 years ago. Use of the ice-free corridor would not have been (14) .... as it did not then exist. That discovery led to several new migration theories, focusing on both route and genetic (15) ....

	A	B	C	D
1	localities	settings	landscapes	sites
2	moulded	carved	formed	configured
3	tradition	custom	habit	ritual
4	antiques	antiquities	artefacts	accessories
5	environments	communes	habitats	settlements
6	knowledge	view	claim	theory
7	set	put	place	rest
8	extended	expanded	crossed	transferred
9	course	duration	schedule	term
10	ruins	remains	deposits	relics
11	evaluation	expedition	assessment	excavation
12	searching	foraging	gathering	seeking
13	habitation	territory	occupancy	civilization
14	workable	feasible	potential	credible
15	pathways	origin	lineage	networks

2 Complete each sentence with the most appropriate word from the box.

~~abandoned~~	spread	expanded	founded
collapsed	dispersed	invaded	conquered

1 The ancient city was abandoned by its people, perhaps because of disease.
2 It is more accurate to say the Roman Empire slowly fell apart than quickly ....
3 The town was .... in the late 18th century when the settlers decided to stay.
4 Several foreign armies .... the island but the extreme climate forced them to retreat.
5 Researchers now know that the disease .... far more rapidly than previously believed.
6 When the society was .... , many of its people became slaves to the new rulers.
7 Civilization .... greatly once people knew how to create fire.
8 It is thought that tribes may have .... across the desert in search of water.

3 Complete each job definition with a word from the box.

~~historian~~	anthropologist	genealogist	archaeologist	geneticist
geologist	palaeontologist	Egyptologist	etymologist	

1 A(n) historian studies or writes about events in history.
2 A(n) .... studies ancient societies by looking at old tools, bones, and buildings that have been discovered or dug up.
3 A(n) .... studies how individual characteristics and behaviour are passed on through genes, from generation to generation.
4 A(n) .... studies the history of families and how they are related.
5 A(n) .... studies ancient Egypt, its culture, history and language.
6 A(n) .... studies the origin and development of particular words.
7 A(n) .... studies the development of human societies, beliefs and customs.
8 A(n) .... studies the history of the Earth by looking at fossils.
9 A(n) .... studies the way the Earth was formed and how it has changed.

4 <u>Underline</u> the most suitable word in each sentence.

1 A person's DNA can be used to discover their *<u>ancestors</u>/predecessors/descendants*.
2 *Ancient/Antique/Prehistoric* man used stone tools for approximately 3,000 years.
3 As a(n) *indigenous/nomadic/tribal* people, they would have constantly been travelling and following their herds.
4 Archaeologists often look for a *trace/trail/deposit* of evidence to solve a mystery.
5 The *hieroglyphics/characters/tokens* on the walls of the pyramid are well preserved.
6 Frequently found near rivers or coasts, *middens/tombs/digs* contain the kind of rubbish that is invaluable to archaeologists.
7 Small wooden *amulets/carvings/statues* of animals were hung from the walls.
8 Researchers will examine the *skull/fossil/skeleton* to see what diseases the man may have suffered.

5 Replace the phrases in *italics* with the most appropriate phrase from the box.

~~golden age~~	era	decade	antiquity
dynasty	prehistory	lunar calendar	millennia

1 During the *most successful period* of Arab science, great discoveries were made in medicine and engineering. golden age..
2 Some of the books on display date back to *ancient times*. ....
3 The Industrial Revolution was an important *long period of time* in the development of technology. ....
4 The professor has spent a *period of ten years* trying to decipher the meaning of the symbols. ....
5 The city was built *thousands of years* ago and its ruins are still visible. ....
6 The *28-day phase of the moon* was used by many people as a means of establishing the date. ....
7 The cave paintings go back to *a time not recorded in writing*. ....
8 This *period when members of the same family ruled* saw the development of major trade routes across the Asian continent. ....

6 Underline the correct word in *italics* to complete the collocation in bold.

1 Ancient Greece is often referred to as the ***cradle/crib* of Western civilization.**
2 Man has sought to colonize new territory **since the *dawn/sunrise* of time.**
3 **At the *heart/key* of the mystery** lies the question of how the city was destroyed so quickly.
4 Some researchers now see a(n) ***imperfection/flaw* in this argument.**
5 Why the people abandoned the caves is **at the *core/centre* of the debate.**
6 Anthropologists believe that surplus food supplies were **the *root/key* to their success.**
7 **Evidence has been found at the *opening/mouth* of the river** that indicates human habitation.
8 The ancient city of Sumeria is said by some to be **the *source/birthplace* of writing.**

7 Match the human achievements (1–7) with their consequences (a–g).

1 The development of agriculture ...e.......
2 Knowledge of metalworking ....
3 Seafaring and navigation skills ....
4 Technological innovation ....
5 The use of irrigation systems ....
6 Advances in medical knowledge ....
7 The invention of writing ....

a ensured that people made progress in simple machine making.
b revolutionized the way that knowledge was transmitted.
c resulted in the creation of weapons and utensils that were more durable.
d facilitated greater life expectancy.
e meant that people could cultivate crops rather than forage for food.
f encouraged people to explore new territory and trade across oceans.
g meant that farmers could water their land more effectively.

5

VOCABULARY

The mind

1 Choose the answer (A, B, C or D) that best fits each space.

A cognitive capacity humans possess is the the ability to recognize (1) .... states in ourselves and in others, and to recognize differences in belief, desire and intention. This makes us better able to explain the actions of people around us and (2) .... what they may do next. We can learn to communicate more effectively and also to (3) .... others. This ability is known as 'Theory of Mind'. A (4) .... in Theory of Mind development is the ability to recognize that others may have beliefs about the world which are (5) .... Neuroscientists often test this ability in a child by showing them two dolls. One doll has a basket and the other a box. The basket contains a ball. The researcher tells the child one of the dolls is leaving the room, removes the doll and then moves the ball from the doll's basket to the second doll's box. The researcher brings back the first doll and asks the child where the doll will look for the ball. Children who say the doll will look for the ball in the basket pass the test. Most children under the age of four will answer 'the box' because they cannot (6) .... that the first doll wouldn't know what they have just (7) .... Children diagnosed with autism are also likely to fail this test of (8) .... with other people or characters.

Neuroscientist Rebecca Saxe recently conducted experiments amongst both sighted and non-sighted volunteers to test the (9) .... that Theory of Mind is acquired through visual observation of others over time. She found that identical brain regions in both groups became active when they were asked to (10) .... on the beliefs of others. This seems to indicate that visual observation has little to do with Theory of Mind acquisition after all.

	A	B	C	D
1	A knowledge	B brain	C thinking	D mental
2	A presume	B guide	C assume	D predict
3	A deceive	B mislead	C lie	D cheat
4	A milestone	B signpost	C landmark	D marker
5	A fake	B pretend	C false	D artificial
6	A imagine	B dream	C suppose	D expect
7	A participated	B witnessed	C regarded	D attended
8	A comprehension	B realization	C empathy	D trust
9	A hypothesis	B subject	C research	D case
10	A consider	B reason	C speculate	D guess

2 Replace the words in bold with a synonym/phrase from the box. Then circle the correct option A–D.

instinctive
helpful
intellectual
operational

1 What are we told about the ability known as Theory of Mind in the first paragraph? ....
- A It is a **cognitive** ability found only in mankind. ....
- B People use it primarily for **cooperative** purposes. ....
- C It shows the order in which the brain undergoes **functional** development. ....
- (D) It is an ability that is **innate** within humans. instinctive

understand
control
weaken
determine

2 The aim of the test conducted by neuroscientists is to
- A **undermine** the concept of Theory of Mind. ....
- B illustrate how adults may **manipulate** children. ....
- C **ascertain** the age at which children develop Theory of Mind. ....
- D establish who children are more likely to **empathize** with. ....

disputed
suggested
responded
told

3 What does the writer say about Rebecca Saxe's experiment?
- A The participants were not **informed** about its overall purpose. ....
- B It **indicated** that sight did not play a role in Theory of Mind development. ....
- C The brains of sighted and non-sighted volunteers **reacted** differently to it. ....
- D It **challenged** the views Saxe had previously held about Theory of Mind. ....

3 Complete each sentence with a form of the word in CAPITALS.

1. The researchers are working with teenagers with behavioural problems. BEHAVE
2. The child's poor .... awareness was a concern to his teachers. SPACE
3. The brain has to constantly deal with a huge amount of .... input. SENSE
4. The subjects first had to .... a series of black and white images. MEMORY
5. Some people claim to know .... when danger is present. INTUITION
6. Our .... experience of the world may not be the same as others'. PERCEIVE

4 Underline the two words or phrases in *italics* which are similar in meaning.

1 People with insomnia are *prone to/addicted to/susceptible to* hallucinations and anxiety.
2 Anyone who has had a traumatic experience may be *overcome/overrated/overwhelmed* by sadness.
3 It is *a tendency to/an addiction to/a craving for* caffeine that makes it hard to stop drinking coffee.
4 Rapid eye movement is a(n) *accidental/subconscious/involuntary* action during the process of lying.
5 The need for social interaction is an *instinctive/interior/innate* human desire.
6 In some people, gambling becomes a(n) *forceful/uncontrollable/compulsive* habit.
7 Under such stress, Chris isn't capable of making a *logical/rational/cerebral* decision.
8 Nicotine can *activate/stimulate/enliven* the brain's pleasure centres, making it hard to give up smoking.
9 Nuha's ability to remember thousands of dates was a remarkable *trait/mood/attribute.*
10 Researchers questioned whether the *cognition/mindset/mentality* of violent criminals was connected to their early childhood.

5 Complete the definitions with a word from the box.

~~willpower~~	hallucinations	well-being	IQ	amnesia
disorder	obsession	dementia	hypochondria	phobia

1 Some who is determined to succeed has a great deal of willpower .
2 Someone who perceives images which do not exist is experiencing ....
3 Someone who is unable to stop thinking about the same subject has a form of ....
4 Someone who performs very well in an intelligence test has a high ....
5 Someone whose behaviour is anti-social may be suffering from a mental ....
6 Someone whose brain no longer functions properly as they get older has ....
7 Someone who treats people for depression wants to improve their emotional ....
8 Someone who has no memory of the recent and/or distant past is suffering from ....
9 Someone who has an extreme fear of something, for example, spiders, has a ....
10 Someone who often believes they are ill when they are healthy suffers from ....

6 Replace the words or phrases in brackets with a more academic word from the box.

~~consolidate~~	provoke	convert	monitor	stimulate
resemble	store	retrieve	modify	relate

The hippocampus helps to (1) consolidate..., (connect and strengthen) learning and (2) .... (change and transfer) information from working memory via electrical signals to longterm storage. It constantly checks information that is sent to working memory and will then instantly (3) .... (compare) it to stored experiences.

The amygdala appears to play an important role in emotions. When a person's experiences (4) .... (excite) the amygdala, it can produce rage but can also (5) .... (cause) fear or pleasure. It encodes an emotional message, if one is present, when learning is transferred from working memory to long-term storage. So, if a person happens to (6) .... (get back) that kind of memory, an emotional message will also be recalled.

The role of the cerebellum is to coordinate every movement. For example, it can (7) .... (make changes to) and coordinate commands to swing a golf club, and allow a hand to bring a cup to the lips without spilling its contents. It may also (8) .... (save) the memory of rote movements, such as touch-typing and tying a shoelace.

The brain stem is the oldest and deepest part of the brain and neuroscientists often refer to it as the 'reptilian brain' since it appears to (9) .... (look like) the entire brain of a reptile. It is the centre of sensory reception, and is used to (10) .... (check) vital body functions such as heartbeat and body temperature.

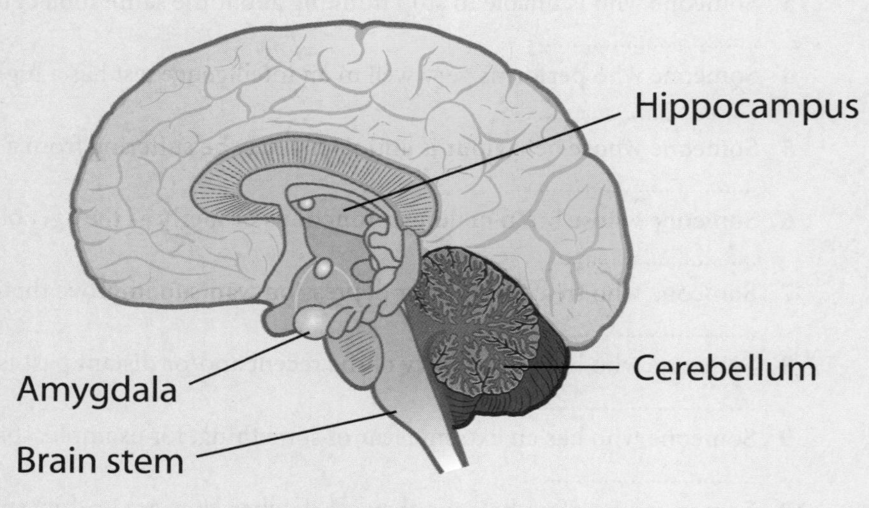

6

VOCABULARY

Technology

1 Choose the answer (A, B, C or D) that best fits each space.

I'm sure that many people in this lecture hall have, at some time, attempted to open up an image file in order to (1) .... their photos onto a social (2) .... site, only to find the file has been (3) .... You find there's no way to (4) .... your digital memories as you've already (5) .... the photos from your memory card. Worse is the realization that your entire hard drive has (6) .... and that you never made back-up copies of your dissertation, years of research, and so on.

Right now, I'm afraid, there's no guarantee that any of our data will survive in the (7) .... currently available. You see, manufacturers want to (8) .... the speed and capacity of drives, but aren't worried about long-term stability. Flash memory drives are not a reliable alternative as they have an estimated (9) .... lifespan of ten years. Top-end CDs with the gold and the phthalocyanine dye layers will (10) .... longer. The other issue of course, is that technology is constantly becoming (11) ....

Many of your parents will have video cassettes at home but unless you have a video player still in (12) .... , you are unlikely to ever view the content. The same goes for any documents saved on floppy disks; no modern PC comes with a (13) .... drive. It's ironic, of course, that paper, the old (14) .... of transferring information, is actually more durable than its modern equivalents.

	A	B	C	D
1	upload	paste	share	display
2	meeting	discussion	networking	chatroom
3	disturbed	disrupted	spoilt	corrupted
4	retrieve	return	retrace	reform
5	rubbed	cancelled	withdrawn	erased
6	collapsed	crashed	fallen	broken
7	formats	shapes	means	types
8	excel	build	boost	uplift
9	top	maximum	peak	upper
10	spend	act	produce	last
11	terminal	obsolete	expired	invalid
12	operation	order	function	occupation
13	fitting	required	compatible	matched
14	opportunity	medium	source	technology

2 Complete the sentences by writing a word from the box in each space.

~~microchip~~	feature	gadget	switch	wire
sensor	glitch	application	device	console

1 The tiny silicon microchip has completely changed the way computers work.
2 It was an innovative safety .... that other cars had yet to incorporate.
3 At the flick of a .... , electricity brings power into our homes.
4 By manipulating their .... , video games players may actually be developing coordination skills.
5 Women were the key consumers of this new kitchen .... in the 1950s.
6 It was a complex .... that was used to calculate astronomical positions.
7 At that time, the same telephone .... ran from house to house.
8 The session will enable you to use the new spreadsheet ....
9 The engineers believe that the .... is small and can easily be fixed.
10 Even the smallest movement is picked up by a nearby ....

3 Replace the definition in brackets with a word or phrase from the box.

~~state of the art~~	durable	waterproof	handy	complex	faulty
mobile	revolutionary	heat-resistant	synthetic	commercially viable	

1 The surgeons will use state of the art (the most advanced) technology to carry out the operation.
2 The designers believe that their product will be .... (at a price consumers can afford).
3 The tool is made of a material that is strong and .... (will not break for a long time).
4 Any instrument they used had to be made of material that was .... (able to exist in hot temperatures without melting).
5 The fabric used to make their clothes needed to be .... (able to keep out rain or moisture).
6 If the product is .... (not working correctly), please return it to the manufacturer.
7 In 1939, the first .... (made from artificial materials) fibre to be produced was nylon.
8 A portable GPS system is .... (useful) in emergencies.
9 The printing press was an invention that allowed the public access to written texts, and can easily be described as .... (completely changing the way something is done).
10 Users found the instructions to be .... (detailed and not simple).
11 The robot is .... (able to move around) on flat surfaces only.

4 Underline the most suitable option in each sentence.

There's little point working on new robots and developing (1) *artificial/fake* intelligence unless the finished product is reliable. When roboticists and the companies funding them create (2) *automated/self-driven* robots for auto assembly lines, they need to keep checking that the powerful (3) *magnetic/hydraulic* arms are doing what they were programmed to do. If they become (4) *misguided/misaligned*, they could cause great damage to cars and profits, not to mention human employees. With mobile robots, the problems that robotocists need to (5) *overcome/oversee* are even greater; firstly a robot needs to know how to (6) *drive/navigate* its way around obstacles and also how to move over uneven (7) *terrain/landscape*; skills that are instinctive to even the lowest lifeforms. Another issue is the robot's object (8) *recognition/comprehension* capacity. You see, robots (9) *perform/enact* their limited functions well in specific environments; so for example, if they are (10) *formulated/designed* to pick up a box from a particular location, that's what they'll do. But imagine the scenario when a child moves to that location; the absence of (11) *logic/wisdom* in a robot means that they could also move the unknown object. Can it then be (12) *taken/held* responsible for the child's injury or death? When it comes to unexpected (13) *interaction/exchange* with humans, robot behaviour is unpredictable.

5 Complete the lecture notes below by writing a word from the box in each space.

~~data~~	databases	image	installation	traits
irises	hackers	scanners	fingerprints	

Biometrics in border control
Electronic passports
These now store:
- personal (1) ...data...
- digital photo (2) .... – at the airport, (3) .... verify they match the passport holder's.

Facial recognition devices
The (4) .... of 'smart gates' at airports is increasing (Australia and the UK). You can bypass queues when the system compares your face with the (5) .... in your e-passport microchip.

Other biometrics
Scientists are working on recognition systems for voiceprint and also a person's (6) .... as these are unique to the individual.
Criticisms from privacy groups.
Hidden cameras may record a person's physical (7) .... without their knowledge.
(8) .... may steal information from centralized (9) ....

7

VOCABULARY

Business and marketing

1 Choose the answer (A, B, C or D) that best fits each space.

Let's look first at small businesses. It's estimated that 56% (1) ....A.. under before their fourth year. Incredible! So, why do so many fail to (2) .... ? First of all, many entrepreneurs don't have an adequate business plan, so they have no clear idea of how much (3) .... will be required to keep their start-up going. So they start spending in a way that unfortunately leads to (4) .... In other cases, people haven't kept enough money in reserve to survive a time of market (5) .... Essentially, it's being prepared for the unexpected, for uncontrollable (6) .... , such as energy rate increases.

What else (7) .... to failure? Well, no matter how excited you are about your product, it's essential to (8) .... your expenses as much as you can. For instance, there's no need to (9) .... expensive office space or to buy designer uniforms. These kinds of unnecessary (10) .... should be avoided. What you need to be (11) .... in is research, i.e. ensuring there is actually customer (12) .... for your product.

Location is also vital. You need to check out the accessibility of any (13) .... you're interested in. Is there parking or public transport? And how about your (14) .... ? In other words, are there stores nearby that may threaten your success? Finally, good customer service is essential. So, (15) .... the right staff and provide the right kind of training, and it'll have a great impact on customer (16) .... and they'll return again and again.

	A	B	C	D
1	**A** go	**B** work	**C** dive	**D** fail
2	**A** bloom	**B** accomplish	**C** thrive	**D** achieve
3	**A** savings	**B** capital	**C** currency	**D** donation
4	**A** debits	**B** debt	**C** dues	**D** sums
5	**A** downsizing	**B** downshift	**C** downfall	**D** downtrends
6	**A** costs	**B** fees	**C** receipts	**D** charges
7	**A** causes	**B** results	**C** produces	**D** leads
8	**A** reduce	**B** decline	**C** diminish	**D** lessen
9	**A** borrow	**B** lease	**C** owe	**D** let
10	**A** overheads	**B** bills	**C** accounts	**D** payments
11	**A** focusing	**B** investing	**C** following	**D** spending
12	**A** choice	**B** interest	**C** opportunity	**D** demand
13	**A** estate	**B** domain	**C** position	**D** premises
14	**A** finances	**B** marketing	**C** competition	**D** management
15	**A** hire	**B** take	**C** arrange	**D** sign
16	**A** relationship	**B** connection	**C** loyalty	**D** devotion

2 Match a person or group of people (1–10) with the correct definition (a–j).

1 the founder ..j......
2 a supervisor ....
3 a project manager ....
4 a public relations officer ....
5 a rival ....
6 a colleague ....
7 the workforce ....
8 a counterpart ....
9 an executive ....
10 an analyst ....

a all the people employed by a company or within an industry
b someone who carefully examines information e.g. about the economy
c someone in charge of a group of workers
d someone who leads a team working on a task or plan
e a person or company who is in competition with you
f someone doing a similar job to you in a different organization or company
g someone you work or cooperate with in the same company
h someone who has a very senior position in a company
i someone who manages communication between a company and the media ....
j the person who started a company

3 Complete the phrasal verbs in *italics* with the correct preposition. Then match each phrasal verb with a synonym from the box.

~~established~~
postponed
planned
became a trend
resolved
chose
anticipated
rejected
collapsed
received
hired
prepared

1 The company was *set* ..up... in the 1990s and has thrived ever since. established
2 Communication had clearly *broken* .... between management and the workforce. ....
3 This popular product first *caught* .... in Europe and then Asian consumers began to take an interest. ....
4 The company said they *looked* .... *to* a rise in profits. ....
5 Employees who reportedly *dealt* .... problems immediately suffered far less stress than employees who *put* them .... , ...
6 For a long time the company *worked* .... new ways to grab our attention. ....
7 Last year, plans were *drawn* .... to restructure the company. ....
8 The advertising industry sometimes *came in* .... a great deal of criticism. ....
9 In the past, most employees *went* .... jobs that offered the most security. ....
10 More organizations *took* .... older workers rather than younger ones. ....
11 Nicolas *turned* .... the job and instead decided to head back to university. ....

4 Choose the correct meaning for the words or phrases in *italics*.

1 It takes a great deal of time to *run* a business properly. ...c...
A work for **B** find the necessary capital for **C** manage

2 The company intend to *implement* the policy early next year. ....
A complete **B** begin to use **C** change

3 Employees are encouraged to *take the initiative* rather than wait for instructions. ....
A make decisions for themselves **B** ask for advice **C** cooperate with others

4 The project was *launched* early in the 1990s. ....
A started **B** proposed **C** rejected

5 It seems that the company have now *set the benchmark* for customer service. ....
A set some specific rules **B** set a high standard **C** set up research

6 Since shift work was introduced, *absenteeism* has dropped considerably. ....
A produced goods **B** people not attending work **C** company morale

7 The *pilot* project will run for three months before the executives make their decision. ....
A global **B** experimental **C** joint

8 The new design was the *brainchild* of Jeff Waterman. ....
A creation **B** hobby **C** ambition

9 The *focus group* gave rather negative feedback on the transport system. ....
A group of customers making complaints **B** a group of executives
C a small group asked for their opinions

10 Many senior personnel said that *doing overtime* was expected of them. ....
A receiving a higher salary **B** making quick decisions
C working long hours

5 Complete each sentence with a form of the word in CAPITALS.

As the number of (1) ..redundancies.. rises, and the concept of job REDUNDANT
(2) .... is disappearing, so the challenges facing job-seekers SECURE
are growing. One issue is modern (3) .... procedure. In the RECRUIT
past, (4) .... sent in a professional-looking curriculum vitae, APPLY
were interviewed by someone from the (5) .... team, and were MANAGE
shortly informed if they were to be a new (6) .... or not. Today, EMPLOY
when a job (7) .... arises, the advert is often placed by an agency VACANT
via an online notice board. The initial (8) .... procedure is then SELECT
carried out by a software programme that recognizes key words in the
CV. Even if the job-seeker is a (9) .... in their field, or they SPECIAL
have increased a firm's (10) .... by 100%, they may never hear PRODUCT
back from the server if it doesn't spot the key words required. In
some ways, this can be worse than receiving a (11) .... letter. REJECT

6 Complete the dialogue by writing an appropriate word from the box in each space.

~~campaigns~~	admen	loyal	segment	endorsement	
catch	target	brands	billboards	promote	pop-ups
tailor	means	audience	profiles	logos	placement

Tanya: OK, what notes have you made for the advertising presentation?
Yves: Well, I started with roadside (1) campaigns , you know, posters and (2) ....
Tanya: Aren't they a bit outdated now?
Yves: I don't think so. They really (3) .... your eye, especially when you're stuck in traffic. The (4) .... know that in most city streets, you're going to have a captive (5) .... !
Tanya: I suppose it's true that you do reach a greater number of people, but surely it's more economical to (6) .... the particular (7) .... of society your product has been designed for? Anyway, I guess I was more interested in the psychology of advertising. So, for example, how new (8) .... are created and what they mean to people, and what makes people remain (9) .... to one and not another.
Yves: Well I think a lot of young people are persuaded through celebrity (10) .... , you know, when they (11) .... a product.
Tanya: I don't know if that's true. Teenagers are fairly sophisticated nowadays. They're probably influenced by product (12) .... , though. I mean, all you see in the movies these days are company (13) ....
Yves: I read that the Internet has taken over from the radio and TV as a (14) .... of advertising, even though most people hate those annoying (15) ....
Tanya: Yes, and I think a lot of companies are building up customer (16) .... through the websites they visit. I think the idea is that in the future, we'll be sent adverts that they (17) .... just to our tastes.
Yves: I'm not sure I like the sound of that!

7 <u>Underline</u> the correct word in each sentence.

1 The annual *revenue/salary* from oil exports continued to rise during the 1990s.
2 The disposable *wages/income* of unmarried employees was mainly spent on travel.
2 *Tax/Fees* on food items increased from 13% to 15% in early 2010.
3 The *economic/economical* trend in the first quarter was a gradual decline in exports.
5 Profit *lines/margins* on luxury goods have been lowered in order to attract customers.
6 *Discounts/Sales* of electronic goods peaked in December last year.
7 Overall *money/wealth* increased by 11% as export markets continued to grow.
8 Average *earnings/takings* per household in 2008 were just over $95,000.
9 A typical weekly *price/budget* for food soared from $171.83 to over $250 last year.

8

VOCABULARY

Science and discoveries

1 Choose the answer (A, B, C or D) that best fits each space.

Phobias, such as an extreme fear of spiders or heights, can cause genuine suffering. In the past, one (1) .... to treatment involved the use of mind-(2) .... drugs, although these often caused undesirable (3) ....- effects in the patient. Another common method still in use is behavioural therapy. This involves exposing people to their particular phobia under controlled (4) .... The (5) .... behind this is that a new memory can be created which says the feared object or situation in (6) .... is safe. In most cases, the effects seem to be more positive than those achieved through chemical intervention.

Most recently, in 2009, a series of (7) .... experiments led by Elizabeth Phelps at New York university looked at the way 'fear memories' were retrieved and the way they could be manipulated. Originally, the experiments had been (8) .... on laboratory rats. Every time the rats were exposed to a certain sound, they were given an electric shock, so they learnt to fear the sound. Scientists (9) .... it was possible to eliminate that fear through 'extinction training', in which the rats were then exposed repeatedly to the sound without any electric shock.

The timing of this training was (10) .... Fear of the sound was only erased in those rats that were trained after an interval of a few minutes but no longer than a few hours after the fear memory was revived. Phelps' study, on human (11) .... given electric shocks when shown coloured cards, was (12) .... on the rat tests. A year after the experiments, nineteen of her (13) .... took part in further tests. Those who had received 'extinction training' more than six hours after the fear memory was revived still showed signs of fear towards the coloured cards. Those who had been trained quickly showed no signs of fear – (14) .... that the fear memory had been eradicated. The research team's (15) .... seemed to offer hope for a new form of phobia treatment.

	A	B	C	D
1	way	means	method	approach
2	altering	changing	adapting	transferring
3	other	after	side	over
4	examples	conditions	cases	rules
5	action	theory	practice	process
6	front	mind	question	point
7	pioneering	leading	main	breaking
8	found out	taken part	looked into	carried out
9	gained	discovered	acquired	wondered
10	meaningful	urgent	crucial	foremost
11	volunteers	nominees	candidates	applicants
12	derived	aimed	designed	based
13	members	interviews	subjects	people
14	indicating	pointing	noting	gesturing
15	findings	intentions	options	summaries

2 Complete each statement about the text in exercise 1 with a form of the word in CAPITALS. Then decide if the statement is true (T), false (F) or not given (NG) according to the text.

1 Spiders are the most common cause of severe ...anxiety..... . ...NG......... ANXIOUS
2 Behavioural therapy is more .... than treatments using drugs. .... BENEFIT
3 The rats suffered .... to electric shocks during 'extinction training'. .... EXPOSE
4 'Extinction training' in rats was .... carried out only if it was done within a short time period. .... SUCCESS
5 There was no .... between the ways that rats and humans responded to 'extinction training'. .... SIMILAR
6 Phobia sufferers have shown a positive .... to Dr Phelps' new form of treatment. .... RESPOND

3 Underline the two words or phrases in *italics* which are similar in meaning.

1 The natural sciences focus on the study of natural *reactions/facts and events/phenomena*, for example, volcanic eruption or plant growth.
2 The social sciences are concerned with the study of human *behaviour/actions/knowledge* and societies.
3 There is a great deal of *speculation/conjecture/worry* about the future uses of the drug.
4 The research team hope that the *data/specimens/information* will prove that their suspicions were correct.
5 An amazing *theory/breakthrough/advance* regarding the treatment of phobias has just been published.

4 Complete each sentence by choosing the most suitable adjective from the box that collocates with the noun in *italics*. More than one answer may be possible.

~~underlying~~	controversial	reliable	concrete	feasible
biased	ground-breaking	empirical		

1 So far we have not discovered the ...underlying.... *cause* of this behaviour.
2 The team's .... *work* resulted in the first ever animal to be cloned.
3 Genetic engineering is still a .... *issue* and causes a great deal of debate.
4 Science depends on .... *data*, which is information gained through observation, experience, or experiment.
5 The side-effects of the drug are uncertain but we will have more .... *results* after a further study.
6 One day it may be *technically* .... to use the water on the moon and turn it into rocket fuel.
7 Some researchers feel that Dr Connor's anti-smoking views may have led to a .... *interpretation* of the study's findings.
8 US scientists have found .... *evidence* of a direct link between light and the rhythms of the human body.

5 Choose the answer (A, B, C or D) that best fits each space.

Looking into space

Outer space has intrigued mankind ever since we first gazed upward. It was easy enough to see stars in the night sky with the (1) ..A.... eye and many early civilizations also noticed that certain groups appeared to form familiar shapes. They used these (2) .... to help with navigation and as a (3) .... of predicting the seasons and making calendars. Ancient astronomers also perceived points of light that moved. They believed they were wandering stars and the word 'planet' (4) .... from the Greek word for 'wanderer'. For much of human history, it was also believed that the Earth was the centre of the Universe and that the planets (5) .... the Earth, and that falling meteorites and (6) .... eclipses were omens of disaster.

It wasn't until the 16th century that Polish mathematician and astronomer Nicolaus Copernicus presented a mathematical (7) .... of how the sun actually moved around the Earth, (8) .... the prevailing understanding of how the solar system worked. The Italian physicist and astronomer Galileo Galilei then used a telescope to (9) .... this theory to be correct.

Many technological advances have allowed us to probe into space since then, and one of the most pioneering was when the first (10) .... spacecraft, the Apollo 11, successfully broke through (11) .... and touched down on the moon's surface. Nevertheless, much of our research must be done from far greater distances. The Hubble Space Telescope was carried into (12) .... by a space shuttle in April 1990 and it has allowed cosmologists to gather incredible data.

Most significantly, it has provided a great deal of evidence to support the Big Bang theory, that is, the idea that the Universe (13) .... as a hot, dense state at a certain time in the past and has continued to (14) .... since then.

	A	B	C	D
1	**A** naked	**B** bare	C clear	D plain
2	**A** systems	**B** constellations	C arrangements	D classifications
3	**A** process	**B** course	C measure	D means
4	**A** calls	**B** bases	C derives	D develops
5	**A** spun	**B** circled	C surrounded	D enclosed
6	**A** sun	**B** sky	C day	D solar
7	**A** form	**B** model	C mould	D copy
8	**A** disagreeing	**B** objecting	C arguing	D challenging
9	**A** prove	**B** state	C claim	D display
10	**A** staffed	**B** manned	C occupied	D controlled
11	**A** gravity	**B** pressure	C space	D layers
12	**A** air	**B** orbit	C atmosphere	D galaxy
13	**A** occurred	**B** happened	C originated	D sprung
14	**A** extend	**B** lengthen	C expand	D enlarge

9

VOCABULARY

The arts

1 Choose the answer (A, B, C or D) that best fits each space.

Some people believe arts subjects such as literature and music have little importance in schools today. To what extent do you agree with this?

In education there has always been (1) .... opinion regarding the arts and more (2) .... subjects such as maths and science. Today that debate continues even as the nature of education is altered by technological and social changes. The question is whether arts subjects are outdated or whether they still (3) .... the purpose of keeping alive creativity and reminding us of the value of beauty.

In most societies, the teaching of the arts encourages students to (4) .... the power of aesthetics. In turn, this helps them to define and understand their own and other peoples' traditions and way of life. It has a unifying influence that has a beneficial effect on humanity; consider the Japanese student who is inspired by Van Gogh's (5) .... to visit Europe.

A criticism often (6) .... at the arts is that they do not develop real skills. However, many arts subjects are the starting points for varying professions: design is a (7) .... that offers a huge range of careers. The study of literature enables students to (8) .... themselves clearly, developing necessary skills for any job requiring good communication.

However, it can also be argued that the arts are (9) .... Can we allow young minds this luxury when there are so many economic and environmental threats to the safety of humankind? Once, an appreciation of the arts was seen as necessary in order for the upper classes to prove their sophistication and higher status. Society now is much more (10) .... so the study of music and painting might be pursued by students with genuine (11) .... – for others, it might be a relaxing hobby rather than a waste of vital study time.

Clearly, the clash between the arts and science subjects will always be present. It is the battle between abstract (12) .... and concrete facts. In short, it is the left brain arguing with the right brain as to which of them should take charge in the challenge to make the world a better place. In (13) .... of learning, perhaps the best attitude we can take is to see them as inseparable and equally (14) .... to the development of civilization.

1	**A** split	**B** divided	**C** opposed	**D** different
2	**A** practical	**B** thoughtful	**C** actual	**D** doable
3	**A** offer	**B** deliver	**C** provide	**D** serve
4	**A** apprehend	**B** accomplish	**C** appreciate	**D** distinguish
5	**A** items	**B** products	**C** goods	**D** works
6	**A** balanced	**B** levelled	**C** pointed	**D** stated
7	**A** field	**B** group	**C** theme	**D** scope
8	**A** speak	**B** express	**C** articulate	**D** describe
9	**A** invalid	**B** impractical	**C** unbelievable	**D** incredible
10	**A** egalitarian	**B** equivalent	**C** identical	**D** alike
11	**A** capacity	**B** proof	**C** talent	**D** facility
12	**A** concepts	**B** plans	**C** sketches	**D** outlines
13	**A** addition	**B** view	**C** particular	**D** terms
14	**A** true	**B** vital	**C** right	**D** current

2 Complete each statement about the text in exercise 1 with a form of the word in CAPITALS. Then decide if the statements are true (T), false (F) or not given (NG) according to the text.

1 Students now prefer .... subjects to arts subjects. .... TECHNOLOGY

2 An interest in the arts may expand people's .... awareness. .... CULTURE

3 There is little .... that arts students will develop real world skills. .... LIKELY

4 In the past, a .... of arts subjects showed a person's superiority. .... KNOW

5 There will probably be .... in the number of students taking arts subjects. .... GROW

3 Match the words in the box with the arts below. Some words may be used more than once.

~~a memoir~~	a blow-torch	charcoal	a stage	a cast	design
a pigment	canvas	a portrait	a metaphor	a melody	a poem
bronze	non-fiction	a composition	an orchestra		
a sketch	durability	function	an instrument	a rehearsal	
a builder	an installation	rhythm	a genre	improvisation	

1 Literature a memoir, ...

2 Music ....

3 Sculpture ....

4 Drawing and painting ....

5 Architecture ....

6 Drama ....

4 Complete each sentence with a form of the word in CAPITALS.

1 The book sometimes suffers from over-long descriptions . DESCRIBE

2 He was one of the most .... writers of the era. INFLUENCE

3 It is .... that many artists are worth more dead than alive. IRONY

4 The actors perform well, but the end of the play is sadly .... PREDICT

5 All the sculptures on display are highly .... IMPRESS

6 The .... will run from March 1st–14th. EXHIBIT

7 The lecture will focus on Islamic Art and its .... patterns. GEOMETRY

8 My university programme will focus on the .... arts. VISION

9 In my opinion, the value of an arts degree is .... RATE

10 The .... will take place at the Civic Theatre. PERFORM

11 Márquez developed his .... style after reading the Czech writer Franz Kafka. LITERATURE

12 I prefer .... to fantasy whenever I choose a film. REAL

5 Complete the lecture notes below by writing an appropriate word from the box in each space.

~~biography~~	metaphors	version	editorials
fiction	plot	reviews	translations

Gabriel García Márquez

(1) ..Biography.......... :
- Born Columbia, March 1928, and raised by grandparents.
- Worked for newspapers – wrote columns, (2) .... and film (3) ....
- Began writing (4) .... e.g. short stories.

Most famous novel was '100 Years of Solitude', published in 1967.
- The original (5) .... was written in Spanish - now there are 27 (6) .... so the book is known worldwide.
- The (7) .... is about the influences of the outside world on a small village.
- The style: lots of (8) .... and the use of irony.

6 Both options are correct. Underline the one that is more suitable in the context.

Welcome, everybody. Well, today we're looking at one of the most (1) *iconic/worshipped* buildings in our city, that is, the National Museum. As an example of modern architecture in an (2) *urban/industrial* environment, it does two things. With its use of beautifully (3) *carved/marked* native wood, it stands out as a structure that reflects our history and cultural (4) *inheritance/heritage*. Furthermore, its architects have won many (5) *rewards/awards* for its unique form and the way it allows in so much natural light. They knew they had a social (6) *requirement/responsibility* to its visitors so they designed a structure that belonged to a community. All architects follow the principle that the form of a building depends on its (7) *function/operation*. In the case of our museum, this seems to be especially true. The architects say they had a clear (8) *concept/hypothesis* from the start: that the museum must provide a sense of open (9) *space/room* so that visitors could clear view each exhibit and not be distracted by overcrowding. What you may not know is that the current museum was not the first on this (10) *ground/site*. An earlier 4-storey museum constructed in the 1970s (11) *met/encountered* with universal criticism. It had few architectural (12) *merits/pros* – the steel decoration on the (13) *facade/face* was ugly and the public found the inside of the structure dark and depressing. However, as the number of exhibits grew, so it was decided to build a large (14) *addition/extension*, another (15) *branch/wing* to the west side. Fortunately, serious structural (16) *imperfections/flaws* were found in the existing museum, meaning that it had to be (17) *pulled/taken* down and new plans had to be (18) *drawn/made up*, that was, um, in the late 1990s.

10

VOCABULARY

Social issues and the media

1 Choose the answer (A, B, C or D) that best fits each space.

Some people believe that children can be better educated by being taught at home rather than by attending lessons at school. To what extent do you agree with this idea?

Education is now generally regarded as a basic human (1) .... In most countries, children from 5–11 receive (2) .... primary school education, and in others, they also receive secondary education during their (3) .... However, there are some children who are (4) .... to go to school but whose parents prefer to homeschool them. In some countries this is a growing (5) .... In this essay I will explore the reasons for this (6) .... and the advantages of both approaches.

First of all, in (7) .... education, pupils not only gain knowledge in a range of academic subjects, but they also learn valuable social (8) .... such as cooperation and team work, which can be used in their adult life. Secondly, staff have acquired (9) .... which means they can use effective teaching (10) .... They can also set benchmarks; in other words, they know exactly what children at different ages should be able to (11) ....

Home schooling, on the other hand, can allow a child to receive (12) .... attention, develop at their own pace and also concentrate more as they will not have to deal with (13) .... fellow students. Another point in favour of home schooling is that more lessons may involve e-learning and the use of (14) .... media.

Continuous innovation in education is providing students with many learning options. If an option helps students to be (15) .... , it should not be ruled out.

	A	B	C	D
1	aspect	right	desire	need
2	compulsory	required	legal	urgent
3	progress	growth	adolescence	maturity
4	entitled	approved	granted	enabled
5	population	attitude	trend	choice
6	event	occurrence	fact	development
7	common	typical	average	mainstream
8	skills	manners	qualities	abilities
9	diplomas	qualifications	certificates	licenses
10	methods	systems	schemes	routines
11	achieve	make	perform	succeed
12	separate	individual	unique	private
13	disruptive	preventing	destroying	prohibitive
14	mutual	interactive	communicative	relating
15	motivated	capable	profitable	improved

2 Underline the two words in *italics* which are similar in meaning.

1 Many people are dependent on *charity/aid/resources* for survival.
2 People living in *suburbs/shanty towns/slums* often have no access to electricity.
3 It is particularly hard to escape the vicious *cycle/chain/circle* of poverty.
4 A vast number of people were suffering from *starvation/malnutrition/mortality*.
5 Women still face gender *discrimination/prejudice/distinction* in many workplaces.
6 Several studies have shown that boys tend to *underachieve/underperform/underrate* in mixed-sex classes.
7 More must be done for the *underprivileged/inconvenient/disadvantaged* in our society.
8 The government launched a *policy/campaign/crusade* to improve eating habits.
9 Scientists believe they have found a link between *anti-social/harmful/wrongful* behaviour and food additives.
10 Children from poor backgrounds are especially *vulnerable/likely/susceptible* to a range of health problems.

3 Choose the answer (A, B, C or D) that best fits each space.

In today's lecture, I'd like to begin with a simple (1) ..B....... of the meaning of poverty. Basically, anyone (2) .... from poverty cannot afford basic human needs such as clean water, food, clothing and (3) .... – that is, somewhere they can stay safe and warm, the things many of us (4) .... for granted. We can make a distinction between absolute poverty, that is, when people are completely (5) .... , I mean they have absolutely no access to the basic needs I described before; and then there is (6) .... poverty, where people have far less income than others in the same society. What some people do not realize is that poverty has actually been the (7) .... for most of human history. People have continuously faced food (8) .... and many other kinds of terrible (9) ....

	A	B	C	D
1	A draft	B overview	C sketch	D speech
2	A hurting	B dealing	C experiencing	D suffering
3	A qualifications	B employment	C shelter	D medicine
4	A have	B take	C feel	D require
5	A destitute	B scarce	C underpaid	D worthless
6	A relative	B reasonable	C similar	D contrastive
7	A situation	B practice	C norm	D state
8	A lack	B shortages	C famine	D rarity
9	A issue	B obstacle	C hardship	D drawback

4 Underline the correct options to complete the dialogue.

Stan: So what do you want to do for the media studies project?

Kathy: How about (1) *freedom/restriction* of the press? We could look at (2) *banning/censorship* in different countries and see what kind of news items are forbidden.

Stan: It's interesting, isn't it? I guess that's why more and more people are turning to blogging, as a way of (3) *disseminating/propagating* and receiving information.

Kathy: Hmm, I'm not sure that that's a reliable way of hearing about (4) *current/real* affairs. On the net, people are unlikely to be objective about what they write.

Stan: But you can say the same about journalists. They're bound to be (5) *inclined/biased*. If you believe in man-made climate change, for instance, you're not going to be (6) *impartial/equal* if you're reporting on an anti-climate change conference.

Kathy: I still think you're going to get better quality (7) *inquiring/investigative* journalism in a newspaper, not the Internet. It's so easy for online news (8) *agencies/societies* to just copy each other's articles with no attempt at verification. Maybe the so-called facts in the original article were true ... or maybe not!

Stan: Well, perhaps some of the respectable (9) *broadsheet/editorial* newspapers are reliable, but you can hardly say that the tabloids are. They just come up with sensational headlines and take a very (10) *external/superficial* look at politics and crime.

Kathy: Well, sure. So why don't we look at the kind of newspaper stories that get (11) *published/broadcast* and why? Is the swing away from serious journalism driven by consumer (12) *request/demand*, for instance?

Stan: Oh, you mean that editors just want the (13) *ratings/circulation* figures to go up?

Kathy: Yes, so they print all those (14) *exposés/reviews* on the private lives of celebrities, rather than inform us about serious issues.

Stan: I guess that's the trend with the (15) *mass/general* media – it's happening everywhere.

5 Change the form of the words in bold to complete the sentences.

1 The company held a press ..*conference*.. to answer questions about what had caused the cars to break down. CONFER

2 Television programmes were originally supposed to be .... rather than purely entertaining. INFORM

3 As a television .... , I have a duty to uncover the truth. CORRESPOND

4 I intend to enrol for a course in .... next year. JOURNALIST

5 Does the public really need these kind of .... stories which invade an individual's privacy? INTRUDE

6 The amount of media .... given to sporting events is substantial. COVER

7 Television has a highly .... effect on young minds. INFLUENCE

8 The spread of North American television across the globe has no doubt had a .... impact. CULTURE

9 Personally, I prefer the kind of .... that lets you know about current affairs. DOCUMENT

10 Can small children differentiate between programmes which are fiction-based and programmes which are .... ? FACT

11

VOCABULARY

The body and health

1 Choose the answer (A, B, C or D) that best fits each space.

An effective health care system should encourage people to take preventative measures against illness and disease, rather than encourage them to rely on treatment.

To what extent do you agree with this statement?

Over the last few centuries, great (1) .... have been made in the field of medicine. More treatments have become available, so that a range of illnesses can be (2) .... and the life (3) .... of people in developed countries has extended. It is still a matter of debate, however, whether governments should focus on prevention or cure.

Nowadays the media is used to promote a (4) .... approach to preserving health. In other words, people are encouraged to look after not only their bodies, but also their mental and emotional (5) .... We have had anti-smoking campaigns and advice on nutrition for decades, and many people have quit their nicotine habit or reduced their fat intake. Thus, there has been some decline in lung and heart disease. The government also supports childhood (6) .... programmes. Thus, few children (7) .... from previously fatal illness such as rubella or hepatitis B. Now we also have leaflets available in doctor's waiting rooms on relaxation (8) .... to reduce stress. Alongside these are posters recommending how much exercise should be taken.

There is no doubt that the measures above help people keep their health to some extent. However, when it comes to most forms of cancer and inherited genetic (9) .... , the only option available is treatment and so it is vital that governments continue to (10) .... research into medication. More effective pain (11) .... and drugs with fewer (12) .... effects should be available to all citizens, not just to the minority who can afford the prices that (13) .... companies charge. Prevention only works when a person has active control over the way their body functions.

	A	B	C	D
1	**A** stages	**B** advances	**C** results	**D** answers
2	**A** healed	**B** cured	**C** dealt	**D** aided
3	**A** expansion	**B** longevity	**C** period	**D** expectancy
4	**A** holistic	**B** conservative	**C** supplementary	**D** detailed
5	**A** aspects	**B** situation	**C** well-being	**D** background
6	**A** injection	**B** antidote	**C** antibiotics	**D** immunization
7	**A** suffer	**B** complain	**C** ensure	**D** bear
8	**A** manners	**B** behaviour	**C** practice	**D** techniques
9	**A** faults	**B** syndromes	**C** disorders	**D** malfunction
10	**A** pay	**B** fund	**C** donate	**D** afford
11	**A** delay	**B** relief	**C** support	**D** assistance
12	**A** side	**B** extra	**C** margin	**D** down
13	**A** chemistry	**B** medicinal	**C** pharmaceutical	**D** surgical

2 Complete the sentences below by writing a word from the box in each space.

~~lungs~~	veins	cochlear	bones	tendons	muscles
arteries	joints	cells	metabolism	retinas	hormones

1 A persistent cough is a sign of damage to the ...lungs..... , often caused by smoking.
2 The two .... are responsible for carrying blood away from the heart.
3 An adult human is estimated to be made up over 100 trillion ....
4 Without calcium, human .... become weak and fragile.
5 .... often become damaged or inflamed during excessive sports practice.
6 Adolescents may suffer changes in mood due to fluctuations in their ....
7 After a long period in hospital, unused .... become weak and stiff.
8 Even the most experienced doctors cannot always find .... quickly when they need to give injections.
9 The elderly often suffer pain in their .... , in particular the wrists and knees.
10 Many people wrongly blame their weight gain on a slow ....
11 Damage to the .... may lead to permanent blindness.
12 Children who are hearing-impaired are now offered .... implants to allow them to have a sense of sound.

3 Complete the definitions of human body systems by writing a word from the box in each space.

~~cardiovascular~~	respiratory	musculoskeletal	reproductive
immune	endocrine	digestive	nervous

1 The cardiovascular system is made up of the heart, arteries, veins and capillaries.
2 The .... system allows the body to process food and transform nutrients into energy.
3 The .... system is made up of a network of cells called neurons that coordinate actions and transmit signals between different parts of the body.
4 The .... system is made up of both internal and external sexual organs, sperm and ova (eggs).
5 The .... system is made up of airways, lungs and diaphragm.
6 The .... system is made up of bones, joints, muscles, tendons etc.
7 The .... system protects the body from bacteria and viruses.
8 The .... system produces chemicals called hormones in the body which are responsible for the control of metabolism, mood, growth and development.

4 Complete the table below by writing an appropriate word from the Symptoms and Treatment boxes in each space.

Symptoms

~~inflammation~~	temperature	
headaches	cough	damage
pneumonia	breathing	thirst
vision	throat	fatigue

Treatments

high-risk	fat	specimen
inhalers	quinine	insulin
exercise	allergens	antibiotics
vaccination		

Disease	Symptoms	Treatment
Asthma	– Sudden (1) inflammation of the airways – Difficulty with (2)	– Use of (3) .... to open up airways to the lungs – Avoidance of (4) .... such as pollen and dust – Avoidance of changes in temperature
Malaria	– High (5) .... , then shivering – Joint pain – Severe (6) .... – Muscle (7)	– Collection of blood (8) .... to confirm presence of malaria – Anti-malarial drugs, often (9) .... -based
Diabetes	*Early signs:* – Excessive (10) .... and fatigue *Long term complications:* – Heart disease – Kidney (11) .... – Stroke – Damaged (12) .... , or even blindness	– Maintenance of healthy blood glucose levels through a balanced diet, (13) .... and medication – Avoidance of refined sugars & diet must be low in (14) .... (15) .... injections may be necessary
Influenza ('the flu')	– Fever, (16) .... , headache – Lack of energy – A sore (17) .... , in bad cases – (18) .... affecting the lungs, which can be fatal for the young and elderly.	– (19) .... is often recommended for (20) .... groups, such as children and the elderly – Plenty of rest and intake of liquids (– note that (21) .... don't work on viral infections)

5 Match each person (1–8) with the statement that describes their job (a–h).

1 a carrier ...g....
2 a physiotherapist ....
3 a surgeon ....
4 a midwife ....
5 a general practitioner (GP) ....
6 an acupuncturist ....
7 a pharmacist ....
8 a homeopath ....

a 'During a pregnancy, I check the baby's growth and measure the mother's blood pressure.'
b 'I carry out several major operations a week with the help of the team.'
c 'I treat my patients using needles which I have to insert into various key points of their body. This treatment can relieve headaches, muscle pain, and other disorders.'
d 'As well as the symptoms of a patient's disease, I also take their physical and psychological state into account. The remedies require many stages of dilution.'
e 'I've designed a new exercise and stretching programme for the player, and we believe he'll overcome the injury in time for the next game.'
f 'At this time of year we're writing out a huge number of prescriptions for antiobiotics, mainly for throat infections.'
g 'I was completely unaware I had the disease. I had no symptoms. It wasn't until I had a routine blood test that I found out I could pass on hepatitis C.'
h 'One of our roles is to ensure that people are taking the right dosage. We don't want people feeling drowsy while they're driving to work!'

6 Underline the most appropriate word in each sentence.

1 Washing hands thoroughly helps prevent the *stretching/spreading/passing* of germs.
2 *Chronic/Acute/Durable* describes serious pain over a long period of time.
3 Repetitive stress injury (RSI) may occur in the *wrists/ankles/knuckles* of mouse users.
4 Health officials doubt the disease will reach *peak/national/epidemic* proportions.
5 Smallpox was finally *expelled/eradicated/terminated* in 1979.
6 The disease is *popular/contagious/transportable* so patients must remain isolated.
7 During the first six weeks of life, a baby is known as a(n) *fetus/embryo/infant.*
8 People dissatisfied with conventional medicine are turning to *alternative/secondary/replacement* medicine, such as homeopathy.
9 Scientists have carried out tests to check the placebo *effect/result/cause* in patients.
10 The inability to fall asleep is known as *amnesia/insomnia/anorexia.*
11 An early *diagnosis/examination/survey* of the disease is vital.

12

VOCABULARY

Attitude and opinion

1 Choose the answer (A, B, C or D) that best fits each space.

The invention of the mobile phone has (1) ...D.... revolutionized the way people communicate and influenced every aspect of our lives. The (2) .... is whether this technological innovation has done more harm than good.

In order to address the question, we must first turn to the type of consumer. (3) .... most parents buy mobile phones for their teenagers to track their whereabouts and ensure their safety. We can also (4) .... that most teenagers want mobile phones to avoid missing out on social contact. In this context, the advantages are clear. However, we cannot (5) .... the fact that text messages have been used by bullies to intimidate fellow students. There is also (6) .... evidence that texting has affected literacy skills.

The ubiquitous use of the mobile phone has, (7) .... question, affected adult consumers too. What employee, on the way home from work, would be (8) .... to answer a call from their boss? (9) .... only 18% of us, according to a recent survey, are willing to switch off their phones once we've left the office.

(10) .... , mobile phones can be intrusive but there are obvious benefits to possessing one. (11) .... speaking, they are (12) .... when it comes to making social or business arrangements at short notice. (13) .... to a recent survey, they also provide their owners with a sense of security in emergency situations.

In conclusion, mobile phones do have their drawbacks, but these are (14) .... by the benefits. I would (15) .... that it is not the tool that chooses its purpose, but the user.

	A	B	C	D
1	**A** improbably	**B** impossibly	**C** uncertainly	**D** undoubtedly
2	**A** topic	**B** issue	**C** subject	**D** case
3	**A** Accordingly	**B** Presumably	**C** Commonly	**D** Traditionally
4	**A** expect	**B** believe	**C** assume	**D** reckon
5	**A** deny	**B** reject	**C** refuse	**D** disallow
6	**A** unarguable	**B** indisputable	**C** doubtless	**D** unhesitating
7	**A** no	**B** past	**C** beyond	**D** without
8	**A** reluctant	**B** stubborn	**C** unenthusiastic	**D** resistant
9	**A** Knowingly	**B** Apparently	**C** Surely	**D** Seemingly
10	**A** Admittedly	**B** Incidentally	**C** Generally	**D** Regrettably
11	**A** Truly	**B** Individually	**C** Personally	**D** Honestly
12	**A** worthy	**B** priceless	**C** significant	**D** invaluable
13	**A** Citing	**B** According	**C** Referring	**D** Concerning
14	**A** outweighed	**B** overcome	**C** overrated	**D** undervalued
15	**A** continue	**B** pursue	**C** argue	**D** follow

2 Underline the word or phrase in *italics* which has a different meaning.

1 *Advocates/Opponents/Supporters/Champions* of this theory are growing in number.
2 Researchers have recently found *compelling/convincing/undeniable/scant* evidence.
3 Professor Taylor *dismisses/concurs with/supports/backs* the idea of earlier migration.
4 There is considerable *conjecture/speculation/supposition/proof* concerning this subject.
5 When it comes to the potential use of biofuels, Schuman is a well-known *detractor/skeptic/campaigner/critic.*
6 The team *concedes/admits/confesses/refutes* it may have misinterpreted the results.
7 Chan continued to *doubt/insist/claim/contend* that the manuscript was authentic.
8 These *findings/summaries/conclusions/results* suggest that dogs were domesticated much earlier than previously thought.
9 Many of the principles behind behaviourism were *refuted/contested/defended/opposed* in the latter half of the twentieth century.
10 If the tomb had been defaced so badly, Collins *reasoned/rejected/inferred/deduced* that it must have been done for political reasons.
11 What Alexey did not *contradict/foresee/predict/envisage* was the speed at which the cells began to die.
12 What began as a(n) *assumption/theory/hypothesis/denial* soon became established fact.

3 Complete each sentence by choosing the most suitable adjective from the box that collocates with the noun in *italics*.

~~common~~	good	empirical	implausible	heated
prevailing	anecdotal	unanimous	convincing	incorrect

1 It is a ..common.. *misconception* that some people have naturally superior memories.
2 Boyd makes a .... *case* against the increasing use of pesticides.
3 There has always been a great deal of .... *opposition* to the theory of evolution.
4 Williams found this *explanation* to be highly .... , and set out to disprove it.
5 Sociologists may begin their research based on .... *hearsay*, and then look for .... *evidence.*
6 The notion that sharks are naturally aggressive is an .... *assumption*, though many believe it.
7 There was a .... *decision* amongst all the team members to continue the project for another two years.
8 We have .... *reason* to believe that the virus originated in an animal species.
9 The .... *opinion* amongst researchers is that 'mother' originated from the Sanksrit word 'ma'.

4 Match the comments in direct speech (1–8) with the explanations in reported speech (a–h).

1 'I am of the same mind ...' ...e........
2 'I am reluctant to draw a conclusion ...' ....
3 'I am still troubled ...' ....
4 'I have a hunch ...' ....
5 'I have a different take on it ...' ....
6 'I was immediately struck by ...' ....
7 'I still hold out hope ...' ....
8 'I think you have to take it as given that ...' ....

a Professor Johannson said he strongly suspected ...
b Professor Johannson said he was surprised ...
c Professor Johannson said that it was acceptable to think that ...
d Professor Johannson said he was optimistic that ...
e Professor Johannson said he agreed ...
f Professor Johannson said he wasn't sure ...
g Professor Johannson said he was worried ...
h Professor Johannson said he disagreed ...

5 Replace the word or phrase in *italics* with a form of the phrasal verb or phrase from the box.

~~take aback~~	lean towards	go along with	win over	point to
fathom out	bear out	write off	rule out	puzzle over

1 The researchers were *completely surprised* by the results of the test. taken aback
2 Edwards now *thinks there is more truth in* the idea of upbringing being more important than genetics in the 'Nature vs Nurture' argument. ....
3 Other scientists in the field have not yet been *convinced* by Simond's claims. ....
4 Physiognomy, the study of head shape in relation to personality, was *dismissed* as pseudoscience in the late nineteenth century. ....
5 Archaeologists have long *been confused by* the layout of the huge stones. ....
6 The team's initial findings were *confirmed* by a second series of tests. ....
7 Werhli *has the same opinion as* Khan on this subject. ....
8 Ericsson *says no to* the possibility of treating the bugs with pesticide. ....
9 Both researchers *regard* deforestation as the primary cause of extinction. ....
10 We have finally *come to understand* how this complex process works. ....

6 Complete each sentence with a preposition that collocates with the word or phrase in italics. Then decide if the sentence expresss agreement (A), uncertainty (U), or disbelief/disapproval (D).

1 Pearce *cautions* ..against...... the idea that the drug will delay the effects permanently. ..D.....
2 The Czech researchers say their findings are *consistent* .... the Swiss team's. ....
3 When the team came up with their hypothesis, it was *greeted* .... *scepticism*. ....
4 There seems to be a strong *correlation* .... birth order amongst siblings and how ambitious they each tend to be. ....
5 Lee *subscribes* .... the idea that podcasting will have a leading role in education. ....
6 The question of whether online gaming really improves hand–eye coordination is *open* .... *debate*. ....
7 The particular design of this urban development has been *called* .... *question*. ....
8 *The jury is still* .... on whether such a form of therapy is beneficial or not. ....
9 In my opinion, this new evidence provides *another tick* .... *the box* to support the theory. ....
10 Reed's careless approach to journalism meant that the newspaper *fell* .... *disrepute*. ....

7 Complete each sentence with a form of the word in CAPITALS.

1 This hypothesis has come in for a great deal of ..criticism... . CRITIC
2 These latest findings have confounded all .... EXPECT
3 It seemed .... to people in the Middle Ages that our planet could be round. CONCEIVE
4 Her findings challenge the .... that elderly people necessarily become forgetful. ASSUME
5 Lanser remains .... and insists that there is insufficient proof. SCEPTIC
6 .... speaking, it is possible to clone any living organism. HYPOTHESIS
7 There seems to be little .... amongst researchers that the cure will be found soon. CONVINCE
8 Martens shares his colleague's .... for fieldwork. ENTHUSE
9 Most marketing professionals seem to be in .... on this point. AGREE
10 Freud's work was highly .... for many early psychologists. INFLUENCE
11 Rossi's .... with volcanoes has nearly cost him his life on more than one occasion. OCCUPY
12 Kozima willingly .... there are risks associated with this kind of experiment. KNOW

13

VOCABULARY

Academic encounters

1 Choose the answer (A, B, C or D) that best fits each space.

Good morning everyone. As you know, your presentations are (1) .... for the week after next. I hope that, by now, you've (2) .... a section of the presentation to each member of your group, and that each person knows exactly what they're going to (3) .... in their section. As in a (4) .... assignment, I hope to see an introduction with clearly (5) .... aims. When you present the results from the research you've (6) .... out, these should be explained with a good (7) .... of detail. Obviously include a (8) .... at the end. Anyway, for each claim you make in the presentation, provide (9) .... evidence. This can be in the form of a graphs or tables, and make sure the (10) .... of this data is visible on your slide. The same goes for (11) .... you use – ensure you acknowledge the author, the book, the year and so on. If you can do all that, you'll be on your way to fulfilling the (12) .... for the presentation.

What else? Visual (13) .... is good, but don't overcrowd a slide with too many photos as it can (14) .... your audience. I'd also advise you to (15) .... your listener and you can do this in several ways. First, include some (16) .... questions; by that I mean ask questions to (17) .... their attention, and then give the answer yourself. Of course, you need to deliver your presentation at the right (18) .... – not too fast, not too slow. Make eye-contact with your listeners – you'll see when they're interested, confused, when they've switched off. Leave time at the end to (19) .... any questions. And just to make it completely clear to you, the assessment is (20) .... towards content, rather than speaking skills.

	A	B	C	D
1	designed	operated	programmed	scheduled
2	divided	allocated	contributed	donated
3	deal	cover	form	involve
4	written	paper	text	visual
5	intended	mentioned	stated	recommended
6	worked	carried	made	taken
7	example	grade	number	level
8	closing	finale	conclusion	culmination
9	supporting	bearing	aiding	helping
10	source	origin	cause	supplier
11	expressions	sayings	quotes	critiques
12	criteria	regulations	standards	legislation
13	pictures	input	impressions	layout
14	distract	disturb	prevent	interrupt
15	invite	involve	connect	keep
16	metaphorical	expressive	rhetorical	instructive
17	involve	create	attract	show
18	timing	moment	way	pace
19	respond	take	reply	conduct
20	biased	transferred	weighted	pointed

2 Match the people (1–12) to their descriptions (a–l).

1 tutor ..d...
2 teaching assistant ......
3 lecturer ......
4 professor ......
5 undergraduate ......
6 technician ......
7 union representative ......
8 peer ......
9 mentor ......
10 author ......
11 opponent ......
12 graduate ......

a someone whose job involves using special equipment or machines, often in a university
b someone who has written a book, article or other publication ....
c someone with experience who helps a less-experienced person with their work
d a teacher in a college or university
e someone who argues against you in a formal discussion
f a member of an organization that speaks for and looks after the needs of students at each university or college
g a teacher at the most senior level at college or university
h a person who gives an academic talk on a particular subject to a large group of students
i someone who may help the university teacher with their marking or who leads the discussion in a small group of students
j a person in the same group or at the same level of ability
k a person who has completed their first degree at university
l a person who has not yet completed their first degree at university

3 Complete the text by writing a word from the box in each space.

~~degree~~	master's	papers	certificate
electives	programme	prospectus	major

I left China for New Zealand when I was 16 and finished my high school education there. I was fairly certain about which bachelor (1) ...degree..... I wanted to take, the Bachelor of Commerce and Administration, and I quickly decided to do my (2) .... in International Business because that was my particular interest. All the individual (3) .... looked interesting; there were about seven a year, but then, when I started reading the online (4) .... in more detail, I realized there was a list of (5) .... , I mean, extra subjects, and that I had to choose which ones I wanted to do during the (6) .... for each year. Anyway, I made my choice and finally received my degree (7) .... at the graduation ceremony last June. My mother was very proud and put it in a frame! The next step is a (8) .... , but I'm going to stay with my company in Auckland for a few years first.

4 Replace the explanation in *italics* with a word or phrase from the box.

~~bibliography~~	thesis statement	recommendations	case study
project	dissertation	first draft	

1 At the end of your essay, don't forget to include the *list of all the books you used to find your information*. bibliography
2 Most students give their tutors their *unfinished essay for feedback and suggestions* and then give the tutor the improved essay. ....
3 Wei is in the middle of writing a *long piece of written work as part of her undergraduate degree*. ....
4 Their *piece of research that recorded details of how the situation developed* took five years to carry out and complete. ....
5 You must make your own opinion clear in the assignment and include some *ideas and suggestions for improvement*. ....
6 Your introduction should contain a *section where you describe the aims of your long essay and what you will include in it*. ....
7 Third year students must work in groups to complete a *piece of research on a topic of their choice*. ....

5 Underline the two possible verbs in *italics* in each sentence.

1 Do you think it will be possible to *fulfil/meet/extend* the deadline?
2 You'll need to *undertake/carry out/ perform* some of the research at the museum.
3 500 new students are expected to *involve/attend/take part in* orientation week.
4 I think we have to *submit/pass over/hand in* our essays by Friday next week.
5 I'm not satisfied with my conclusion so I think I'll have to *amend/redo/affect* it.
6 This time next week we'll be *sitting/passing/taking* the final exam!
7 To improve your *grades/credits/marks*, you'll need to improve your accuracy.
8 In our latest experiment, we found that over 24% of the *recipients/sample/subjects* were unable to remember the brand names correctly.
9 I'm looking for someone to *proof-read/approve/go through* my thesis for typing errors before I give it in.
10 You missed a really useful *seminar/tutorial/appointment* last week; we had a really good discussion with the tutor.

6 Complete each sentence with a form of the word in CAPITALS.

1 I'm hoping to get an extension on the deadline for my essay. EXTEND
2 The final .... date for dissertations is the 8th May. SUBMIT
3 I'm not sure how the .... of credits works for this paper. ALLOCATE
4 What are the .... for enrolling for this degree? REQUIRE
5 In his presentation he gave a detailed .... of the results of the experiment. ANALYSE
6 Copying someone else's work without admitting it is known as a .... PLAGIARIZE
7 I think we should present our .... to the class on Friday. FIND
8 I think we receive a written .... of our presentation tomorrow. ASSESS

14

VOCABULARY

Graphs, charts, trends

1 Choose the answer (A, B, C or D) that best fits each space.

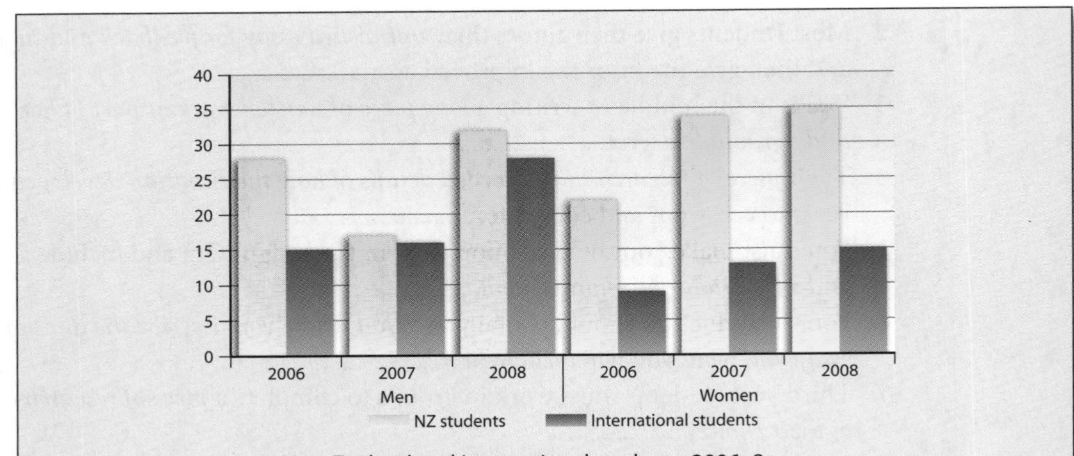

New Zealand and International students, 2006–8

The bar chart (1) ..D...... the number of male and female students (2) .... science subjects at Northland College, New Zealand (3) .... three years, and also (4) .... whether they were New Zealanders or international students. (5) .... to the number of New Zealanders, the number of international students was (6) .... smaller. Nevertheless, there was clear statistical growth in the (7) .... group from 2007–2009. Furthermore, the number of female students from New Zealand eventually (8) .... the number of males from the same country, (9) .... a high of 35 students in 2009. 2008 (10) .... the most dramatic developments, (11) .... the number of male New Zealanders dropping from just (12) .... 30 students to 17, and the number of female New Zealanders increasing from 23 to 34. There was also (13) .... growth in the number of male students from overseas, climbing from15 in 2007 to 27 in 2009. Overall, we can see a(n) (14) .... trend in the number of students at the college.

	A	B	C	D
1	**A** points	**B** draws	**C** examines	**D** illustrates
2	**A** study	**B** studies	**C** studying	**D** studied
3	**A** during	**B** over	**C** through	**D** since
4	**A** indicates	**B** tells	**C** regards	**D** underlines
5	**A** Compared	**B** Comparing	**C** Comparison	**D** Comparative
6	**A** slightly	**B** really	**C** significantly	**D** marginally
7	**A** last	**B** least	**C** latter	**D** later
8	**A** outweighed	**B** overtook	**C** extended	**D** upturned
9	**A** getting	**B** aiming	**C** finding	**D** reaching
10	**A** met	**B** existed	**C** happened	**D** saw
11	**A** and	**B** with	**C** for	**D** but
12	**A** under	**B** less	**C** minus	**D** before
13	**A** noticed	**B** noticing	**C** notable	**D** noted
14	**A** upward	**B** general	**C** irregular	**D** stable

2 Add synonyms to each verb in 1–7 below.

~~go up~~	dive	be unpredictable	climb	stay constant
drop	plunge	shoot up	hold steady	reach a high point
slump	rise	grow	rocket	fall	jump

1 to increase ....go up..........
2 to decrease ....
3 to remain stable ....
4 to fluctuate ....
5 to soar ....
6 to plummet ....
7 to reach a peak ....

3 Underline the two adverbs that have a similar meaning.

1 Sales figures dropped *sharply/suddenly/gradually* in April of 2007.
2 The amount of time spent on leisure activities was *exactly/approximately/roughly* 20%.
3 Membership rose *steeply/slightly/significantly* during the summer months.
4 The number of accidents fell *rapidly/steadily/progressively* during 2009.
5 The percentage was *relatively/comparatively/marginally* higher in the following year.
6 The figure in 1997 was *vastly/somewhat/rather* lower compared to the 1996 figure.

4 Rewrite the first sentence by changing the verb in *italics* into a noun, any adverb in *italics* into an adjective, and making any other necessary changes.

1 The number of people owning mobile phones *rose dramatically* between 1990 and 1995.
There ..was a dramatic rise in.. the number of people owning mobile phones between 1990 and 1995.
2 Migration from rural regions to urban centres *has levelled out* over the last ten years.
Over the last ten years there .... migration from rural regions to urban centres.
3 The amount of time spent on leisure activities *fell slightly* in 2008.
2008 saw .... the amount of time spent on leisure activities.
4 Newspaper circulation during the 1990s *fluctuated considerably.*
There .... newspaper circulation during the 1990s.
5 The rate of applications for the nursing profession *plateaued* between 2001 to 2007.
The rate of applications for the nursing profession .... between 2001 to 2007.

5 Choose the answer (A, B, C or D) that best fits each space to complete the information about the pie chart.

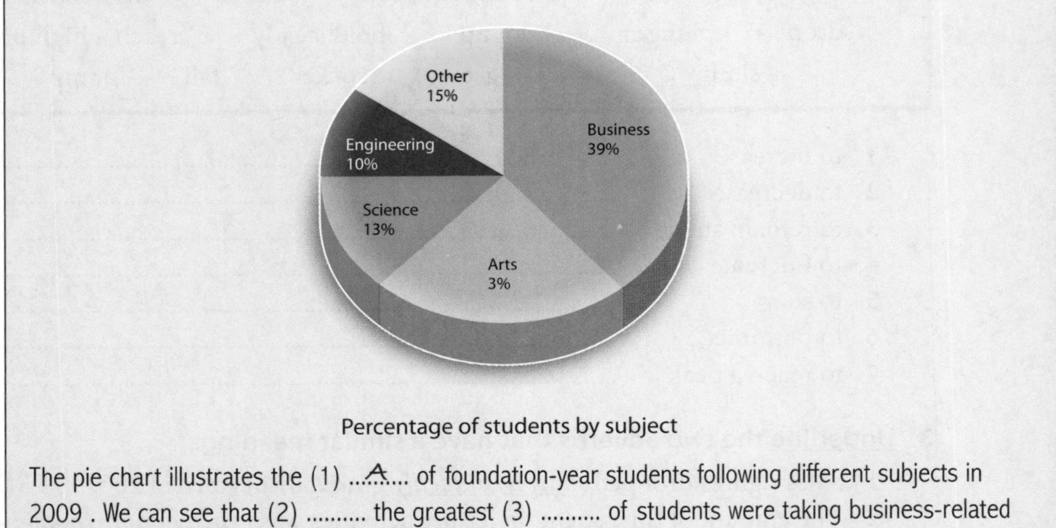

Percentage of students by subject

The pie chart illustrates the (1) ...A... of foundation-year students following different subjects in 2009 . We can see that (2) .... the greatest (3) .... of students were taking business-related courses. The (4) .... highest group were students taking Arts subjects, and these (5) .... 23% of the total. Science-programme students made (6) .... 13%, and the smallest group, the Engineering students, (7) .... 10%.

1	**A** proportion	**B** sector	**C** size	**D** variety
2	**A** as for	**B** by far	**C** much more	**D** about
3	**A** amount	**B** part	**C** fraction	**D** percentage
4	**A** following	**B** less	**C** after	**D** second
5	**A** added up	**B** worked out	**C** accounted for	**D** counted towards
6	**A** with	**B** up	**C** by	**D** from
7	**A** contained	**B** composed	**C** comprised	**D** consisted

6 Underline the two or three linking words in *italics* which make sense.

1 *Whereas/Although/While* the number of students taking Business subjects remained approximately the same, the number taking Arts subjects rose from the previous year.

2 *Comparing/Compared/In comparison* with the previous year, the number of Engineering students fell slightly, from 10 to 6%.

3 The number of female students slowly declined *while/but/whilst* the number of male students went up sharply.

4 *Regarding/Concerning/As for* the number of international students, the trend was unpredictable throughout the period 1995-2005.

5 *In total/All in all/Overall*, there was a generally downward trend in the number of students enrolling for Social Sciences.

7 Look at the language for describing a trend in bold in the first sentence. Choose the correct meaning in *italics* in the second sentence.

1 In the 1960s, we began to see **a swing away from** the traditional view that women should be homemakers.
People were *holding on to*/*beginning to reject* their traditional view.

2 There has been **a backlash against** the government response to the flu pandemic.
The public are generally *supportive*/*critical* of the government's response.

3 Critics of biometric data collection suggest it **is a move towards** the loss of personal freedom.
The loss of personal freedom is *becoming more likely*/*will now occur.*

4 Figures continued to rise steadily throughout the 1990s. **An exception to** this trend was a brief dip in the first quarter of 1994.
The first quarter of 1994 was *a good example of*/*not included in* this trend.

5 Over the last few years, there has been **a resurgence** of interest in Gothic literature.
People have *gradually become less* /*suddenly become more* interested.

6 It remains to be seen whether this new approach to weight loss will **catch on**.
This approach may *become popular*/*disappear rapidly.*

7 There is **a tendency amongst** men in this age group to neglect their health.
The pattern of behaviour of men in this age group is *predictable*/*unpredictable.*

8 The **long-term outlook** for this species is still uncertain.
The possible *future*/*past* situation regarding the species is not known.

9 In some countries, long-term partners are choosing not to have children. **What is behind this development**?
How can we explain this change?/*What will the result be?*

10 Since the 1970s, there has been **a** gradual **drift away from** the practice of the eldest son taking over the family farm.
It is becoming increasingly *common*/*rare* for the eldest son to take over the farm.

15

VOCABULARY

Synonyms for academic essays

1 Complete the text giving advice by writing a word from the box in each space to replace the word in brackets.

~~recommended~~	employ	appropriate	allocated	required
basic	further	paraphrase	intended	heed	key
reproduce	identical	broad	limited	impacted on	ensure

In order to do well in the IELTS Academic Writing test Part 2, it is (1) ..recommended.. (suggested) that you (2) .... (follow) the advice below.

- (3) .... (Make sure) you read the first part of the question carefully. Often the topic is fairly (4) .... (narrow), so, for example, if the question is about how the environment is (5) .... (affected) by tourism, do not write about the environment in general.
- Make a (6) .... (rough) plan before you start writing. Start by making notes about the (7) .... (main) statements or claims you plan to include. Then each statement/claim needs one or more supporting examples, so add (8) .... (more) notes for those.
- Do not (9) .... (copy) the question and (10) .... (use) it in your opening paragraph because you will not impress the examiner. It's better to find a way to (11) .... (reformulate) the question.
- Include your opinion. At university, students are often (12) .... (asked) to do this in the introduction and the conclusion. However, during the IELTS test, you are (13) .... (given) a time limit. It is probably better to write your opinion only in the conclusion, so you are not repeating the same points and using (14) .... (the same) language in two stages of your essay.
- Use a (15) .... (wide) range of grammatical structures and vocabulary which are (16) .... (suitable) for academic writing. This unit is (17) .... (designed) to help you learn synonyms that will give you greater flexibility in expressing yourself.

2 Read the essay question and the following sentences. Decide whether the statements indicate advantages (A) or disadvantages (D).

Some educational systems are now focusing on the teaching of practical skills to high school students, rather than on theoretical knowledge.

What are the advantages and disadvantages of this development?

1 One benefit of learning practical skills at school is ... ..A.......
2 A further argument in favour of focusing on practical skills is ... .
3 In the long run, there may be certain negative outcomes. ....
4 A major downside to this form of education might be that ... .
5 Learning practical skills may also be beneficial because ... .
6 A practical education may also be advantageous because ... .

7 A secondary drawback is that ... .
8 Such training may be invaluable later on in life. ....
9 This kind of education may be of considerable benefit in the way that ... .
10 One other unfortunate aspect of this trend is that ... .

3 Read the essay question and the following sentences. Decide whether the statements indicate cause (C) or measures that need to be taken (M).

Many people who live in urban areas are suffering increasingly from stress. What do you think are the causes of this problem and what measures could be taken to reduce it?

1 The first step would be ... .M....
2 One key factor behind urban stress is ... .
3 Inner city stress may also derive from ... .
4 Another potential solution would be ... .
5 There is another approach that could be considered. ....
6 Feelings of anxiety may also result from ... .
7 To some extent, urban transport may also contribute to a sense of stress. ....
8 Another underlying reason for this form of nervous tension is ... .
9 An alternative strategy could be ... .
10 A further way to tackle this issue could be ... .
11 One possible way to address this problem is ... .

4 Underline the two words in *italics* in the second sentence which are similar in meaning to the word or phrase in bold in the first sentence from different parts of an essay.

1 Free healthcare is certainly a **matter of debate**. (in the introduction)
As we have seen, free healthcare is a *divisive/argumentative/controversial* issue. (in the conclusion)
2 Censorship of the media is certainly a **complex** issue. (in the introduction)
As the arguments above illustrate, the subject of media censorship is highly *confusing/complicated/multifaceted.* (first line in the conclusion)
3 In this essay, I will **evaluate** the pros and the cons of introducing higher tax on unhealthy foods. (last sentence in the introduction)
After *measuring/assessing/weighing up* both sides of the argument, it seems clear that a tax would certainly bring about considerably more benefits than problems. (first line of conclusion)
4 Over the last few years, there has been a **steady** increase in violent crime. (claim)
Cases of assault have *constantly/continuously/sharply* been going up and robbery is now more likely to result in injury. (evidence)
5 When deciding whether art should be a compulsory subject, we have to **take into account** the personal interests of the students. (first claim)
We also need to *wonder/consider/bear in mind* how relevant art may be to a student's future working life. (later claim)
6 There are **some** situations in which a competitive personality would benefit a person. (claim)
There are also *varied/certain/particular* situations in which this kind of behaviour may be harmful. (opposing claim)

7 There is **little likelihood** of people voluntarily giving up their cars. (claim)
It is also *improbable/incredible/unlikely* that public transport networks will be able to transfer commuters to the precise locations they require. (later claim)

8 If we do not tackle the issue of homelessness now, we will have to face the **consequences** later. (claim)
Greater levels of ill-health and depression are just two of the likely *repercussions/ influences/outcomes* of failing to deal with this problem. (evidence)

5 Complete the second sentence with an appropriate word from the box with a similar meaning to the words in *italics* in the first sentence.

~~depending~~	~~information~~	question	violent	operate	afford
immense	construction	the case	elderly	pleasure	company
selection	countryside	reply	anxious	contentment	impact

1 People are no longer *relying* on paper-based *research*. Instead they are depending on the Internet for their information .

2 Consumers are *heavily influenced* by advertising, whether they realize it or not. The .... of television and billboard commercials on our decision-making in the supermarket is ....

3 In some societies, there is growing *concern* about the treatment of the *older generation*. The .... and their middle-aged children are .... about who will look after them when they can no longer take care of themselves.

4 If we continue to extend our cities and *build* in *rural areas*, the decline of certain animal species is certain. New .... should be located in waste land within urban areas, rather than the ....

5 Is it true that money can *buy happiness*? In my opinion, it cannot by itself lead to real .... , but it means that people can .... shelter, warmth and food. Without these essentials, it is a challenge to find any .... in life.

6 It is *true* that recent graduates may bring fresh ideas to an *organization* that will improve its *performance*. Nevertheless, it is also .... that older employees have the kind of knowledge and experience that allows a .... to .... successfully in the long term.

7 If you *ask* the older generation if books will become obsolete, their *response* is a definite 'no'. But put the same .... to a group of younger people, and the .... is a unanimous 'yes'.

8 If a child is allowed to *choose* their own video games, they may be exposed to *extreme and disturbing images*. Careful .... by parents instead should mean that games brought into the house are less ....

16

VOCABULARY

Linking words and phrases for academic essays

1 Complete the essay by writing a linker from the box in each space.

~~consequently~~	yet	as for	so that	provided	such as
in the case of	despite	even though	however	in terms of	

Genetic engineering is a dangerous trend. It should be limited.
To what extent do you agree?

Over the last few decades, remarkable advances have been made in the field of genetic engineering. (1) Consequently... , scientists now have the ability to manipulate genes for a range of purposes, from making improvements in agriculture to experimentation with human genes. The question, (2) .... , is whether there should be any limitations on this development. Is this essay, I shall examine both sides of the argument.

Firstly it is clear that genetic engineering has brought about certain benefits (3) .... crop production. Now plants, for example, can produce more fruit more quickly. This achievement mean that greater harvests are guaranteed, (4) .... more people can be fed. (5) .... the impact of genetic engineering on healthcare, advocates claim it could be used to cure a range of health-related problems, (6) .... cystic fibrosis and Alzheimer's. Children and adults with these diseases endure terrible suffering,
(7) .... with gene therapy, there is a possibility of a better quality of life.

(8) .... these advantages, there are some aspects of genetic engineering which require ongoing consideration. Critics claim that genetically modified plants have little nutritional value and that they will lead to the eradication of weeds, which many insect species depend on. (9) .... gene therapy, it is still uncertain how the alteration of one gene, (10) .... it may be faulty, could affect the functions of the human body in the long term.

In my opinion, the benefits of genetic engineering can outweigh the drawbacks, (11) .... governments and scientists consider the consequences carefully, and put people before profit.

2 Structure: use the linkers to complete the sentences.

even	also	not only	but	in addition to

1 Poor nutrition can lead to obesity, heart disease, ... death.
2 .... obesity and heart disease, poor nutrition can lead to death.
3 .... can poor nutrition lead to obesity and heart disease, ... death too.
4 Poor nutrition can lead to obesity, heart disease and .... death.

3 Meaning: add linkers from the box to the correct category.

in spite of	in addition to	not only/but	concerning	even	while
moreover	finally	furthermore	on the other hand	having said that	
to begin with	nevertheless	regarding	secondly		

Ordering ideas	Introducing an idea	Addition	Contrast	Concession
first of all	in terms of as for in the case of	also	but however yet	despite even though

4 Complete each sentence using a linker from the box. Two answers are possible for each gap.

~~nevertheless~~	in spite of	having said this	despite	while	even though

1 As we have seen, there are many advantages of home schooling. Nevertheless /.................... , it does not work well for all kinds of learner.

2 ..../.................... the many advantages of home schooling, it does not work well for every kind of learner.

3 ..../.................... there are many advantages of home schooling, it does not work well for every kind of learner.

5 Complete the paragraph using a linker from the box. Two or more answers are possible for each gap.

~~first of all~~	as for	in the case of	furthermore
moreover	to begin with	regarding	in terms of

Raising taxes on imports may have both a positive and negative impact on the economy and employment. In this essay, I shall examine both types of effect. (1) ..First of all.... , (2) .... the economy, it may encourage people to buy domestically-produced goods. The profits would then remain within the country. (3) .... employment, greater demand for domestic products would create more job opportunities for the workforce. (4) .... , these new employees would then be able to afford to spend more on domestic consumer goods themselves.

6 Meaning: add linkers from the box to the correct category.

like	as long as	in order to	for instance	as a result
therefore	hence	so as to	subsequently	so if

Showing condition	Showing result	Showing purpose	Exemplification
provided	consequently	so that	for example such as

7 Structure: underline the correct linker in each sentence. Then answer the question.

1 a Many adolescents enjoy taking risks, *so/hence/therefore* the greater likelihood of accidents amongst teenagers.
  b Many adolescents enjoy taking risks. *So/Hence/Therefore* teenagers are more likely to have accidents.
  c Many adolescents enjoy taking risks *so/hence/therefore* teenagers are more likely to have accidents.

In which of the examples above can you use *consequently* or *as a result*, followed by a comma?

2 a There are many reasons why we need to be careful with Internet research. A frequent lack of accuracy, *such as/for example*, is a common problem with online texts.
  b There are many reasons why we need to be careful with Internet research, *such as/for example*, a frequent lack of accuracy in online texts.
  c There are many reasons why we need to be careful with Internet research. *Such as/For example*, there is often a lack of accuracy in online texts.

In which of the examples above can you use *for instance*?

3 a The influence of foreign television will not transform our culture *as long as/in order to* we take steps to protect our own traditions.
  b *So that/In order to* protect our culture, we must limit the influence of foreign television.
  c We must limit the influence of foreign television *so that/as long as* we can protect our culture.

In which of the examples can we use *so as to*? In which can you use *if*?

8 Complete each sentence 1–3 with a linking expression to explain its use. Then use the expression in the correct sentence 4–6.

on the other hand	on the contrary	whereas

1 '...................' is used to compare two situations, activities, groups, etc and to look at the differences.
2 '...................' is used to compare advantages and disadvantages, or to introduce the other side of the argument.
3 '...................' is used to say that the previous statement or claim is untrue.
4 It is a common belief that the world is unable to produce enough food to feed everyone. .... , much of the food we produce is actually wasted and thrown away.
5 It is certainly a good idea to grow biofuel plants on this land. .... , the land could also be used to grow crops to feed the poor.
6 .... the land used to be fertile and produce good harvests, it is now barren and dry.

9 Structure: underline the correct linking expression in *italics* indicating 'reason' in each sentence. More than one answer may be possible.

There are numerous reasons (1) *about/why/for* more people are suffering from allergies. First of all, we can lay the blame partly on pollution. Cases of asthma, for example, have risen dramatically (2) *because/because of/due to* poor air quality. The local environment may also be contaminated with pesticides, and (3) *for this reason/the cause of this/because of this*, certain people may be suffering from skin allergies or breathing difficulties.

Secondly, we can probably attribute the rise in allergies to particular products that are sold on supermarket shelves. Many people clean their kitchens with antiseptics (4) *since/as/because of* they believe they must kill all forms of germ. However, this action may actually increase the risk of allergy (5) *since/owing to/on account of* the fact that young children in these households are never exposed to the bacteria that will later provide them with immunity.

17

VOCABULARY

The Academic Word List: sublists 1 and 2

1 Sublist 1: complete each sentence by writing a noun from the box in each space.

sector	process	estimate	research	definition	income
response	legislation	policy	authority	benefit	theory

1 'In my experience, applying to university is actually an extremely complicated ....'
2 One .... that possibly explains the disappearance of dinosaurs is that a meteorite hit the earth millions of years ago.
3 After the interviews with staff were completed, the company realized it would have to change its .... regarding maternity leave.
4 'The export .... in my country is beginning to really grow, so the future is looking bright.'
5 'I would say that most jobseekers are looking for a significant increase in ....'
6 According to intensive .... involving thousands of future tertiary students, many expect to be in debt after they graduate.
7 'At the beginning of your presentation, make sure you provide a clear .... of what you mean by 'green policy'.
8 There was a very negative .... from customers when the company rebranded its existing products.
9 Scientists have given a rough .... of 50 years before the oil reserves run out.
10 One .... that tourism brought to my region was greater employment opportunities.
11 The government introduced new .... to help control the lending of money by banks.
12 'In my culture, the teacher is seen as someone with .... , and deserving respect.'

2 Sublist 1: complete each sentence by writing an adjective or verb from the box in each space.

available	similar	involved	specific	derived	established
major	economic	consistent	legal	required	significant

1 There are some general recommendations in your essay but you must be more ....
2 Two .... types of insects live in the same ecosystem, alike in appearance and feeding habits.
3 'Part of my research .... travelling to Latin America.'
4 In the early 19th century there were several .... earthquakes in the region.
5 The first British colonies in the US were .... in the 17th century.
6 The first step after a natural disaster is to ensure water is ....
7 Many medicines are .... from plants and trees.
8 The end of 2008 was a time of serious .... disaster, with many banks and companies going bankrupt.
9 Although the company claimed to be concerned about the environment, its actions were not .... with its words.
10 'If you want to gain promotion in my industry, you are .... to speak at least one other language well.'
11 Whether it is .... to download certain Internet content remains a grey area.
12 It was .... that the increase in disease amongst the local community began soon after the opening of the chemical factory.

3 Sublist 1: complete each sentence by writing a noun or verb from the box in each space.

individual	principle	labour	method	data	contract
export	source	assessment	create	assume	evidence

1 There is no .... of human habitation here before 750 BC.
2 This new .... of protecting paintings from bacteria is relatively cheap.
3 The grade students receive is based on continuous .... and the final test.
4 Bampton has recently won a .... to provide training for Human Resources staff.
5 I support the .... that health care should be free for all members of society.
6 It is wrong to .... that young criminals all come from bad backgrounds.
7 Once the .... was entered into the computer, a pattern began to emerge.
8 'The company I worked for used to .... cars to Australasia.'
9 It is debatable whether the rights of the .... outweigh the rights of the society he or she lives in.
10 Biofuels were already a .... of energy in the early 20th century.
11 Earthquakes which occur on the sea bed often .... tsunamis.
12 Cheap goods are only made available to consumers when .... is also cheap.

4 Sublist 1: complete each sentence by writing a noun or verb from the box in each space.

indicate	variables	environment	period	factors	procedures
concepts	occur	per cent	interpretation	structure	issues

1 Accidents in workplaces often occur as a result of staff not following proper ....
2 There has been increasing pressure on businesses to do more to protect the ....
3 At the end of the meeting there were still a number of unresolved ....
4 The assignment requires you to examine the history of the company and describe the .... that caused it to go bankrupt.
5 Early European explorers of Australia encountered a people for whom the .... of ownership and trade were completely unknown.
6 Unlike annual flu epidemics, pandemics rarely ....
7 Fewer than sixty .... of those questioned could identify the current Prime Minister.
8 Weather forecasting is not an exact science as so many .... are involved.
9 The seashells discovered in this area .... that it was once underwater.
10 The 19th century was a .... in which great technical advances were made.
11 'Your .... of the novel and its purpose is similar to mine.'
12 'I think you need to .... your essay in a more logical way.'

5 Sublist 1: complete each sentence by writing a word from the box in each space.

financial	identified	formula	section	constitutional	role
analysis	distribution	function	area	approach	context

1 For many decades, black American musicians have played an important .... in the development of the US music industry.
2 'I will start by explaining the .... in which these historical events occurred.'
3 It is clear that the .... of wealth in society is not equal.
4 One of the most important .... institutions is the New York Stock Exchange, also known as 'Wall Street.'
5 One .... to tackling the threat of global warming is to tax carbon-producing businesses.
6 The museum has a .... devoted to the study of prehistoric fossils.
7 In the USA, freedom of the press has long been a .... right.
8 The team needed to find a remote .... in which to test the rocket.
9 The key .... of the human liver is to cleanse the blood,
10 Further .... of the results is required before the findings can be made public.
11 The plant samples the researchers collected were later .... as types of moss.
12 Most parents know there is no perfect .... for creating the ideal child.

6 Sublist 2: complete each sentence by writing a word from the box in each space.

community	resident	construction	conclusion	text	computer
evaluation	assistance	distinction	chapter	survey	purchase

1 .... students account for around 25% of the student population.
2 In the last .... of the book, Lansbury speculates on the islanders' economic future.
3 Every online .... that a consumer makes is recorded and stored in the database.
4 The language in a literary .... is quite dissimilar to the style used in a scientific one.
5 The international office offers .... in setting up student exchanges.
6 After each presentation, you are expected to submit a written self- ....
7 Most people can make a .... between moral and immoral behaviour.
8 There is often little sense of .... amongst people living in urban areas.
9 Anthropologists have come to the .... that the statues at Easter Island represented the ancestors of the indigenous people.
10 A recent .... indicated that more people are suffering from stress.
11 The poor .... of the houses meant they were easily destroyed by the hurricane.
12 The .... has had a huge impact on the way we share information.

7 Sublist 2: complete each sentence by writing a noun from the box in each space.

range	strategies	elements	security	consequences	features
commission	regulations	items	injury	resources	categories

1 Becker recommends several .... that can be used to improve memory.
2 A criticism often directed at younger people is that they tend to take risks without thinking of the possible .... of their actions.
3 Collecting and cataloguing rock samples are two .... of a geologist's work.
4 Australia is a country rich in natural ....
5 Images showing previously unseen .... of the planet have been sent back.
6 According to Kagan, the lies people tell often fall into two different ....
7 There should be far stricter .... concerning embryonic research.
8 The university offered a broad .... of courses in computer technology.
9 The chance of severe .... resulting from car accidents has been reduced by new safety measures introduced by car companies.
10 Archaeologists found many personal .... that had been buried with their owner.
11 We are looking at ways of improving the .... of our website in order to protect it from hackers.
12 The government set up a .... to investigate ways to reduce health problems among the general public.

8 Sublist 2: complete each sentence by writing an adjective or verb from the box in each space.

previous	final	positive	normal	relevant	obtained
cultural	primary	complex	restricted	perceived	traditional

1 The problem is a .... one with no clear solutions.
2 Anthropologists concluded that the .... inhabitants of the island had been wiped out by disease.
3 Global warming is .... by many people as a serious threat to mankind.
4 Do not include anything in your essay which is not .... to the question.
5 The team are .... that a breakthrough will soon be achieved.
6 Oil is the .... reason for the country's wealth.
7 To protect the native flora and fauna, access to the reserve is ....
8 Modern medicine has learned a lot from .... medical practices from other countries, such as acupuncture.
9 Children with learning difficulties may exhibit behaviour which is not considered .... or acceptable to society.
10 After the DNA was analysed, the team finally .... the proof they needed.
11 From a .... perspective, eye contact may have many different interpretations.
12 There is one .... point I would like to make in favour of including art in the curriculum.

9 Sublist 2: complete each sentence by writing an adjective or verb from the box in each space.

investment	acquisition	focus	region	impact	equation
participation	potential	consumer	site	journal	institute

1 The process of language.................... is still not fully understood by scientists.
2 The .... of Darwin's discoveries on the scientific world was immense.
3 Any tertiary .... usually has a wide range of student services.
4 The question is whether advertising informs or manipulates the ....
5 The full .... of all students in seminar discussion is required.
6 Archaeologists discovered a large burial .... deep under the ground.
7 Einstein's most famous .... is probably $E=mc^2$.
8 There are fascinating accounts of the explorer's experiences in Africa based on a .... he kept throughout his travels.
9 In this part of the course, the .... is on the effects of the Industrial Revolution.
10 The competition is an opportunity for young athletes to demonstrate their ....
11 The two entrepreneurs are hoping to attract .... in their new invention.
12 This form of sculpture was common across the northern .... of Greece.

10 Sublist 2: complete each sentence by writing a noun or verb from the box in each space.

aspects	achieve	appropriate	transfer	select	credit
affect	seek	administration	maintenance	design	conduct

1 In terms of architectural .... , the building is second to none.
2 The first week of the term is usually spent dealing with .... , such as enrolments, timetables and payment of fees.
3 A course in time management teaches you the value of organizing your life in order to .... your goals.
4 One of the reasons the economy crashed was that banks were offering easy .... to their customers, and borrowing increased to dangerous levels.
5 A new version of the equipment was produced which was easier to use and required very little ....
6 It is a training course that provides students with a range of skills they can .... to a variety of jobs.
7 'There are certain .... of my job which I find quite challenging.'
8 Evans intends to .... a series of tests to prove the hypothesis correct.
9 The subjects were asked to .... the patterns they believed were symmetrical.
10 The researchers will begin to .... further clues next year.
11 How the pollution will .... the health of the local community is not yet known.
12 To request an extension to your essay deadline, please complete the .... form.

18

VOCABULARY

The Academic Word List: sublists 3 and 4

1 Sublist 3: complete each sentence by writing a noun from the box in each space.

reaction	technique	minority	core	criteria	contribution
validity	philosophy	compensation	sex	proportion	task

1 Every ethnic .... should be encouraged to vote in the election.
2 Several speakers at the conference questioned the .... of climate science.
3 The dogs in the experiment carried out the .... faster than expected.
4 The new .... allows scientists to confirm a person's identity faster.
5 The .... of hybrid cars on the road is still relatively low.
6 The patients' .... to the treatment was immediately positive.
7 To be described as 'sustainable', a product needs to meet certain ....
8 A lack of motivation lies at the .... of the pupils' problems.
9 The Persian astronomer Al-Birjandi made a significant .... to his field.
10 According to modern educational .... , a child should be allowed to develop at their own pace.
11 Current thinking suggests that a person's .... should not be relevant when applying for a job.
12 The idea that the blind have improved hearing as .... for impaired sight is a myth.

2 Sublist 3: complete each sentence by writing a verb from the box in each space.

consented	specified	shifted	illustrated	commented	removed
excluded	demonstrated	registered	published	ensured	implied

1 The earthquake .... 5.1 on the Richter scale.
2 'In his feedback, I think the tutor .... I wasn't speaking clearly enough.'
3 Over the voyage, van Duk .... his journal with drawings of sea birds.
4 Charles Darwin .... his theory of evolution in *On the Origin of Species*.
5 By concealing the brand of the soft drink, the researchers .... that the test group made an objective choice about their preferred flavour.
6 Sufferers of diseases such as leprosy were often .... from society.
7 After Jennings died, his family .... to his brain being used for research.
8 Although researchers .... the way the gate could be opened, the apes were unable to copy them.
9 The team .... all dirt from their equipment before drilling into the ice.
10 'The project criteria clearly .... that we needed to carry out a survey.'
11 The population has .... from the south to the capital city.
12 'I'll have .... on your assignment by Friday.'

3 Sublist 3: complete each sentence by writing a noun from the box in each space.

framework	justification	deduction	partnership	constraints	funds
convention	location	link	reliance	coordination	outcome

1 There is absolutely no .... for the ridiculous amount of money the government spent on this campaign.
2 The obvious .... of a bad education is a lack of employment opportunities.
3 George Sand was a 19th century French woman and novelist who rebelled against .... by dressing in men's clothes and smoking tobacco.
4 Politicians are discussing the .... for the reduction of greenhouse gases.
5 There will be fewer .... on your creativity in your final film project.
6 Students are expected to arrive at the right answer simply through a process of ....
7 .... for the project have already gone and more money will be required.
8 Our .... on the car as a means of transport has led to serious congestion.
9 The Chinese team are working in .... with the Russians.
10 The exact .... of the original building is unknown.
11 Researchers are trying to establish a .... between allergies and the length of time a child is breast-fed.
12 With age, some people lose their .... and can no longer move easily.

4 Sublist 3: complete each sentence by writing a noun from the box in each space.

scheme	emphasis	technology	circumstances	instance	sequence
interaction	volume	component	layer	immigration	document

1 Researchers are hoping to work out the .... of events that led to the collapse of the civilization.
2 The government's previous .... to reduce unemployment failed to work.
3 During the case study, there was one .... in which I had to conduct the interview by email.
4 Employees were asked to focus on improving their .... with customers.
5 Modern .... has allowed us to communicate at ever faster speed.
6 .... from Europe to the USA peaked in 1907 when 1,285,349 people applied to enter.
7 A faulty .... prevented the machine from working properly.
8 To improve the lives of these children, greater .... needs to be placed on providing them with long term education.
9 'What were the .... that led to the company's collapse?'
10 The .... of fat around the animal's body protects it from the cold.
11 Listening to music at this .... can lead to long-term damage of the ear drum.
12 Archaeologists believe that the .... may describe a battle.

5 Sublist 3: complete each sentence by writing an adjective from the box in each space.

considerable	sufficient	dominant	alternative	constant	technical
physical	corporate	maximum	corresponding	initial	negative

1 'There were no jobs in my field so I needed a new and .... career.'
2 The response was fairly .... when they asked for volunteers.
3 The .... male will challenge outsiders if they enter his territory.
4 Sufferers of arthritis may be in severe and .... pain with this disability.
5 There was no .... evidence of the species on the island, but only eye-witness reports.
6 The team then experienced an unexpected .... problem with their software.
7 'My .... impression of London was that it was very crowded but then I got used to it.'
8 Between January to March, use of mobile phones was 15% higher than in the .... period in the previous year.
9 Currently, the .... penalty for this kind of offence is two years in prison.
10 A .... number of subjects reported feelings of nausea after the experiment.
11 Mules were needed to ensure .... food and water was taken along for the expedition.
12 A .... decision was taken to relocate the headquarters to Delhi.

6 Sublist 4: complete each sentence by writing an adjective from the box in each space.

apparent	annual	prior	principal	civil	ethnic
domestic	obvious	subsequent	adequate	internal	approximate

1 'My .... reason for taking an IELTS course is to enter university here, although I'm also taking it to improve my general writing ability.'
2 'The company are looking for an .... candidate, and will not be recruiting from outside the firm.'
3 It is believed that the .... age of the ship is 500 years old.
4 In a multicultural society, it is vital that the various .... groups socialize.
5 There is low .... rainfall in this dry region.
6 After a while, it became .... to researchers that their strategy had failed.
7 Without .... oxygen, it would not be possible to reach the summit.
8 The tsunami hit the port and the .... clean-up operation took months.
9 .... dogs and cats are not the norm in Saudi Arabia, although they may be used on farms.
10 .... to the earthquake, there had been little sign of it coming.
11 In a democracy, it is your .... right to be able to express your views freely.
12 Karol's experience in Antarctica made him the .... choice for team leader.

7 Sublist 4: complete each sentence by writing a verb from the box in each space.

contrasted	emerged	granted	predicted	undertook	implemented
retained	imposed	labelled	promoted	attributed	accessed

1 'I'd like to begin with one of the key findings that .... from the research.'
2 Japan's economic success is frequently .... to a strong national work ethic.
3 Despite the impact of foreign television programmes, the country has .... its cultural identity.
4 In order to tackle the problem, the government .... tough new laws.
5 Children who are .... 'slow learners' may lose all motivation to succeed.
6 At that time, no-one .... how the use of pesticides would destroy local ecosystems.
7 In the late 19th century, a group of explorers .... a risky expedition to travel across the desert.
8 Schools have recently .... healthier ways of eating to the children.
9 Anderson finally .... the information he needed in the British Library.
10 The team were .... permission by the authorities to examine the mummy.
11 My expectations of life in this region .... sharply with the reality.
12 The university .... the new enrolment policy at the beginning of term.

8 Sublist 4: complete each sentence by writing a noun from the box in each space.

investigation	goal	integration	mechanism	summary	commitment
hypothesis	option	regime	conference	stress	parallel

1 Diabetics may be able to control their disease through a strict dietary ....
2 The Japanese have traditionally eaten a great deal of fish, so the recent .... of meat into their diet may have an impact on health.
3 Far more research is required to understand the memory .... and how the different parts of the brain are involved.
4 There is a clear .... between the behaviour of the ants and certain aspects of human society.
5 'At this stage, the idea is only a .... , and we need to find proof.'
6 The .... was attended by physicists from all over the world.
7 The .... into the source of the pollution took months to complete.
8 Placed under enormous .... , many people fail to make logical decisions.
9 'If you want to make sure you have a place on the next course, your best .... is to enrol now.'
10 The government needs to make a .... to improving healthcare facilities.
11 'The .... in your assignment is too brief and needs extending.'
12 'I'd say that my .... in life is to achieve a comfortable standard of living.'

9 Sublist 4: complete each sentence by writing a noun from the box in each space.

series	output	parameters	sum	code	phase
concentration	status	job	project	professional	occupation

1 The .... to build an irrigation system will begin next year.
2 'My current .... is "student" but I hope to be employed soon.'
3 A considerable .... of money has been spent on renovating the library.
4 'Entering all of our information into the database is not a .... I wanted.'
5 Parents may have their own views on child-rearing, but they must still act within the .... of the law.
6 A high level of additives in food has been linked to a loss of .... in children.
7 In recent years, there has been a .... of riots in which people have protested over rising food costs.
8 'We ought to hire a .... to fix all the software problems.'
9 The ancient Greeks used a secret .... to send messages between armies.
10 Her .... as a writer has been huge; over 35 books in 22 years.
11 We will shortly be entering the final .... of the project, so the new library should be completed by October.
12 In my culture, if a man becomes unemployed, it leads to a loss of social ....

10 Sublist 4: complete each sentence by writing a word from the box in each space.

despite	implications	cycle	attitudes	error	overall
hence	dimension	communication	resolution	debate	statistics

1 'Parts of my thesis could have been improved, but .... , I was pleased with it.'
2 .... towards work and career have changed over the last ten years.
3 Recent .... indicate that heart disease is on the rise again.
4 It is almost impossible to break the .... of poverty that affects many families in this country.
5 A lack of .... between partners is one of the fundamental reasons for an unhappy relationship.
6 Sunderland admitted to making a basic .... in one of his early calculations.
7 Mining in this kind of terrain is dangerous, ... the need for better equipment and safety measures.
8 The entry of this pest into the country could have serious .... for agriculture.
9 The causes of climate change are still a matter of great ....
10 Smokers continue their habit, ... knowing it can lead to premature death.
11 'We've discussed the situation, but there's an additional .... we haven't yet mentioned.'
12 Unfortunately, the two sides have not yet found a .... to their problem.

1

Words and phrases

1 Family and relationships

Complete the monologue by writing a word from the box in each space.

~~extended~~ remarried nuclear stepsister divorce blended only child

'In the past, people used to live together as an (1) extended family, grandparents, parents and all the children, but nowadays, (2) .... families are more the norm, just parents and their offspring. My family is a little different. My parents decided to (3) .... and my mother (4) .... Her new husband also has a daughter from a previous marriage, so we've become a (5) .... family. Having a (6) .... is great as before I was an (7) ....

first-born groom kinship arranged marriage ceremony siblings

'(8) .... is the custom in my country. It just means that your family does a lot of research to match you up with a partner from a respectable family. Our wedding (9) .... is very different to the Western one as male and female guests are separated. The (10) .... goes to the women's room to take his bride home. Anyway, my wife and I are expecting our (11) .... , and hopefully, he or she will have lots of (12) .... The idea of (13) .... is very important in our society. When I needed help finding a job, for example, I turned to my uncle and he found me a position in his company.'

adoption single parent upbringing child rearing

'My father died when I was very young, so my mother was solely responsible for our (14) .... Some people suggested she put us up for (15) .... , but my mother refused. She was quite strict and I think my own ideas about (16) .... are quite different, but I admire the way she coped as a (17) ....'

emotional fulfilment in-laws institution relatives

'In my country, marriage is still regarded as an important (18) .... And when you get married, in fact you are gaining not only a husband or wife, but a large set of (10) .... and distant (20) .... Having said that, marriages are no longer arranged for economic gain but more for (21) .... That's quite a big shift in social attitude.'

2 Ways of dealing with people

Underline the two words in *italics* which are similar in meaning.

1 Researchers are still *debating/arguing/interacting* over the origin of the ancient text.
2 Erikson *advised/contacted/approached* others in his field to seek their opinions.
3 The team *recommend/propose/demand* that the government invest in adult education.
4 The participants were *questioned/interviewed/surveyed* about the effects of advertising on their consumer habits.
5 Researchers from the two universities are *teaming up /mediating/collaborating* on the project.
6 Professor Ha will be *coordinating/assisting/organizing* the other team members.
7 The boys observed in the case study were unable to *interact with/relate to/network with* members of their family.
8 You will need to *liaise/debate/cooperate* more with the other students in your presentation group.
9 The company decided that they had to appoint someone to *contest/mediate/arbitrate* between management and the workforce.
10 Several scientists have *contested/interrogated/questioned* Wang's claims.

3 *Come*

Complete each sentence with a word or phrase from the box.

~~fire~~	conclusion	up	across	long way	surprise	down
against	together	contact	decision	criticism	down	

1 Several companies have *come under* ......fire....... for their misleading advertising.
2 I've finally *come to a* .... about the subject for my thesis.
3 At the end of your essay, *come to a* .... about the causes of the problem.
4 The result *came as a* .... to the research team.
5 Matthews *came into* .... *with* other geologists also gathering data.
6 Medicine has *come a* .... since the twentieth century.
7 I think I *came* .... *as* a little nervous when I gave my presentation.
8 There are many aspects of the fuel crisis to consider, but what it all *comes* .... *to* is the fact that the supply of oil will finally run out.
9 Davis has sometimes *come in for* .... regarding the way he collects evidence.
10 The team from China and France have *come* .... on this project.
11 Without formal qualifications, people in my country will *come up* .... serious obstacles when they try to find a job.
12 Many elderly people *come* .... *with* flu at this time of year.
13 The small team of scientists believe they have *come* .... *with* a solution.

4 Prefixes *anti-, post-, pre-, pro-*

Complete each sentence using one of the prefixes above.

1 Psychologists point to the increasingly ..anti-.. social behaviour of young men.
2 In the ....war years, many economies took time to gradually recover.
3 ....-smoking campaigners say that it is their right to smoke.
4 The tutorial will be held on Tuesday instead as I have a ....-arranged meeting with other staff.
5 For people who are ....-nuclear energy, the advantages outweigh the risks.
6 In the novel, it is the ....-hero that the author clearly favours.
7 The continents as we know them today separated during ....history.
8 The ....-communism era saw great fluctuations in the economy.
9 The editorial section of the paper tends to be ....-government and rarely contains any criticism.
10 ....-heated food tends to have little nutritional value.
11 The areas we have to research were ....defined by the course tutor.

5 *In*

Complete each sentence with a word from the box.

~~case~~	contrast	response	practice	advance	conclusion
view	retrospect	accordance	order	addition	comparison

1 Please finish your presentation by 2.30 in ...case......... anyone wants to ask questions.
2 After further research Adams now says 'In .... , I think we were wrong to recommend this diet.'
3 In .... to its negative effects on the ecosystem, pollution can also damage the health of children and adults.
4 In .... to anyone who supports higher taxes, I would argue that not everyone is able to afford them.
5 In .... with 2008, 2009 saw a slight improvement in sales.
6 In .... of the need to reduce crime, I feel that tougher penalties are required.
7 The fabric is then taken to the dyeing room in .... to change its colour.
8 In .... with the terms of their contract, staff were allowed to work flexitime.
9 In .... to the consumer spending patterns of men, those of women were far more consistent.
10 In theory, it is advisable to exercise regularly, but in .... , people cannot often find the time.
11 The fees for the term need to be paid four weeks in ....
12 In .... , it can be seen that the benefits outweigh the drawbacks.

2

Words and phrases

1 City life

Complete each sentence with a form of the word in CAPITALS.

1 Its diverse nationalities make London a ...cultural... city. CULTURE
2 The old parts of the city were .... last year. MODERN
3 On the outskirts of the city are the .... areas. INDUSTRY
4 .... areas in my country often suffer high unemployment. SUBURB
5 An .... rail network allows commuters to get around easily. EXTEND
6 My city is a major .... centre and most banks are located there. FINANCE
7 There's an .... range of amenities, for example, the new mall. IMPRESS
8 All the main tourist attractions are quite .... within the city. CENTRE
9 Some people worry that the city has become .... POPULATION

2 Words meaning 'part'

Complete each collocation with a word from the box.

~~stage~~	quota	constituent	feature	period	fraction
fragment	phase	component	branch	layer	

1 ...stage... in a child's development/in rock formation/in a process
2 .... of rock/of clothing/of meaning
3 bone/manuscript/pottery ....
4 .... of history/of economic recovery/of drought
5 .... of the exhibition/of the landscape/of the new mobile phone
6 .... of the moon/of adolescent behaviour/of the project
7 machine/course/microchip ....
8 .... of the original value/of the cost/of a second
9 .... of science/of a company/of a tree
10 fish/sales/daily ....
11 .... of oil/of blood/of medicine

3 Suffixes *-ance, -ence, -ment, -ness*

Complete each sentence with the word in CAPITALS, using one of the suffixes above. Make any other spelling or form changes that are needed.

1 In summary, it is vital we preserve the ...uniqueness... of every culture. UNIQUE
2 It is essential that the .... fits the crime. PUNISH
3 The .... of education cannot be underestimated. IMPORTANT
4 Our .... on fossil fuels cannot be sustained. RELY
5 .... can affect the elderly if they are apart from their family. LONELY

6 We must improve public .... of this issue. AWARE
7 There have been significant .... in the field of medicine. IMPROVE
8 Genuine .... is a rare and infrequent state of mind. HAPPY
9 All babies possess the potential to develop their .... INTELLIGENT
10 The .... of some languages is sad, but inevitable. DISAPPEAR

4 *Under*

Complete each sentence with a word from the box. In some cases *under* is part of the word.

~~control~~	eighteen	review	staffed	law	developed
estimate	lying	nourished	privileged		

1 The company claim that they now have the problem *under* ....control.... .
2 The children in the survey were frequently ....under.................... and tired.
3 Visitors *under* .... are admitted free of charge.
4 In several ....under.................... countries, the new medicine is proving effective.
5 *Under* Australian .... , no food may be brought into the country.
6 The test is now *under* .... after several international students complained it gave Canadian students an advantage.
7 The government ought to provide more housing for the ....under.................... .
8 In my opinion, we should not ....under.................... the seriousness of this issue.
9 The office is currently ....under.................... and is looking for a new receptionist.
10 Scientists believe they have found the ....under.................... cause of the problem.

5 *Give*

Complete each sentence with a word or phrase from the box.

~~rise~~	in	credit	away	try
birth	off	grounds	encouragement	way

1 The use of detergents in the home may have *given* ....rise.... *to* the increase in allergies.
2 An effective teacher should always *give* .... *to* their students.
3 I'm not really into adventure sport but I might *give* sky-diving *a* ....
4 Tiny movements in the facial muscles often *give* .... a person who is lying.
5 The plant *gives* .... a strong smell which attracts a wide range of insects.
6 When do we have to *give* .... our assignments?
7 Researchers believe this dinosaur *gave* .... *to* live young, not eggs.
8 This medical breakthrough *gives* .... *for* optimism in the search for a cure.
9 In my department, we were *given* little .... *for* all the work we did.
10 It is likely that CDs will shortly *give* .... *to* downloaded music.

3

Words and phrases

1 Groups

Underline the options which make sense. More than one answer may be possible.

1 There is a *variety/sub-species/rank* of fern on the island which grows nowhere else.
2 The department was split into three *subdivisions/classes/sectors.*
3 People whose income does not allow them to meet the cost of living fall into the *classification/category/personnel* of 'working poor'.
4 Within their social hierarchy, the older female wolves have a high *rank/status/class.*
5 The team chose a *breed/race/class* of dog that was easy to train.
6 Members of the *tribe/clan/clique* would have used a range of weapons for hunting.
7 All the *personnel/workforce/hierarchy* in the company were surveyed.
8 Mammals are a *class/species/variety* of animal with backbones and which usually give birth to live young.
9 Genetic engineers are working on a new *breed/strain/variant* of rice.
10 The first people to arrive on the island established a small *colony/herd/settlement.*
11 More must be done to integrate new immigrants into the local *community/society/neighbourhood.*

2 *Take*

Complete each sentence with a word from the box.

~~measures~~	account	risk	place	give	course
lead	power	dive	responsibility	hours	

1 It is often believed that the government should *take* tougher ...measures... to prevent the spread of serious crime.
2 I *took a* .... in International Relations as I hope to become a diplomat.
3 It *took* .... before I could find the information I needed in the library.
4 The current government *took* .... in 2006 after a general election.
5 Reynolds knew he was *taking a* .... by travelling to the region alone.
6 We have created a society where fewer people seem willing to *take* .... for their own actions.
7 The expedition will *take* .... between April and July next year.
8 Large corporations must *take the* .... in fighting global warming.
9 When choosing a course, *take into* .... how likely it is to lead to a career.
10 The number of tourists booking 'green holidays' *took a* .... in 2009.
11 Scientists are interested in how the concept of .... *and take* has developed in human communities, and its impact on their survival.

3 Time and duration

Complete the second sentence in each pair with an adjective from the box so that it means the same as the first sentence.

~~provisional~~	chronological	simultaneous	prolonged	futuristic
historical	current	contemporary	previous	temporary

1 Ali's offer of a place at Massey University depends on him achieving IELTS band 6.5.
Ali has a .provisional... offer of a place at Massey University.

2 The opinion that scientists have at the moment may soon change.
.... opinion amongst scientists may soon change.

3 News reports happened at the same time across the world.
There were .... news reports across the world.

4 The presentation I did before didn't contain enough visual material.
My .... presentation didn't contain enough visual material.

5 This period of Korean art occurred over the same period as the European Renaissance.
This period of Korean art was .... with the European Renaissance.

6 In the past, Simón Bolívar played an important role in developing South America.
Simón Bolívar is a key .... figure in the development of South America.

7 The novel is about a time in the future when computers dominate the world.
The novel offers a .... view of the world where computers dominate.

8 Just for a short while, the exhibition is showing in the Terrace Room.
The .... exhibition is showing in the location of the Terrace Room.

9 People whose exposure to smoke continues over a long time may be harmed.
The effects of .... exposure to second-hand smoke may be harmful.

10 Archaeologists are hoping to work out in which order the events happened.
Archaeologists are hoping to work out the .... order of events.

4 At work

Match a verb (1–10) with the rest of the sentence (a–k).

1	I work .g.	a	the senior manager with setting up events.
2	I handle	b	after patients, mostly the elderly.
3	I'm responsible	c	with the other team members once a week.
4	I assist	d	up meetings for everyone involved in the project.
5	I meet	e	out my boss's schedule for the week.
6	I'm in charge	f	customer enquiries, mainly from overseas callers.
7	I look	g	on educational projects and training materials.
8	I sort	h	of a group of five other people.
9	I send	i	for training new staff.
10	I set	k	out letters or emails to our clients.

5 Prefixes *bi-, co-, mono-, semi-*

Match each prefix in the box to its meaning and the example below.

~~co~~	semi	mono	bi

= half	= one	= two/twice	= together
..........-circular	..........poly	..........annual	...co....education

Now complete each sentence using one of the prefixes.

1 The two countries finally signed a ...bi...*lateral* agreement.
2 In Parts two and four of Listening Test, you will listen to a ....*logue*.
3 There is a shortage of .... -*skilled* workers in this industry.
4 Ensure that you ....*operate* with the other members of your team on this project.
5 Many young adults leaving home are only ....-*independent*.
6 Christianity, Islam and Judaism are the main ....*theistic* religions.
7 Jackson discussed the overtime problem with his ....*workers*.
8 Having a Spanish father and German mother, I grew up ....*lingual*.

6 Words with a similar meaning

Underline the correct words in each pair of sentences.

1 The lecture today will *range/cover* the main advantages of hydroponic farming.
The period of history covered in the course *ranges/covers* from the Middle Ages to the present day.
2 The disease quickly *spread/stretched* across Asia and into Europe.
The main line of the Trans-Siberian railway *stretches/spreads* over 9,000 kilometres from St Petersburg to Vladivostok.
3 Although the two archaeologists disagree about the function of the ancient site, their opinions *unite/converge* about the way it should be protected.
Researchers are *united/converged* in their belief that the drug may have long term side effects.
4 The university has recently *diversified/widened* the choice of courses on offer.
The company originally sold medicinal drugs and then *diversified/widened*.
5 In the middle of the summer, local temperatures can *rise/raise* to 40°C.
The campaign aims to *rise/raise* awareness of the dangers of speeding.
6 The number of business students has *enlarged/multiplied* over the last few years.
We hope to *enlarge/multiply* the conservation area by up to another 200 square kilometres.

4

Words and phrases

1 Traditional events

Underline the correct word in each sentence.

1 The Hindu wedding *celebration/ritual* I like best is when the priest ties the end of the bride and groom's clothing together.
2 A typical wedding *ceremony/custom* in my country is quite long and complicated.
3 Most of the *festivals/occasions* in my country involving singing, dancing and eating.
4 On the *birthday/anniversary* of our country's unification, people take the day off.
5 Most religions have a period of *fasting/dieting* when food restrictions apply.
6 On this day we *celebrate/commemorate* the lives of the soldiers who died in the war.
7 For Muslims, it's their duty to go on a *pilgrimage/worship* to Mecca at least once.
8 The wedding ring *symbolizes/reflects* the eternal union between husband and wife.
9 It's the *habit/custom* in my culture to give money to the poor during this time.
10 I think Christmas is a special *occasion/occurence* for children, but perhaps not for their busy parents.

2 *On*

Complete each sentence with a word from the box.

~~behalf~~	reflection	contrary	loan	agenda
hand	basis	average	verge	point

1 I'm learning English so I can do business *on* ...behalf... of my father with American clients.
2 The first item *on the* .... for discussion is the proposal for the new library.
3 The team were *on the* .... *of* giving up when they made an amazing discovery.
4 The number of smokers has not decreased. *On the* .... , the figure actually rose last year.
5 Dividing school children into classes according to their ability may help them to work at their own pace. *On the other* .... , it may also lead to a lack of motivation amongst students in the lower class.
6 *On* .... , we can see from the graph that men spent more on luxury goods than women.
7 People who exercise *on a regular* .... tend to suffer less from heart disease.
8 When I gave my presentation, I thought it was all right, but *on* .... , I think I should have provided more specific examples.
9 It is a species of lizard which is sadly *on the* .... *of* extinction.
10 The paintings in the exhibition are currently *on* .... from The Louvre.

3 Prefixes *cent-, pan-, multi-, tri-*

Match each prefix in the box to its meaning and the example below.

~~tri~~	pan	centi	multi

= three	= many	= hundred	= all
...tri...angle	..........national	.... metre	..........theism

Now complete each sentence using one of the prefixes.

1 The economic downturn was a ..pan..-European issue.
2 Do you know how to convert Fahrenheit into ....grade?
3 The final book was certainly the best of the ....logy
4 My city has become increasingly ....cultural.
5 The ability to ....task is a requirement of the job.
6 The carnivorous plants feed mainly on beetles and ....pedes.
7 The last ....mester of the academic year seems the hardest.
8 The ....demic was responsible for a dramatic fall in the population.

4 *Put*

Complete each sentence with an expression from the box. More than one answer may be possible.

~~at risk~~	forward	another way	through	at a disadvantage	down to
under pressure	across	an end to	off	in control of	

1 We are *putting* our own health ..at risk..... by allowing toxic waste to reach the ocean.
2 'I was *put* .... the project when the team leader resigned.'
3 Pupils are *put* .... enormous .... by their parents to perform well in tests.
4 'If you don't speak English in my field, it *puts you* .... when you're applying for work.'
5 We need to *put* .... to slavery which still exists in parts of the world.
6 'It is time we recognized the contribution of women to science. To *put it* .... , more attention must be given to women who have made scientific discoveries.'
7 'I thought you *put* .... your ideas quite clearly in the presentation.'
8 Researchers initially *put* the collapse of the civilization .... war, but now they believe the reason was disease.
9 One solution to crime that is often *put* .... is longer prison sentences.
10 'I was planning to take my IELTS test in May but then I *put it* .... till June.'
11 The people taking part in the experiment were *put* .... a series of medical tests.

5

Words and phrases

1 Character traits and emotion

Complete each sentence with a form of the word in CAPITALS.

1 I like to take .... in my work. PROUD
2 Most subjects showed an .... response to the video clip. EMOTION
3 Extreme .... can quickly lead to an increase in blood pressure. ANGRY
4 Advertisers deliberately try to make consumers feel .... of others. ENVY
5 Most people suffer from a degree of .... before an interview. ANXIOUS
6 Young employees often lack .... in such situations. ASSERT
7 Does natural .... exist more strongly in some people? INTELLIGENT
8 One in four of the interviewees had a sense of .... about the planet's future. PESSIMISTIC
9 People with a more .... nature are less likely to question the decisions of their managers. CONFORM
10 My decision to come to Australia was rather .... IMPULSE

2 Student text types

Match each instruction from a tutor (1–8) to the way a student reports it later (a–h).

Tutor:

1 'You'll need to keep a log during the field trip.' ..h.......
2 'Write a critique on the character development in Salinger's Catcher in the Rye.' ....
3 'Write a summary of the ideas behind free trade policy.' ....
4 'We would like you to keep a weekly journal.' ....
5 'We would like to ask you to present a paper at the conference.' ....
6 'You'll need to narrow down the scope of your dissertation.' ....
7 'Ensure that you include a full bibliography with your essay.' ....
8 'You will need to contribute a posting to a discussion forum each week.' ....

Student:

a 'I have to write briefly about the main ideas and not the details.'
b 'I have to write down my thoughts and personal experience on a regular basis.'
c 'I have to read and examine it carefully and give my opinion.'
d 'I have to look at other students' ideas and comments on-line and respond to them.'
e 'I have to add all the names of authors, book titles, publishers and page numbers at the end of my work.'
f 'I have to write about my research and give a talk on it.'
g 'For my final long research essay, I have to reduce the range of what I intended to cover.'
h 'I have to record the details of each day's events and any important information.'

3 Prefix *in-*

Complete each sentence with a form of a word from the box, using the prefix *in-*. More than one answer may be possible.

~~accurate~~	conceive	signify	appropriacy	defend
access	convenience	advice	numeracy	

1 As an accountant, inaccuracy is something I really have to avoid.
2 Medical treatment is often .... to the poor in society.
3 There was a small and .... rise in student numbers in 2009.
4 More must be done to educate the illiterate and ....
5 The fact that children are dying from starvation is ....
6 For many people, public transport is rather ....
7 Adults affected by extreme autism may demonstrate behaviour that others find ....
8 It's .... to include too many graphs in your presentation.
9 I find it .... that the elderly can be so badly neglected.

4 *Make*

Complete each sentence with a word from the box.

~~time~~	use	suggestion	adjustment	mistakes	progress
gestures	perfect	difference	decision	living	

1 Our hectic modern lifestyle does not always allow us to *make* .... *for* the important things in life, such as friends and family.
2 Many people are struggling to *make a* .... and cannot even afford basic health care.
3 After food which contained these chemicals was removed from the children's diet, it *made all the* .... *to* their behaviour.
4 To reach professional level in sport, it is true that *practice makes* ....
5 'I feel that we're *making slow* .... with this project.'
6 'Did you find it easy to *make the* .... to study in New Zealand?'
7 'I'd like to *make a* .... Perhaps we could start the presentation with some visual material?'
8 'Please *make* .... *of* the Internet for your research but make sure you include the website address in your bibliography.'
9 Kirk discovered that he had *made* a couple of .... when entering the data.
10 Researchers observed that the chimpanzees were *making* similar .... when asking for food.
11 Immigrants often have to *make* a quick .... *to* the culture and lifestyle of the new country.

6

Words and phrases

1 Transport and transportation

Replace each definition with a group of people from the box.

~~cyclists~~	passengers	commuters	urban planners	pedestrians

1 Every year a growing number of *people who ride bicycles* are injured when motorists knock them off their bikes ...cyclists... .
2 Thousands of *people who travel to work* find the traffic stressful. ....
3 More inner city areas should be allocated to *people who walk* only. ....
4 *People who design our cities* should make the roads safer for cyclists. ....
5 *People paying to use the bus* in Switzerland know they can rely on an efficient service. ....

Complete each sentence with a term from the box.

electronic fuel injection	a hybrid	an electric vehicle	a catalytic converter

6 .... relies on a battery and outlets where it can obtain electricity.
7 .... relies on a smaller battery and a conventional car engine.
8 .... removes pollutants from exhaust gases before they leave the car.
9 .... reduces the volume of pollutants by making combustion more efficient.

Match 10–17 with a–h to make suitable compound nouns.

10	traffic ..e.......	a	recall
11	rush	b	network
12	fuel	c	efficiency
13	driver	d	limit
14	product	e	congestion
15	emissions	f	alertness
16	bus	g	hour
17	speed	h	laws

Complete each sentence with one of the compounds from 10–17 above. Some of the compounds will not be used.

18 Our tough .emissions laws.. have reduced the number of old cars on the road.
19 Accidents caused by faulty wiring led to an immediate ....
20 The question is whether the legal driving age should be increased or the .... reduced instead?
21 .... will only be reduced if fewer private cars are on the road.
22 Manufacturers claim the car is second to none in terms of its ....
23 New technology will prevent collisions often caused by failures in ....

2 Priority and order

Underline the correct option. Sometimes both are correct.

1 Amelia Earhart was a *pioneering/ground-breaking* female aviator and the first woman to fly solo across the Atlantic Ocean.
2 When offered a choice between a job that was creatively satisfying but low-paid and a job that was mundane but paid well, most people chose the *latter/second.*
3 Students were chosen *at random/out of order* to take part in the experiment.
4 The government must give *priority/precedence* to improving the conditions of the underclass.
5 Our old buildings with traditional architecture should be preserved for *posterity/ afterwards.*
6 In this case, the benefits clearly *outweigh/overtake* the drawbacks.
7 As a *former/prior* criminal himself, David was able to understand some of the attitudes held by the young offenders.
8 *Preliminary/Early* findings suggest that the vaccine has been effective.
9 Sijbren observed that the birds came back to the island for four *consecutive/ successive* years, and then failed to return.
10 The neoclassical style of art dominated European art for almost a half-century and is one of the *precursors/predecessors* of modern painting.
11 It was a style of music that was considered *ahead of its time/avant garde.*

3 Confusing words

Underline the correct words in each pair of sentences.

1 The chemical had no *affect/effect* on the majority of the test group.
Few people cannot be *affected/effected* by the sight of a hungry child.
2 Would you mind if I *lent/borrowed* your notes from the lecture?
I hope the bank will *lend/borrow* me enough money for my tuition fees next term.
3 We *require/request* you to show your passport before you take the exam.
I *requested/required* an extension for my essay from my tutor.
4 We must take measures to *reduce/decline* the amount of waste we produce.
The amount of waste has been *reducing/declining* over the last few years.
5 So far, I have *avoided/prevented* taking a test in English.
My job *prevented/avoided* me from coming to England to study before now.
6 In my country, I *live/stay* in Riyadh with my parents and sisters.
I'll be *living/staying* in a hotel in Riyadh when I visit Saudi Arabia.
7 We have to *find out/find* an alternative source of energy instead of fossil fuel.
I expect to *find out/find* the results of my test on Friday.
8 It is the duty of parents to *educate/bring up* their children with a sense of social duty.
More people need to be *educated/brought up* about good eating habits.

4 Prefix *un-*

Complete each sentence with a form of the word in CAPITALS, using the prefix *un-*. Make any other spelling or form changes that are needed.

1 In many respects, the future of civilization is unpredictable . PREDICT
2 People may .... consume GM food as it not clearly labelled. KNOW
3 It may be the case that true equality in society is .... ATTAIN
4 Allowing urban development to spread onto land set aside for conservation purposes is .... JUST
5 Last year, the number of .... fell by 3%. EMPLOY
6 It would be .... to expect a reduction in government spending. REAL
7 Another factor is that some practitioners of alternative medicine are .... QUALIFICATION
8 It is impossible to remain .... by the sight of so much poverty. AFFECT
9 It is .... that television has a huge influence over young minds. DENY
10 There is still some .... as to whether the project will go ahead. CERTAIN

5 *Meet*

Complete each sentence with a word from the box.

~~criteria~~	deadline	demand	halfway
opposition	standards	needs	obstacles

1 'Make sure your essay *meets* all *the* criteria .'
2 Self-confidence allows a person to overcome any .... he or she may *meet*.
3 'I decided to study academic English because it *meets my* .... more.'
4 'I'm worried that I won't *meet* next week's .... *for* the assignment.'
5 Whenever the government proposes to raise the legal driving age, this proposal is often *met with* strong .... from rural populations.'
6 Legislation was passed to ensure all imports *met the* minimum safety ....
7 Production was increased to *meet the* .... *for* the new vaccine.
8 After long negotiations, the two countries agreed to *meet* .... *on* the new trade agreement.

6 Suffixes *-able, -ial, -ive*

Complete each sentence with the word in CAPITALS, using one of the suffixes above. Make any other spelling or form changes that are needed.

1 I think my city is relatively.. safe compared to others. RELATE
2 That's quite a .... issue, I think. CONTROVERSY
3 Personally, it would be .... to live abroad for ever. IMAGINE
4 I don't have to work .... hard, so I don't mind my job. EXCESS
5 I think .... journalism has a duty to show you the truth. INVESTIGATE
6 My goal is to run a .... successful company, one day. COMMERCE
7 It's .... whether 'fame' means the same thing as 'success'. DEBATE
8 I used to have a .... position in my last job. MANAGER

7

Words and phrases

1 Rubbish and waste

Complete each sentence with a word from the box.

~~tax~~	biodegradable	packaging	toxic	accumulate
disposable	landfill	recycling	leftover	

1 The government is proposing to ....tax......... households per bag of rubbish produced.
2 Statistics suggest that .... accounts for over 50% of household waste.
3 Most tins, cans, and bottles can be collected for ....
4 It is greener to use metal cutlery rather than .... plastic items.
5 Plastic bags are not .... yet we dispose of millions every day.
6 Most kinds of .... food can be thrown onto the garden compost heap.
7 The amount of rubbish that one household can .... weekly is astonishing.
8 The number of .... sites is growing across the country as our rubbish increases.
9 Most domestic waste gives off .... emissions when burnt.

2 Industry

Complete each definition with the correct kind of industry from the box.

~~pharmaceutical~~	textile	consumer electronics	retail	
energy	aviation	construction	food processing	dairy

1 The ..pharmaceutical. industry develops and sells drugs for medical purposes.
2 The .... industry produces and sells petroleum, natural gas and electricity.
3 The .... industry processes and sells animal milk and derived products.
4 The .... industry designs, develops and operates aircraft.
5 The .... industry produces and distributes different fabric such as cotton and also designs and sells clothing.
6 The .... industry designs, manufactures and sells products such as personal computers.
7 The .... industry is involved in the planning and building of new structures, e.g. apartments and car parks, as well as infrastructure, e.g. roads.
8 The .... industry transforms raw ingredients or animals killed for their meat into the kind of product that appears on supermarket shelves.
9 The .... industry buys large quantities of goods from manufacturers, mostly via a wholesaler, and sells them to customers, or 'end-users'.

3 Suffixes *-ify, -ize*

Complete each sentence with the word in CAPITALS, using one of the suffixes above. Make any other spelling or form changes that are needed.

1 The rock that forms the Earth's surface can be classified into three types. CLASS
2 Regional population growth .... by the mid 1900s. STABLE
3 The molten iron slowly cools and .... SOLID
4 It is hard to .... a world in which we no longer depend on cars. VISION
5 Before answering this question, it is necessary to .... what is meant by the term 'community'. CLEAR
6 Researchers are .... their efforts to find a cure for the disease. INTENSE
7 During the next stage, the .... glass is poured into funnels. LIQUID
8 In ancient civilizations, the moon frequently .... a god. SYMBOL
9 The team are hoping that the government will .... further funding of their work. AUTHORITY
10 We can .... three key factors behind this situations. IDENTITY

4 *Carry* or *hold*

Complete each sentence with the correct form of *carry* or *hold*.

1 The disease can be passed to children by mothers who carry the gene.
2 Travelling by plane .... less risk than a journey by car.
3 'Our lecturer is good at .... everyone's attention.'
4 'We'll be .... a meeting to discuss the problem.'
5 In my country, murder .... a sentence of life imprisonment.
6 'I hope to .... on the work that my father started.'
7 The researchers believe that this algae may .... the key to the biofuel issue.
8 More research needs to be .... out before a decision can be made.
9 'Who knows what the future may .... ?'

5 Word formation

Complete each sentence with the word in CAPITALS. Make any other spelling or form changes that are needed.

1 Theoretically speaking, there is no reason why solar power can't be used. THEORY
2 Most people's .... of political issues is fairly limited. KNOW
3 Further research should provide us with .... proof. STATISTICS
4 For some .... reason, Adams decided to abandon the project. EXPLAIN
5 Unfortunately, the results from the first test were .... CONCLUDE
6 A .... study must take place before the site can be developed. FEASIBLE
7 Personally, I would not object to eating .... modified food. GENE
8 Asking someone their age is not.................... offensive in my country. CULTURE
9 It is a human .... to fear the unknown. TEND
10 The planet's .... conditions would not support life. ATMOSPHERE

8

Words and phrases

1 Crime

Underline the correct word in *italics*.

1 Those people who are guilty of *minor/inferior* crimes should be fined, not imprisoned.
2 If one person kills another by accident, it is *manslaughter/assassination*, not murder.
3 Once a person has been to prison, he will have a criminal *document/record* for life.
4 Violent crimes such as *assault/shoplifting* are on the rise.
5 The current government has been criticized for showing a soft and *tough/lenient* attitude towards criminals.
6 Young people who are sent to prison can easily be influenced by *hardened/strengthened* criminals.
7 The issue of *capital/corporal* punishment is a controversial one, although the majority of people are opposed to the death penalty.
8 Young people often *perform/commit* acts of vandalism when they lack purpose in life.

2 Confirming and denying

Underline the correct meaning in the second sentence for the words and phrases in *italics* in the first sentence.

1 The results from the test *confirmed* Lee's *suspicions.*
What Lee first believed was *correct/incorrect*.
2 Lee said that further research was needed to *corroborate* the *results.*
Lee said thought further research was needed to *support/disprove* the results.
3 Lee *refutes* this commonly held view.
Lee says the view most people have is *wrong/right*.
4 Lee then attempted to *verify the claim* in a series of tests.
Lee tried to show the claim was *true/untrue*.
5 Lee *upheld his position* during the debate.
Lee *admitted he had been wrong/continued to say he was right*.
6 Lee believed he had new evidence that could *undermine the existing theory.*
Lee believed the evidence would *support the theory/make the theory weaker*.
7 Lee *countered* McHugh's *argument* at a recent conference.
Lee *gave his support to/opposed* what Fennemore was saying.
8 Lee *rebutted the allegations* that Fennemore made against his work.
Fennemore criticized aspects of Lee's work and Lee *proved/argued* that Fennemore was wrong.

3 Verbs and nouns with the same form

Complete each pair of sentences with a word from the box.

~~document~~	conflict	input	project	aid
extract	subject	labour	guarantee	

1 As part of our research, we intend to document changes in local temperature.
As a historical document the Treaty is carefully preserved in the museum.
2 Engineers are working on new ways to .... gold from the mountain.
Can I include a short .... from a published report in my essay?
3 The bird may .... on the building of its nest for several days.
There is a shortage of .... in the agricultural sector.
4 The team that will .... Professor Kossoff come from various backgrounds.
It is often perceived that foreign .... does not reach the people it is intended for.
5 Even if divers reach the sunken ship, there is no .... they can retrieve it.
The company claim they can .... the reliability of the product.
6 There is ongoing .... between those who are opposed to GM foods and those who are avid supporters.
The results from the second experiment appeared to .... with the first.
7 It may take some time to .... the data into the programme.
.... from the Japanese engineers will be of great help to us.
8 The team .... that the glacier will be gone by 2030.
The .... looked at the development of speech in twins.
9 Every .... in Young's experiment reported their insomnia had improved.
Many social networking sites .... their users to unwanted advertising.

4 Suffix *-en*

Complete each sentence with a verb formed from an adjective from the box, using the suffix *-en*.

~~strong~~	loose	straight	tight	short
moist	soft	hard	broad	wide

1 The dam is weak and will need to be .... before long.
2 If the person is unconscious, first .... any clothing around their neck.
3 The track was narrow and had to be .... to allow the equipment through.
4 Water is added to .... the firm clay so it can be used more easily.
5 We hope to .... our understanding of the way the solar system was created.
6 Restrictions on human cloning need .... before we go too far.
7 Our prime minister has recently .... his attitude towards immigration, allowing more immigrants to apply for residency last year.
8 Until now, doctors have attempted to .... curved spines using bone grafts.
9 Obesity-related illness can .... a person's life expectancy by over 15%.
10 As people grow older and less tolerant, they tend to .... their attitudes towards others who are less fortunate.

5 *Life/living*

Complete each sentence with an expression from the box.

~~cost of living~~	in living memory	work–life balance
make a living	in later life	standard of living
working life	living language	claims many lives
way of life		

1. Every year, the cost of living.. goes up and not everyone can afford their basic needs.
2. The .... has improved considerably since our grandparents' day, and most people in my country are reasonably comfortable in their homes.
3. Under pressure to spend longer hours at the office, many people fail to maintain a good ....
4. For local people, it was the worst flood ....
5. Emigrating to a new country means adapting to a new culture and ....
6. While poor diet may not have immediate consequences, it may affect people ....
7. Children in certain countries .... by working long hours in factories.
8. Unfortunately, malaria still .... in countries where there are few medical facilities.
9. The campaign to promote spoken Maori in schools and on the television in New Zealand has meant it has become a .... once again.
10. A person's .... should ideally be mentally rewarding, although many employees are focused solely on their salary.

6 Modifying

Underline the correct option. Sometimes both are correct.

1. On some *degrees/levels*, the book can be regarded as a masterpiece.
2. I agree to some *extent/degree* that investment in public transport could improve our urban environment.
3. It was, *by and large/on the whole*, a period in which peace and prosperity reigned.
4. I doubt that Warburg's form of therapy could work. *Knowingly/Admittedly*, I have heard many reports of the therapy being successful.
5. We've all been given an extension for the essay deadline, *apparently/obviously*.
6. Scientists have, in the *main/majority*, been sceptical about robots becoming self-aware.
7. *Generally/Mostly* speaking, students in my country are under considerable pressure to perform well in their high school.
8. In some *aspects/respects*, these early navigators were far more skilled than later sailors attempting the same journey.
9. It is by no *way/means* certain that the tomb contains the body of a Pharaoh.
10. The conservation team believes the species is now extinct, or so it would *appear/seem*.

9

Words and phrases

1 Language and communication

Underline the correct word in each sentence.

1 Humans have the *cognitive/comprehensive* ability to produce and recognize grammar.
2 I was working a part-time *interpreter/translator* of Spanish to English documents.
3 The use of *gesture/indication* is a significant means of communication.
4 Children *attain/acquire* their first language through constant exposure.
5 Ensure that all contracts are in writing as *spoken/verbal* contracts are hard to prove.
6 The common consensus is that the *characters/hieroglyphics* used for writing in China evolved from earlier Neolithic symbols.
7 Sceptics say that chimpanzees can only *repeat/mimic* humans and not genuinely communicate with them.
8 Many *indigenous/domestic* languages are sadly under threat of extinction.
9 Not everyone seems to have the capacity to learn a foreign *tongue/voice.*
10 Early Semitic languages relied on an *oral/aural* tradition rather than a written form.
11 Although Tokyo is the capital of Japan, it has moved away slightly from standard Japanese forms and has developed its own regional *dialect/accent.*
12 Carter had heard *gossip/rumours* of mammoth bones being dug up in the nearby tundra.
13 There was plenty of *anecdotal/mythical* evidence but no concrete proof of the tomb's existence.

2 Importance

Decide if the pairs of words in italics are synonyms (S) or antonyms (A) in the sentences below.

1 It is *vital/crucial* that we take steps to reduce carbon emissions. S/A
2 Education is *fundamental/irrelevant* to a long-term successful career. S/A
3 The *basic/simple* reason for landslides in this region is deforestation. S/A
4 One of the *key/minor* challenges that students face is the amount they have to read in their own time. S/A
5 'You've made a couple of *trivial/significant* errors in your introduction.' S/A
6 Wang has played a *major/substantial* role in the creation of this new technology. S/A
7 The differences between the two sets of results were *negligible/slight.* S/A
8 I think we've spent a(n) *essential/needless* amount of time adding graphs to our powerpoint presentation. S/A
9 'This part of the essay is rather *redundant/unnecessary*, I'm afraid.' S/A

3 Relationships and connection

Replace the words in italics in each sentence with a more academic phrase from the box.

~~was instrumental in~~	was a correlation between	
was the epitome of	was irrelevant to	was consistent with
was symptomatic of	was endemic to	was indigenous to

1 The figure I've chosen is King Abdul Aziz, who *played an important role in* founding modern Saudi Arabia. was instrumental in
2 In my opinion, the rise in crime at that time *provided us with proof of* a society which ignored its social problems. ....
3 Personally speaking, I feel that any language which *originally came from* a country must be preserved. ....
4 If you look at the slide, you'll see that the result of the second experiment *was very similar to* the result of the first. ....
5 The common cold was an illness that *was very common in* Europe before it was transmitted across the world. ....
6 I would say that my grandfather *was the best example of* the hard-working entrepreneur. ....
7 Actually, I thought there *were some similarities between* the Korean attitude to work and the American one. ....
8 I'm afraid this section of your essay *had no connection to* your thesis statement. ....

4 Suffixes *-hood, -ship*

Complete the sentences using one of the suffixes above and a word from the box. Make any other spelling or form changes that are needed.

~~craftsman~~	champion	adult	intern	
child	likely	scholar	life	neighbour

1 Craftsmanship... used to be valued, but now many goods are mass produced.
2 On reaching .... a person must be responsible for their own actions.
3 In small villages, there is more of a sense of community in the ....
4 I hope to receive a .... that will allow me to go to university.
5 Last year I did a brief .... in a company in the USA, which gave me valuable work experience.
6 There seems to be little .... of peace being achieved in our lifetime.
7 Competitive sport encourages young people to reach .... level, which provides them with a sense of purpose.
8 If the factory is moved overseas, this action will threaten the .... of hundreds of local people.
9 I spent my .... in Hong Kong, as my father was working there at the time.

10

Words and phrases

1 Forms of authority and government

Complete each definition with the correct authority word from the box.

~~council~~	executive	democracy	supervisor	regime	anarchist
principal	patriarchy	bureaucracy	minister	watchdog	

1. A ..council... is a group of elected politicians who are in charge of a local area.
2. An .... is a person who believes we should not have a government or laws.
3. A .... is a person in charge of a group of people at work or an activity.
4. A .... describes a system of government in which the public votes for the people they want to govern them.
5. A .... is a person in charge of a government department.
6. A .... is an organization working to prevent illegal or unethical activity in particular areas of society or business, e.g. advertising.
7. A .... describes a government that strictly and unfairly controls a country.
8. A .... refers to a society in which men have all or most of the power and women have none or very little.
9. A .... refers to a complex and annoying system of rules and processes which slow down the action a person wishes to take.
10. A .... is in charge of the academic management of a school or university.
11. An .... is a senior manager in a company.

2 Processes

Match the descriptions of a process (1–12) with the correct terminology (a–l).

1 keeping eggs warm until they hatch ...f......	a transpiration
2 making a liquid less strong by adding another liquid, e.g water	b pollination
3 liquid becoming gas or steam	c desalination
4 gas becoming a liquid	d conversion
5 removing salt from sea water	e disintegration
6 changing from one system, method, form or use to another	f incubation
7 sending power, energy or signals from one place to another	g crystallization
8 taking in a substance, form of energy, or liquid	h dilution
9 placing pollen from one flower on another	i transmission
10 being completely destroyed by breaking into tiny pieces	j evaporation
11 water passing from the surface of a plant into the air	k condensation
12 changing into may tiny solid substances with many sides e.g. ice, salt	l absorption

3 Suffixes *-sion, -tion, -ity*

Complete each sentence with the word in CAPITALS, using one of the suffixes above. Make any other spelling or form changes that are needed.

1	We can see a period of economic ..stability.. during this decade.	STABLE
2	The .... of knowledge should be a lifetime goal.	ACQUIRE
3	The continual .... of low-paid workers must stop.	EXPLOIT
4	The annual .... of the whales begins in late November.	MIGRATE
5	As an artist, he began to express his .... at an early age.	INDIVIDUAL
6	There can be little .... for ignoring the destruction of our natural environment.	JUSTIFY
7	The .... of the city began in the mid 17th century.	EXPAND
8	Reports about corruption now appear with increasing	REGULAR
9	We expect your full .... in weekly seminars.	PARTICIPATE
10	It is human nature to make .... about cultures we are unfamiliar with.	ASSUME
11	As a synthetic material, plastic has incredible	DURABLE
12	Most people have no .... of the full problem.	COMPREHEND
13	There seems to be little .... to his argument.	VALID

4 Adverbs of degree

Complete each sentence with an adverb from the box. More than one answer may be possible.

~~merely~~	reasonably	widely	barely	marginally	increasingly
radically	fully	inextricably	principally	certainly	predominantly

1 Is consumerism ..merely..... a matter of choice, or is it more to do with external influences?
2 After the accident, Sarah could .... remember any personal history at all.
3 I'm taking IELTS .... to get into university in Canada.
4 Zahl was .... certain he had found the source of the pollution.
5 The language .... spoken in this region is Karelian.
6 In its time, the printing press .... changed the way information was spread.
7 Martens believes his counterpart's theory is .... plausible.
8 The ability amongst the children in the survey varied ....
9 Every year, it is becoming .... difficult to prevent the erosion.
10 His desire to work in the laboratory was .... linked with the need to find a cure for the disease.
11 Adolescents are not .... aware of the consequences of their actions.
12 In 2009, the amount of coal extracted from the mine had risen .... from 2008.

Answers

Where answers are marked *suggested answers*, other answers may be possible. Where students provide their own answers, verbs are given in full or contracted form following their use in the question.

Grammar 1

1 1 *d* 2 b 3 j 4 a 5 e 6 c 7 h 8 i 9 g 10 f

2
1 *become*
2 are beginning
3 are removing
4 want
5 believe
6 encourages
7 are losing
8 explains
9 disappears
10 also shows
11 generally ignore
12 makes
13 are taking part
14 no longer contains
15 is going down

3
1 *are you waiting*
2 Does the price of the room include
3 comes
4 Does this laptop belong
5 is getting/'s getting etc
6 are getting on
7 think
8 is taking/'s taking
9 am having/'m having
10 refers

4
1 *are choosing*
2 have
3 is increasing
4 depend
5 is becoming
6 saves, are working
7 sometimes find, suits
8 does it have
9 am working/'m working
10 feel, are all heading

5
1 *involve*
2 consists of five parts
3 do not belong to
4 tend to be taller than their Asian counterparts
5 do you weigh
6 ticket price includes the cost of the meal
7 Professor Sanchez comes from
8 does this word mean
9 two samples appear to be the same
10 resulted from a chemical reaction in a laboratory

Grammar 2

1
1 *was piloting*, took off
2 was still climbing, noticed, was coming
3 collided, lost
4 took over, tried
5 got, was rapidly losing, became
6 made, decided
7 watched, managed
8 followed, left, was travelling
9 quickly rescued, was slowly filling
10 survived, received

2
1 *were you doing*
2 started
3 was getting/growing/becoming
4 did you do after
5 we were waiting we had
6 she died the newspapers described her as
7 caused the crash
8 were you living

3
1 *heard*, looked, was happening
2 waited, decided, was taking
3 was driving, lost, collided
4 wasn't carrying, was saying
5 found, was starting, was falling, was wearing
6 caused, came, was getting

4
1 *feared*
2 believed
3 circulated
4 did not realize
5 was entering
6 was spreading
7 possessed
8 was now rising
9 were doing
10 flowed
11 ended up
12 occurred
13 died
14 was improving
15 were working on
16 completed

5
1 *opened*
2 entered
3 included
4 was attending
5 was travelling
6 stopped
7 decided
8 intended
9 was getting down
10 came
11 was holding
12 knocked
13 carried
14 died
15 occurred
16 was walking

6
1 *the arrival of the Prime Minister*
2 decision to become a pilot
3 invention of the gramophone
4 discovery of America
5 flight
6 death
7 construction of the dam
8 investigation of the robbery

Grammar 3

1
1 *makes*
2 does
3 hold back/keep
4 sets
5 do not require
6 keeps/holds back
7 receives
8 goes out
9 purchases
10 ends up

2 suggested answers
1 *do the text and table present*
2 does the text define
3 happened
4 Did this figure rise or fall

5 occurred
6 Did this trend continue
7 do/did the 2007 arrival figures include?
8 did the emigration figures peak?
9 Did this figure
10 caused

3 1 information about UK population figures between 1998 and 2007
2 someone who changes their country of usual residence for at least a year
3 there was a steady rise in immigration
4 it fell
5 a steep rise
6 no, it did not
7 96,000
8 2006
9 no, it fell the following year
10 a fall in British citizens emigrating to Spain and France

4 1 *becomes visible*
2 separates into different colours
3 causes the light to bend
4 depends on the wavelength of the beam
5 become visible
6 acts as a tiny prism
7 leaves the raindrop
8 sees the range of colours

Grammar 4

1 1 *have recently discovered*
2 has been circling, have detected
3 found
4 quickly melted, was
5 found, it has detected
6 was
7 also believed
8 was, has come from
9 has been monitoring, It has also been studying
10 has shown, cost

2 1 *has announced*
2 have spent
3 told
4 feel
5 held
6 is now considering
7 made
8 has been preparing
9 have already drawn up/ are already drawing up
10 started
11 has also begun
12 have already worked/are already working

3 1 *has provided/has been providing financial services*
2 Fiona Allan has written five
3 Scientists have not discovered life on other planets
4 The construction team has now completed the Olympic Stadium.
5 The company has been producing green vehicles
6 Professor Thompson has been living/has lived in Vancouver
7 Ann Smith has held the post of chief executive
8 of young people entering higher education has been rising/has risen recently.
9 The satellite has been circling the Moon
10 The research team has concluded that

4 1 *consider*
2 have been living/have lived
3 has only recently begun
4 has always been
5 there are
6 have been looking/have looked
7 seem
8 recover
9 have ever owned
10 has changed
11 have met
12 have never felt
13 never thought
14 have also been investigating/have also investigated
15 believe

5 1 *The project hasn't finished yet.*
2 This is the first time there has been such a serious financial crisis.
3 Nobody/No one has proved that the dinosaurs died in this way.
4 The situation has changed since 2008.
5 It is still raining.
6 I've never been/I haven't been to Bulgaria before.
7 Have you met Professor Johnson (before)?

6 1 *designed*
2 bears
3 has been rising/has risen/ is rising
4 have been experimenting
5 has soared/has been soaring
6 was
7 suffered
8 has been
9 begins
10 contains
11 has been using/has used
12 have found
13 works
14 have also been combining
15 has used/has been using
16 seems

Grammar 5

1 1 *destroyed*
2 first noticed
3 were rising
4 had never expected
5 it had been burning
6 were blowing
7 had destroyed
8 had not killed
9 never established
10 put

2 1 *were examining,* noticed, had previously overlooked
2 stared, was still falling, was growing/had grown, had packed, did not think
3 returned, saw, had progressed, had not expected
4 developed, were searching
5 drowned, was trying, had fallen, had removed, had repeatedly stolen

3 suggested answers.
1 *had died*
2 remarried
3 entered
4 had taken
5 had become
6 had listened
7 (had) sent
8 observed
9 had been making
10 looked
11 saw
12 had changed
13 had disappeared
14 came
15 had discovered
16 found

4 1 *used to believe, now think*
2 used to think, now know
3 used to claim, now have to
4 used to ride, are now driving/now drive
5 used to be, now divides
6 used to write, are now using/now use
7 used to sit, now eat
8 used to receive, now take out

5 1 *had started by the time we got into the ground*
2 knew that they had lost the battle
3 arrived at the office I realized (that) I had left my keys at home
4 had eaten/had a Japanese meal before, so I knew what to expect
5 phoned her office Jane had already left
6 hadn't been to/visited Romania before
7 couldn't understand what his letter meant
8 forced to eat their pack animals since they had eaten all their food
9 the injured man had fallen from the window
10 the interview was over they had already decided to give him the job

Grammar 6

1 1 *has risen*
2 fell
3 stayed
4 has been
5 has fallen
6 caused
7 did not receive
8 had probably had
9 had already built up
10 started
11 received
12 had largely eliminated
13 had not acquired
14 had also begun
15 stood

2 1 *has grown steadily*
2 have increased
3 have connected
4 has almost reached
5 has shown
6 has also had an effect
7 has expanded fourfold
8 has completely changed
9 have been complaining
10 had never been online
11 has indicated
12 have remained popular
13 have now discovered
14 have continued
15 have limited

Grammar 7

1 1 *I'll let you know*
2 will be lying
3 will fall/are going to fall
4 will be/is going to be
5 are we going to do
6 won't be leaving/aren't leaving
7 we'll finish/we're going to finish
8 We're all going to miss/We'll all miss
9 will probably have risen
10 I'm going to work/I'll be working

2 1 *will be working*, will be putting
2 will soon be entering, will have made
3 will be replacing, will have returned, will be supplying
4 will also be talking, will be visiting, will have come, will have started

3 1 *process/have processed*, will let
2 leave, will give
3 will begin, have tested
4 takes off/has taken off, switches off/has switched off
5 is, will contact
6 have, will send
7 will meet, finishes/has finished
8 come, will be
9 will be, begins
10 will send, arrive/have arrived

4 1 *artificial organs will be commonplace by the end of the century*
2 car use will have doubled within twenty years
3 most people will be home workers/will work at home in twenty years' time
4 what will happen in the future
5 of future technology will be lower
6 that they will have completed the tunnel by the end of the year
7 90% of us/people will be using mobile phones by the end of the decade
8 it will rain tomorrow
9 people will be eating in the future
10 will have colonized other planets by the end of the century

5 1 *will be introducing*
2 will cause
3 starts
4 will no longer be
5 will have closed
6 passes
7 will record
8 will be able
9 will result
10 is going to make
11 will confuse
12 will prove
13 will pass
14 will end up
15 won't really be
16 will receive
17 will get
18 won't come back

Grammar 8

1 1 *200 years ago*
2 towards
3 on time
4 yet
5 until
6 one day
7 since
8 by
9 Throughout
10 last

2 1 *Up to*
2 later
3 in/during
4 at
5 formerly
6 until
7 In
8 after
9 On
10 before
11 later
12 in
13 finally
14 in
15 for
16 By
17 after
18 Since

3 1 *C* 2 A 3 C 4 D 5 D 6 B 7 B 8 A 9 A 10 D 11 B 12 C 13 B 14 B 15 C 16 A

4 1 *in* 2 ago 3 later 4 longer 5 in 6 later 7 until 8 after 9 for 10 already 11 At 12 Since

5 1 *around*
2 ago
3 at
4 later
5 in/during
6 After
7 until
8 In/During
9 In/During
10 still
11 in
12 at
13 since
14 in/during
15 later
16 in
17 Nowadays

Grammar 9

1 1 *will probably rise*
2 will have increased
3 will be
4 will be living
5 will have sprung up
6 will be struggling
7 will not have been able
8 will be finding
9 will simply not have
10 will be facing
11 will have to address
12 will have improved
13 will have provided
14 will have

2 1 *Nowadays*
2 Over/During/For
3 present
4 Since
5 by
6 Over/Throughout/During
7 ago
8 Since
9 still
10 By

3 1 *the population aged 65 and over*
2 has increased from around 7.5 million
3 the population aged 16 and under
4 between 1971 and the present
5 rose by about 30%
6 fell by about 20%
7 will stand at about the same figure
8 will have risen to around 13 million

Grammar 10

1 1 *B* 4 B 7 A
2 C 5 C 8 C
3 A 6 B

2 1 *When did you decide to be a lawyer?*
2 How long did you have to study?
3 How do you remember all the facts?
4 What interests you most about the law?
5 What kind of law do you specialize in?
6 What kind of law firm do you work for?
7 Do you earn a high salary?
8 Have you ever appeared in a murder trial?
9 What do you like most about your job?
10 What will you be doing in ten years' time?

3 1 *was William Shakespeare when he died*
2 have teams of scientists been working on genome projects
3 developed the first long-lasting practical electric light-bulb
4 did the first astronauts on the Moon bring back
5 was (the French biochemist) Jacques Monod born
6 do birds sing
7 is Maria Montessori best known for
8 will the entire project cost
9 will the next conference take place/be taking place
10 do scientists believe exists at the centre of our galaxy

4 1 *this is the right answer?*
2 what time the train leaves?
3 where the entrance is.
4 how this machine works.
5 who he was.
6 when the final examination takes place?
7 it is going to rain.
8 how thunder and lightning occur?
9 why you told me to wait here.
10 what the meaning of this word is?/what this word means?

5 suggested answers

1 *a* *some birds fly thousands of miles*
2 i some birds stay in the same place
3 e advantages does migration bring?
4 h migration routes become established.
5 b birds manage to migrate over long distances.
6 j strategies birds use on long trips.
7 c birds find their way.
8 g young birds are able to follow migration routes
9 f do these young birds know where to go?
10 d route they should follow.

Grammar 11

1 1 *has been suspended*
2 makes
3 have been completed
4 is determined
5 has been chosen
6 was developed
7 has been recorded
8 published
9 are generally considered
10 is being investigated

2 1 *are being imported from Poland*
2 was invented about a thousand years ago in China
3 of fuel oil is being increased from tomorrow
4 must be completed by 31st March
5 are used to search for extra-terrestrial life
6 while it was being transported from Paris to Rome
7 have been suspended for the next three matches
8 will be published at the end of the month
9 with planets in orbit around them have been discovered
10 is being closed until further notice

3 1 *are known*
2 is used
3 is questioned/is being questioned
4 checks
5 may indicate
6 are administered
7 was depicted/is depicted
8 has been replaced
9 sit
10 are connected
11 is supposed
12 can be detected
13 is sometimes called
14 are limited
15 are frequently employed
16 can be forced

4 1 *Glucose is used by the cells to provide energy.*
2 All the athletes taking part were provided with laptops and video cameras.
3 Everyone is advised to eat 400 grammes of fruit and vegetables per day.
4 It is not known how the fire began.
5 According to reports, the storm has hit coastal areas the hardest.

6 Around $400 million was spent worldwide on advertising last year.
7 If they asked me to rejoin the project, I would refuse./I would refuse to rejoin the project if they asked me.
8 A broken arm has forced Smith to abandon the Tour de France.

5 1 *realize*
2 are being forced
3 has been set up
4 is becoming/has become
5 has doubled
6 are persuaded/have been persuaded
7 is wasted
8 are left on
9 are provided
10 can be cut
11 have been replaced/are being replaced
12 has been fitted/is being fitted
13 has been reduced/is being reduced
14 are collecting
15 have been installed
16 is served
17 applies
18 are given/are being given
19 are not lectured/are not being lectured
20 is encouraged/is being encouraged

Grammar 12

1 suggested answers
1 *What information does the graph show?*
2 During this period did UK visits abroad rise or fall?
3 Was the fall in 2009 as steep as the fall in 2008?
4 Do the figures for overseas visits to the UK show the same trend?
5 Do the figures show any seasonal variations?
6 What was the approximate difference in millions between February 2008 and February 2010?
7 Did the figures for overseas visits to the UK show the same general trend?
8 What was the approximate fall in numbers between February 2008 and February 2010?
9 What probably explains these trends?
10 What are future trends likely to be?

2 suggested answers
1 *then cleaned and dried until the seeds are ready for use.*
2 the seeds are soaked in wine and vinegar to soften them, and to make the husks easier to remove.
3 the seeds are crushed and ground into flour.
4 the flour is passed through sieves to remove the husks.
5 white wine, or vinegar and water, are added and the mixture is blended until a paste is formed.
6 the paste is blended with seasonings and flavourings.
7 the mixture is heated and left to simmer slowly before being allowed to cool.
8 measured amounts of mustard are poured into jars or bottles, the lids are sealed and the jars are packed into boxes.

3 suggested answers
1 *have been constructed*
2 have been repaired/renovated
3 have been supplied/provided
4 have been furnished/supplied
5 have been helped
6 have been renovated/repaired
7 have been fitted out
8 have been provided
9 will be given
10 are being subsidized
11 were wholly funded
12 were trained/were being trained
13 has been distributed
14 has been achieved
15 have been changed

Grammar 13

1 1 *don't act, will be*
2 improves, will go ahead
3 would increase, were available
4 would be, spent
5 had, I'd help
6 are not given, will die
7 had, would they be
8 is postponed, will take
9 don't finish, I'll come
10 were investing, would

2 1 *are*
2 pays, will add/will be added
3 exceed, will not accept
4 lose, will still be
5 do not have, will continue
6 stop, will be
7 is
8 die, will pay

3 1 *The plants won't grow unless you water them.*
2 The machine won't start unless you plug it in.
3 Unless staff are given a pay rise, the union will call a strike.
4 Unless the government acts, there will be a water shortage.
5 The programme is likely to go ahead unless there is a last-minute hitch.
6 Unless there is an examination at the end of the course, some students will not study seriously.
7 People tend not to succeed unless they enjoy what they are doing.
8 Students cannot use the library unless they have a valid library card.
9 Unless measures are taken, the situation will get worse.
10 Unless the patient's condition deteriorates, she should make a full recovery.

4 suggested answers
1 *If I had my driving licence with me I would be able to hire a car.*
2 If there were/was no water on Earth, life would be impossible.
3 If everyone spoke the same language, people would get on well together.
4 If we had a computer it would be easier to do the calculations.
5 If food were/was distributed fairly, everyone would have enough to eat.
6 If people knew the risks involved in smoking, they would probably give (it) up.
7 If aliens landed on Earth, we might not notice them/they might not be noticed.
8 If the library opened on Sunday we could/would be able to go there to study.
9 If more people used public transport, there

would be less pollution from cars/it would cut the amount of pollution from cars.
10 If people ate less and took more exercise they wouldn't be overweight.

5 1 *If*
2 will
3 will
4 are
5 If
6 is
7 will
8 are/were
9 may/might
10 do
11 doesn't
12 is
13 can/should/will
14 are
15 be
16 do/can
17 will
18 is
19 will
20 Unless
21 will
22 unless

Grammar 14

1 1 *hadn't closed*, would have become
2 doesn't make, will continue
3 would have finished, hadn't been
4 would certainly have carried on, had been
5 hadn't collapsed, would have been
6 flooded, would have to
7 would suffer, made
8 had followed, would have noticed, could have been

2 1 *would have happened*
2 had successfully invaded
3 (had) conquered
4 had beaten
5 would have found
6 would have presented
7 might have emerged
8 would not have enjoyed
9 would have proved
10 had not existed
11 would/could not have proceeded
12 would have ended
13 had not entered
14 would have happened
15 had not taken place
16 had been
17 would have remained
18 would not have been

3 1 *If the company had made a profit it might not have reduced its workforce.*
2 If rescue teams had arrived in time, they might have rescued more people/more people might have been rescued.
3 If the government had (been) prepared for the heatwave there might not have been a shortage of water.
4 If the people in the town had been more friendly, we might have stayed there longer.
5 If we hadn't had problems with our computer network, we might have finished the project on time.
6 If the banks had properly understood what they were investing in, they might have avoided the financial crisis.
7 If the two sides had been willing to negotiate, the dispute might not have dragged on for months.
8 If the maintenance staff had carried out routine checks, a breakdown might not have occurred.
9 If the patient had been given the correct dosage of medication, she might have survived.
10 If an engineer had not spotted the cracks in the wing, the plane might have crashed.

4 suggested answers
1 *hadn't lent the company some money, would not be*
2 the bank loan, would have been/gone
3 the economic climate does not worsen, will probably make
4 had not been for the (rise in the) price of oil, would not have risen
5 been for severe weather in the North Sea, would not have been cut
6 would not have been so/as serious, had not been a helicopter crash
7 the weather hadn't been, the helicopter crash would not have
8 had negotiated, would not have been
9 had agreed, would not have decided/would not have taken the decision
10 the management behaves, won't be any calls for strike action

5 suggested answers
1 *Even if we caught an earlier train we still wouldn't arrive before 6.00.*
2 If you were to reconsider our offer, I think you might change your mind.
3 If it hadn't been for the security officer, the robbery would have succeeded.
4 (You should) Use the security code otherwise the computer won't work.
5 If Janet Ward had taken the job, she would be/would have been head of the company.
6 Researchers may access this material on condition that they do not use it for commercial purposes.
7 If it were not for government grants, many students would be unable/would not be able to study.

6 1 *would*
2 was/were not
3 were
4 would
5 would
6 not
7 provided
8 condition
9 unless
10 may/will
11 have
12 if

Grammar 15

1 suggested answers
1 *If you always turn off appliances on standby, you'll save 25% of the energy they use.*
2 If you replace old appliances with new energy-efficient ones, you'll save up to 50% of the energy they use.
3 If you install a home energy monitor, it'll show you exactly how much energy you are using.
4 If you use cold water in your washing machine, you'll save 90% of the energy used to heat water.

5 If you fit double-glazed windows, you'll feel warmer and save money.
6 If you insulate your roof, you'll stop 30% of the heat in your house from escaping.
7 If you bring your heating system up to date, you'll lower your bills by as much as 15%.
8 If you turn down the thermostat of your heating system, you'll save up to 20% of your heating bill.
9 If you swap your old conventional light bulbs for energy-saving bulbs, you'll save money on lighting, and replace the bulbs less often.

2 1 *If houses are built on soft ground, they are more likely to collapse during an earthquake.*
2 If you ask people in developing countries to take precautions against earthquakes, they ignore the warning, as they have their daily survival to worry about.
3 If people knew that an area was situated near a major fault, they would not build their towns and cities there.
4 If governments introduce building regulations in earthquake prone areas, this can reduce fatalities in the event of an earthquake.
5 In California, if building regulations had not been strictly enforced, in recent earthquakes more buildings would have been damaged, and there would have been more casualties.
6 If governments made people more aware of the dangers of earthquakes, and trained them what to do in an emergency, casualties might be reduced.
7 If people in the Pacific in December 2004 had known about the effects of tsunamis, there might have been fewer casualties.
8 If there had been a tsunami early warning system then, as there is now, people would have had the chance to move to higher ground.
9 Even if there had been a warning before the Haiti earthquake in 2010, it might not have made a difference to the number of casualties, as there would not have been enough time to evacuate people.
10 If scientists had the same financial and intellectual resources to use in places like Indonesia and Pakistan as are used in the USA or Japan, they would/might be able to minimize the effects of more earthquakes.

Grammar 16

1 1 *may increase*
2 cannot assume
3 could have been
4 can only get
5 must be
6 should be
7 might have
8 can't have got in
9 must be
10 might as well

2 1 *B* 2 C 3 B 4 A 5 C 6 A

3 1 *This can't be the way to the city centre.*
2 The director may not attend the meeting
3 You might have told me that the library always closes on Fridays.
4 The plane must have struck a flight of birds.
5 That could be why things have been going wrong.
6 We should get some early results by the end of the week.
7 They might have taken the wrong road in the dark.
8 Be more careful! You could have given yourself an electric shock!
9 You must be very proud of your daughter's achievements.
10 There is bound to be a lot of traffic on the motorway.

4 suggested answers
1 *could have hurt*
2 are bound to improve
3 might/should have arrived
4 must have forgetten
5 must have paid
6 might/should have woken
7 can't/might not get
8 might have left
9 might well rain
10 may/might have found

5 suggested answers
1 *The builders can't have constructed all the pyramids in the same way or for the same reason.*
2 A large labour force must have dragged huge blocks of stone over long distances.
3 It was originally assumed that slaves must have performed these tasks.
4 Skilled workers may/might have worked for a salary, or as a way of paying their taxes.
5 This statue may/might have weighed 60 tonnes.
6 Eight to ten workers may/might have been able to move a typical stone building block.
7 The workers must have used large amounts of wood to do this.
8 Eventually a shortage of wood must have restricted pyramid construction.
9 The ancient Egyptians must have possessed great organizational skill.
10 The mathematical knowledge of the builders of the Pyramids must have been considerable.

Grammar 17

1 1 *haven't been able to finish*
2 are not to smoke
3 don't have to pay
4 we'd better start
5 needn't have worried
6 shouldn't study
7 had to go
8 shouldn't have left
9 could swim
10 must not take

2
1 *should/ought to*
2 need not have
3 been able
4 has to/had to/has had to
5 did not have/need to
6 had better/should/ought to
7 should/ought to
8 did not need to
9 should/must
10 must/have to

3
1 *You shouldn't drink too much coffee.*
2 There is plenty of food in the fridge so you/we don't have to go shopping.
3 If you want to hire a car you must have a full driving licence.
4 All visitors are to report to reception.
5 We shouldn't have travelled there by bus.
6 I'll be able to give you more detailed information at the end of the week.
7 It is important that the government calls/call an election as soon as possible.
8 (I think) You'd better try to relax for a few days.

4
1 *There has to be a better way of encouraging*
2 The government really must introduce a scheme that
3 The prosecutor should not have charged
4 then it ought not to delay its decision.
5 Such injuries need not be a problem provided

5 suggested answers
1 *should not have happened*
2 must be/has to be
3 must receive/has to receive
4 was not able to complete/couldn't complete
5 didn't need to take
6 should not have set out/ought not to have set out

6
1 *had to wait*
2 are able to watch
3 don't have to be
4 needn't have bothered
5 has to monitor
6 should watch
7 are only able to
8 should we be
9 should this be allowed
10 must not violate
11 have to think again

Grammar 18

1 suggested answers
1 *might suppose*
2 should know
3 have to use/must use/need to use
4 can be used
5 could/might/will/may be
6 can/may/will/might be
7 will not agree
8 cannot be
9 are bound to/can/will produce
10 have to/need to/must take
11 should be/is
12 had to link
13 could/might/may be
14 must be
15 must/will have to wait

2 suggested answers
1 *The government should/ought to/must improve roads to encourage bicycle use/promote cycling.*
2 The government should/ought to/must improve public transport and make it cheaper.
3 The government should/ought to/must discourage/ban powerful 4x4 vehicles.
4 The government should/ought to/must promote working from home.
5 The government should/ought to/must discourage/ban free car parking at work.
6 The government should/ought to/must discourage/ban the use of disposable batteries/promote the use of rechargeable batteries.
7 The government should/ought to/must promote/improve environmental education in schools.
8 The government should/ought to/must discourage/ban water in plastic bottles.
9 The government should/ought to/must provide more information on energy efficiency of household products.
10 The government should/ought to/must promote electric and non-polluting vehicles/introduce lower taxes for people who drive electric and non-polluting vehicles.
11 The government should/ought to/must discourage parents from taking their children to school by car/promote walking to school/improve road safety so more children will walk to school/provide free school buses to take children to school.
12 The government should/ought to/must introduce awards/lower taxes for companies that have cut carbon emissions.

3

1	*a*	5	h	9	b
2	f	6	l	10	c
3	d	7	j	11	i
4	e	8	k	12	g

Grammar 19

1
1 *An, an, –*
2 The, –, the
3 –, a, a, –, the
4 –, –, –, –
5 –, –, the, –
6 an, a, an, –
7 A, the, a
8 The, the, a, –, a
9 –, a, a, –, a, –
10 A, a, the, –

2
1 *Giorgio is an Italian.*
2 Does a Jane Smith live here?
3 I've got a headache.
4 This (painting) is a Renoir.
5 Maria has been studying the wines of France.
6 The elephant is a herbivore.
7 The head of the bank earns over £10 million/ten million a year.

3

1	*a*	13	the
2	the	14	the
3	the	15	the
4	a	16	a
5	a	17	–
6	a	18	–
7	–	19	the
8	–	20	an
9	–	21	–
10	the	22	the
11	a	23	–
12	–		

4
1 *The three*
2 The names
3 –
4 an easily administered system
5 the ground
6 the/a process
7 –
8 the roots
9 a 25% saving

10 the cost
11 the air
12 A lot
13 the main advantage
14 –

5
1 *a*
2 –
3 –
4 A/The
5 –
6 The
7 the
8 the
9 –
10 the
11 the
12 –
13 The
14 –
15 –
16 –
17 the
18 The
19 –
20 the
21 an
22 The
23 the

6

A will stretch from the St. Pancras,
the Europe's expanding high-speed rail network
reducing a journey times.
in the east London
around the several stations

B he could get the moviegoers
'eat a popcorn'
fears that the governments
the British researchers have shown
instilling the negative thoughts.
about whether the people can process the emotional information

Grammar 20

1
1 *the Greek island of Milos*
2 the moon rising above the Alps
3 a physics textbook
4 the first Tuesday in August
5 coffee to tea
6 on holiday
7 a member state of the European Union
8 the British Library
9 the paper
10 a citrus fruit

2
1 *Susan is an Australian.*
2 I'm afraid that George is still in bed.
3 Anna studied medicine.
4 The sun is hottest in the middle of the day.
5 Helen is at work, but I can give you her number.
6 We get paid on the last Friday of the month
7 Inspector Gorse is on duty at the moment.

3
1 –, the, the, –, –, a, the, –
2 A, a, an, –, an, an, The, a, –
3 a, –, the, The, a/–, an, the, –, a
4 –, a, –, a, a, the, the, the, The
5 The, a, The, The, –, an, –, the

4
1 *A*
2 a
3 –
4 a
5 the
6 the
7 –
8 A
9 the/–
10 The
11 a
12 the
13 the
14 a
15 –
16 The
17 –
18 the
19 the
20 the
21 the
22 –
23 the
24 the
25 a
26 –
27 the
28 the
29 –
30 a
31 a
32 the
33 the

5
1 *the Maya*
2 –
3 the Tumbalá Mountains
4 the ruins
5 –
6 the 18th century
7 the world
8 –
9 of the city
10 –
11 an aqueduct
12 a complex
13 –
14 –
15 the most
16 –
17 –
18 a jade suit
19 –
20 a series
21 –
22 The

Grammar 21

1
1 –
2 –
3 –
4 –
5 –
6 –
7 the
8 –
9 the
10 –
11 The
12 the
13 –
14 –
15 the
16 the
17 the
18 the
19 –
20 –

2
1 *the*
2 a
3 a
4 the
5 the
6 the
7 a
8 the
9 the
10 the
11 a
12 the

3
1 *the*
2 the
3 –
4 a
5 a
6 the
7 –
8 a
9 –
10 the
11 –
12 the
13 a
14 –
15 the

4 requires a notion
the variables plotted
the graph itself
A graph is a presentational device,
in a chosen format.
what a graph shows
about a graph.

Grammar 22

1
1 *any money*
2 little hope/not much hope
3 too many containers
4 help/some help
5 too much
6 enough
7 some advice
8 just enough room
9 isn't very much/isn't a lot
10 millions of litres of wine

2
1 *Some*
2 little
3 many
4 amounts
5 many
6 up
7 some
8 few
9 many
10 hardly
11 few
12 plenty/lots
13 much
14 enough

3
1 *The earthquake made a large number of people homeless.*
2 How much time have we got left?
3 There is little point in carrying on.

4 We've been thinking, and we've come up with a few suggestions.
5 Not enough interest has been shown in the project to make it viable.
6 There isn't any money in the emergency fund.
7 None of the patients reported any side effects.
8 There are hardly any remaining options.
9 A lot of damage has been done to the bridge.

4 1 *much*
2 few
3 little
4 only
5 many
6 enough
7 many
8 number
9 lot
10 hardly
11 some/many
12 lot
13 many
14 too
15 of
16 none
17 enough
18 number
19 few
20 much
21 some/many
22 few
23 number
24 enough/any
25 few
26 much/a lot of
27 number
28 little

5 1 *few companies specialise in this product*
2 me some advice about what I should do
3 many open spaces in this area
4 time you need a break, there's a cafeteria on the next floor
5 much nitrogen is there in the atmosphere?
6 a little more maintenance than the earlier model
7 no cure for this condition
8 many as a hundred police officers were involved in the security operation

6 suggested answers
1 *There is not enough time to deal with this issue properly.*
2 Many thousands of people remain homeless.
3 There was hardly enough room to fit everyone in.
4 A large amount of damage has been reported from the capital.
5 A few troublemakers were arrested.
6 There is plenty of time before the plane leaves.
7 Add a little salt, and stir well.
8 None of the people I spoke to knew where the college was.
9 There are too few parking places.
10 How much water does the reservoir contain?

Grammar 23

1 1 *faster than a car*
2 I've ever seen
3 twice as fast as mine
4 too difficult to do
5 the more appealing it becomes
6 hard enough
7 as much money left
8 more and more demanding
9 like
10 just about as much as I can take

2 1 *most*
2 just
3 as
4 more
5 more
6 than
7 more
8 than
9 not
10 as
11 less
12 as
13 than
14 much/far
15 much/far
16 fewer
17 as
18 as

3 1 *easier problem than we thought it was*
2 worst state the finances have (ever) been in
3 as likely to change his mind
4 more dangerous of the two
5 twice as much profit as last year
6 too late to put out the fire
7 like the bus now
8 a lot more expensive

4 1 *The other research paper is not as detailed as this one.*
2 At weekends, Harry works as a cleaner.
3 This problem is not as easy as I thought it was.
4 This book is the more interesting of the two.
5 This is the wettest summer we've had for ten years.
6 This year there are not so/as many students on the course. There are not so/as many students on the course this year.
7 He didn't feel strong enough to carry on.
8 She tried as hard as she could.

6 1 *just as*
2 more and more
3 as much
4 more surprising
5 drier
6 less water
7 harder
8 higher
9 the best
10 twice as much
11 a lot more
12 the longer
13 shorter and cooler
14 minute less
15 more sense
16 than
17 a little richer
18 as simple as

Grammar 24

1 1 *many*
2 number
3 more
4 than
5 most
6 times
7 fewer
8 more
9 many
10 more

2 1 *most populous*
2 not even
3 largest
4 mostly
5 dominant
6 considerable
7 significant amounts
8 large numbers
9 greater extent
10 highest
11 substantial
12 many
13 extensive
14 large quantities
15 busiest
16 major

3 suggested answers
1 *more*
2 enough
3 too
4 enough
5 than
6 few
7 fewer
8 number
9 many
10 more
11 as
12 not
13 Too
14 sufficiently
15 not
16 few/minority
17 as
18 enough
19 few
20 less

Grammar 25

1
1 *has completed*
2 wherever
3 During the time
4 in the way
5 since
6 anywhere
7 as
8 when exactly
9 arrive
10 before

2
1 *way*
2 Wherever/Anywhere
3 When/While/Whenever
4 When/Once
5 while
6 After/Once
7 When/While
8 whenever/when
9 When
10 wherever
11 By
12 After
13 where
14 Once/When

3 suggested answers
1 *I used glue as it said I should in the instructions.*
2 The moment the match finished, there was a huge cheer.
3 When the tomb was discovered, the archaeologists were astounded.
4 Once the operation had started, it could not be interrupted.
5 They didn't fit the windows in the way we wanted (them to be fitted).
6 This is just how I imagined the village would be./The village is just how I imagined it would be.
7 I won't leave home before six.
8 The refugees found shelter wherever they could.
9 The way of life of the people in the mountains is much as it was in the last century.
10 It sounds as if they are not telling the truth.

Grammar 26

1
1 *As*
2 such a
3 in case
4 In spite of taking
5 Seeing as
6 so rapidly
7 Even if
8 In order that
9 so little
10 whereas

2
1 *so*
2 Although/While
3 as/since/because
4 that
5 even
6 so
7 While/Although
8 As/Since/Because
9 so
10 As/Since/Because
11 although/while
12 so that
13 as/since/because
14 while/whereas/but
15 As/Since/Because
16 so that

3 suggested answers
1 *The headwind was so strong that the flight was delayed.*
2 Since you failed to provide any references, your application has not been accepted.
3 As the meeting was poorly attended, no vote was taken on the proposal.
4 The computer programme had so many errors that it had to be rewritten.
5 Although the weather was bad, the building work was completed on time.
6 I'll give you my phone number just in case you change your mind.
7 Much as I appreciate your offer, I am afraid I have to decline.
8 Classes finished early so that students could attend rehearsals for the play.
9 It is such a dangerous substance that it has to be kept in a special container.
10 Even though they had been advised to turn back, the expedition went on.

4 suggested answers
1 *As the Islands are a tax-neutral jurisdiction, no one there pays income tax.*
2 Since the islands do not produce manufactured goods, everything has to be imported.
3 The government levies a special tax on all imports so (that) it can pay for essential services.
4 So many people want to work there and there is so much tourism that the government is also able to raise large amounts of revenue from work permits and port fees.
5 This policy has been so successful that the Islands are one of the wealthiest places in the world.

5 suggested answers
1 *Although*
2 When
3 so
4 While/Whereas
5 so that
6 so
7 so that
8 Although/While
9 as/since
10 when/whenever

Grammar 27

1

1 *a*	5 k	9 f
2 c	6 d	10 b
3 g	7 h	11 i
4 l	8 e	12 j

2 suggested answers
1 *When*
2 Whenever/When
3 Although
4 as soon as/once
5 as though
6 such
7 The moment
8 In case
9 Since/As
10 As/Since

11 by the time
12 while/even though
13 Even though/While
14 as if

3 suggested answers

1 *So many people in the developing world now use or have access to mobile phones that mobile technology is now a major contributor to economic growth.*
2 It seems that mobile phone use will just keep on rising, until the entire world population owns or has access to a mobile phone.
3 Puerto Ricans top the list of mobile phone chatters, as/since/because many mobile phone plans in Puerto Rico include unlimited calls to the US where many people have relatives.
4 However, although/while people in developing countries may come lower on the list as far as minutes per month are concerned, mobile use is still booming.
5 Many people using mobile phones subscribe to money transfer services, so that they can send money easily by text message.
6 While /Although sales of mobiles have rocketed, sales of landline connections have remained at the same level for some time.
7 In the developing world, which now accounts for over 60% of mobile use, people choose not to have landlines, as/since/because they are more expensive and harder to acquire.
8 Traditionally, effective communications infrastructure has been so poor in developing countries, that they have been held back economically, but mobile technology has changed everything.
9 Nearly everywhere/Wherever you travel, it is now possible to use your mobile phone.
10 Even though there are a few parts of Britain where there is no mobile coverage, it is possible to use your mobile on Mt Everest as/since/because there is a China Telecom mast at the bottom of the mountain!

Grammar 28

1 1 *that/which*
2 whom
3 whose
4 –/that/which
5 whose
6 who/that
7 that/which
8 whose
9 who/that
10 –/that/which

2 1 *that we, that nobody*
2 –
3 that we set up
4 person who, which I had bought
5 who is in charge
6 that we, that everyone
7 somebody here whom
8 –
9 period that, one which is rightly
10 –

3 1 *What*
2 who
3 whom
4 whose
5 whom
6 which
7 which
8 that/–
9 who
10 when

4 1 *I need someone I can rely on.*
2 The doctor phoned back all the patients she had already had interviews with.
3 This is exactly the kind of material we have been looking for.
4 There are two or three matters I want to take issue with.
5 A phenotype contains the genome it originates from.
6 His third film, *Last Time*, is what he will be remembered for.
7 It was not the experiment they were most satisfied with.
8 The sale of its old offices was the transaction the company profited most from.
9 Such a substance can be broken down into the elements which it is composed of.
10 Shakespeare is one of those writers whose personal life there is very little evidence for.

5 1 *which/that*
2 which/that
3 which/that –
4 whoever
5 which/that
6 who
7 whose
8 who
9 which
10 whose
11 which
12 which
13 where
14 which
15 which
16 whose
17 who
18 who/that
19 which/that
20 which
21 who
22 where
23 who
24 which

Grammar 29

1 1 *Taking a deep breath, she dived ...*
2 After considering/ Having considered the new evidence, the judge dismissed ...
3 ... carefully photographing/having photographed each one first.
4 While he was driving to work, a tree ...
5 Having accepted the recommendations of the committee, ...
6 On checking the figures again Foster realized ...
7 It being a public holiday, all ...
8 Since becoming president, O'Hara has been forced ...
9 Although suffering from a paralysis of the right hand, Leonardo ...
10 Having been forced/ Forced to leave Vienna, Freud ...

2 1 *taking a holiday she felt much better*
2 badly damaged, the plane managed to land safely
3 thinking, he deleted the document
4 arriving in Paris, she went directly to her hotel
5 removed his shoes, he walked through the metal detector
6 writing the first *Harry Potter* book, JK Rowling has become a top-selling author
7 daring to breathe, he pressed the button
8 examined the patient, the doctor decided she should be admitted to hospital
9 carbon-dating, the archaeologists established the age of the sword

10 in the wrecked car, she was not discovered for several hours

3 suggested answers

1 *retaining*
2 continuing/developing
3 making
4 turning out
5 studying
6 publishing
7 spending
8 concerning
9 investigating/studying
10 returning
11 going
12 left
13 Noticing
14 carrying out
15 attracting
16 Abandoning/Having abandoned
17 developing
18 having succeeded

4 1 *Before leaving, we locked all the doors/We locked all the doors before leaving.*
2 While checking the photographs, she made an interesting discovery./ She made an interesting discovery while checking …
3 On receiving the news of his appointment, he called a press conference./He called a press conference on receiving …
4 Since starting to take this medicine in June, I have had no recurrence of symptoms./ I have had no recurrence of symptoms since starting …
5 Picking up the papers, she ran out of the room.
6 For students not wishing to attend on Friday, there will be a session next Tuesday./There will be a session next Tuesday for those students not wishing …
7 Having been accused of falsifying the bank's accounts, Jackson was forced to resign.
8 The castle is thought to be of timber construction, there being no traces of masonry.
9 Having been burgled twice, we have decided to install a new alarm system.
10 All trains leaving this station stop at Euston.

Grammar 30

1 1 *who/that*
2 which/that
3 which
4 who/that
5 which
6 who/that
7 which
8 who/that
9 which
10 who/that
11 who/that
12 which
13 which
14 What

2 where participle clauses are not possible, the original clause is shown as the answer.
1 *showing*
2 choosing
3 using
4 travelling
5 carrying
6 giving
7 meaning
8 which tend
9 which may be used
10 causing
11 what we should do
12 unmentioned/not mentioned
13 living
14 needing
15 not included
16 who is elderly
17 what will reduce
18 making
19 providing
20 funding and implementing/able to fund and implement

3 1 *a*
2 r
3 d
4 k
5 n
6 e
7 l
8 h
9 g
10 c
11 p
12 j
13 b
14 i
15 q
16 m
17 o
18 f

Grammar 31

1 1 *nothing*
2 each other
3 every
4 both
5 none
6 someone
7 each
8 nothing else
9 everything
10 both

2 suggested answers

1 *time Smith plays the team wins*
2 of the experiments succeeded
3 of these books are unsuitable
4 person on the project received a bonus
5 was discovered by the expedition
6 proposal/of these (two) proposals will be expensive
7 wrong in this line
8 to sit in this part of the library
9 interesting to tell you
10 else to eat

3 1 *both*
2 something
3 both
4 Both
5 neither
6 anyone
7 one another/each other
8 ones
9 One
10 the other
11 Both
12 neither
13 No one
14 one
15 Others
16 both
17 Neither
18 anyone
19 Some
20 nothing
21 every
22 someone

4 suggested answers

1 *Is there anywhere we can get something to eat?*
2 Neither of us knows the answer.
3 There is nothing in the cupboard.
4 I'll take both of them/ them both.
5 Is there anything/ something wrong (with you)?
6 Everyone needs someone to love.
7 I can't find my wallet anywhere.
8 We can use either of them.
9 Someone else is sitting in my place.
10 These people have nowhere to live.

Grammar 32

1
1. *across, over*
2. under, on
3. in, at
4. inside, on
5. ashore, on
6. On, around
7. abroad, at
8. Among, to
9. behind, ahead
10. up and down, out

2
1 *f* 2 i 3 c 4 a 5 h 6 d 7 b 8 e 9 j 10 g

3
1. *in*
2. on
3. in
4. in
5. to
6. far away
7. in
8. back
9. to
10. to
11. at
12. on
13. opposite
14. beside
15. through
16. beneath
17. down
18. on
19. round
20. to
21. at
22. to
23. under
24. in
25. In
26. among
27. in
28. within
29. to
30. in
31. alongside

4
1. *On average, women live longer than men.*
2. The new bridge is still under construction.
3. Tina is in charge of the sales department.
4. The two men are under suspicion.
5. We are in control of the situation./We have the situation under control.
6. The president is under pressure to change the law.

5 suggested answers
1. *The faculty library is located within a short distance.*
2. We finished the project ahead of schedule.
3. Government spending is out of control.
4. For full information, see below.
5. I am half way through the book at the moment.
6. Above all, Koch is remembered for his work on tuberculosis.
7. Under the circumstances, you'd better leave, and come back next week.
8. Peter is going away on business.

Grammar 33

1
1. *under*
2. up
3. for
4. under
5. under
6. In/By
7. below
8. about/around
9. in
10. out
11. at
12. under
13. in
14. in
15. in
16. in
17. under
18. in
19. On
20. in
21. in
22. on
23. under
24. by

2
1. *Anyone*
2. Among
3. nowhere
4. in
5. None
6. each/every
7. in
8. at
9. for
10. over
11. in
12. back
13. in
14. under
15. In
16. either
17. nowhere
18. above/over
19. out
20. into

3
1 *a* 2 m 3 q 4 d 5 j 6 i 7 n 8 r 9 e 10 f 11 k 12 o 13 b 14 g 15 l 16 p 17 c 18 h

Grammar 34

1
1. *claims*
2. implies
3. found
4. estimates
5. predicts
6. demonstrate
7. explains
8. confirmed
9. suggest
10. commented

2 suggested answers
1. *predicts*
2. implies/suggests
3. point out
4. estimates
5. claim/suggest
6. confirms
7. suggests/implies
8. proves

3
1. *was once believed to circle round the Earth*
2. is thought to have been caused by heavy traffic
3. half a million people are known to be at risk
4. is said to be growing worse all the time
5. was reported to have offered financial assistance
6. is considered to be the best available
7. is said to have been found in the 18th century
8. is believed to be experiencing communication problems
9. is thought to have become extinct at the end of the 19th century
10. is said to be suffering from lack of investment

4 suggested answers
1. *Professor Scott argues that the effects of global warming have been greatly exaggerated.*
2. The Institute has confirmed that Professor Dawking has resigned.
3. The scientists explained that the disease is not transmitted by human contact.
4. The report claims that this kind of medication has little beneficial effect.
5. The UN agency estimates that there are two million people affected by the drought.

Grammar 35

1
1 *involve*
2 meant
3 expects
4 persuaded
5 encouraging
6 imagine
7 complaining
8 regret
9 forgot
10 let

2
1 *misleading*
2 to claim
3 giving
4 to believe
5 not checking/not having checked
6 to deal with
7 getting on with
8 living
9 to cooperate
10 surviving
11 to respect
12 (to) develop

3
1 *I suggest running/that we run/that we should run the experiment again.*
2 I hope you don't mind working late tonight.
3 The rain went on falling for twenty four hours.
4 James regretted not keeping/that he had not kept/not having kept another copy of the data.
5 Helen is learning to fly.
6 They invited him to send in an application.
7 The results need checking/need to be checked twice.

4
1 *This appears to be the solution.*
2 The defendant was made to pay £500 costs.
3 I couldn't help noticing that the other rooms were empty.
4 We would prefer people not to use plastic bags.
5 They arranged to lend the company the money.
6 The company employed a team of researchers to discover what their customers wanted.

Grammar 36

1 suggested answers
1 *want*
2 waiting
3 prefer
4 decide
5 suggests
6 estimated
7 expected
8 needs
9 arrange
10 help
11 shows
12 involve
13 avoid
14 thought
15 risks
16 appears
17 considered
18 argue
19 encouraging
20 advised

2
1 *walking*
2 having
3 worrying
4 to have
5 to pick up
6 to have
7 to make sure
8 doing/to do
9 surfing
10 getting
11 to go
12 being
13 to enjoy
14 being
15 having
16 to walk and balance
17 wondering
18 not having taken/not taking

Grammar 37

1
1 *despite*
2 furthermore
3 to some extent
4 instead
5 as well as
6 In spite of
7 nevertheless
8 apart from
9 in the same way
10 compared with

2
1 *more*
2 Although/While
3 respects/ways
4 comparison/contrast
5 extent
6 hand
7 yet
8 Apart
9 contrary
10 instead

3
1 *These chemicals can cause long-term damage to the environment as well as harming those who come into contact with them.*
2 The victimisation of this ethnic group is increasing and what is more, this is being generally ignored by the media.
3 Fluids are a subset of the different kinds of matter and include liquids, gases, plasmas and, to some extent, plastic solids.
4 The historic centre of the centre is still there more or less as it was in the 17th century.
5 Road communications in the area are extremely good, but rail services, on the other hand, are not adequate.
6 Some Members of Parliament denounced the law as a flagrant violation of human rights, but the government nevertheless continued to enforce it/ but the government continued to enforce it nevertheless.
7 Jefferson always spoke out against slavery, in spite of the fact that he owned slaves himself.
8 The city suffers from terrible traffic congestion, but at least there is an efficient metro system.
9 In general this camera has a very satisfactory design, apart from one small detail.
10 Wages in the country this year are 5% higher compared to last year.

4 suggested answers
1 *Although*
2 To some extent/In some respects
3 As well as
4 Despite/In spite of
5 On the contrary
6 Instead of
7 in spite of/despite
8 In some respects/To some extent
9 on the other hand
10 above all
11 at least
12 also

5 suggested answers
1 *the interest on the account is not high, at least it is tax-free*
2 respects, the government itself was responsible for the crisis
3 providing the reader with a general outline, the book (also) includes

some controversial material
4 the unusually low temperature, weather conditions were good
5 your CV, you must also send a covering letter

Grammar 38

1 1 *in conclusion*
2 For example
3 and thus
4 merely
5 such as
6 simply
7 As far as Africa is concerned
8 Logically
9 that is to say
10 namely

2 suggested answers
1 *utter*
2 sheer
3 number
4 all
5 Examples
6 such
7 simply
8 words
9 Secondly
10 put
11 Interestingly
12 Thus
13 for
14 so
15 say
16 as

3 1 *Obviously, the implications must be considered not only in respect of the management but also the staff.*
2 Unusually, the story is told only from the point of view of a ten-year-old child, who cannot fully understand what is happening.
3 Supposedly, the directors of the company knew nothing of the true financial situation.
4 Politically, the European Union cannot afford to allow the pressure on the Euro to divide the Union into two camps.
5 Financially, there is a huge disparity between the public sector and the private sector.
6 Generally, the results of these experiments match our predictions.

4 1 *Some sectors of the economy, such as manufacturing and heavy industry, have suffered most.*
2 A number of new measures will be introduced.
3 The site will provide pitches for football, rugby, hockey and so forth.
4 People were literally jumping up and down with joy.
5 The project finished on time, and in this respect it was satisfactory.
6 Generally, birds of this species do not migrate as such./Birds of this species generally do not migrate as such.

5 suggested answers
1 *such as*
2 in a way
3 as far as the developing world is concerned
4 simply wrong
5 First of all
6 In other words/To put it another way
7 that is to say
8 Secondly
9 to put it another way/in other words
10 Environmentally
11 Finally
12 Thus
13 in this respect
14 in conclusion

Grammar 39

1 1 *very*
2 it
3 not at all
4 No sooner
5 the former
6 is very much
7 What
8 it
9 not in the least
10 that they realized

2 suggested answers
1 *a*
2 m
3 h
4 g
5 o
6 n
7 l
8 k
9 c
10 e
11 b
12 i
13 f
14 d
15 j

3 1 *Rarely has there been such appreciation and enthusiasm for a conference of this kind*
2 Seldom has such a complex topic been presented with such insight.
3 Only in certain circumstances does this regulation apply to non-residents.
4 Not until there has been time to collect and evaluate all the data will the research project make any contribution to the development programme.
5 Under no circumstances will personal details be made available to commercial organisations or unauthorised members of the public.
6 Never has the pace of technological advance been greater than it is at present.

4 1 *What*
2 this
3 all
4 this/that
5 very
6 former
7 latter
8 What
9 It
10 this
11 least
12 whatsoever
13 do
14 what
15 It
16 were

Grammar 40

1 suggested answers
1 *Increasingly*
2 what
3 it
4 them
5 precise
6 those
7 to
8 However/Nevertheless/Nonetheless
9 number/range
10 well
11 However
12 such
13 besides
14 What
15 it
16 particular
17 words
18 far
19 this
20 Compared

2 suggested answers

1	*a*	5	i	9	g
2	f	6	b	10	c
3	d	7	j		
4	h	8	e		

VOCABULARY ANSWERS

Vocabulary 1

1

1	*C*	5	C	9	D
2	A	6	C	10	C
3	D	7	C	11	A
4	A	8	A	12	C

2
1 *available*
2 double
3 twin
4 unit
5 ensuite
6 facilities
7 access
8 charge
9 reservation
10 contact
11 book
12 conference
13 suite
14 reception
15 participants
16 maximum
17 equipment
18 screen
19 arrangements
20 whiteboard
21 refreshments
22 trip
23 activities
24 canoe
25 guide
26 harbour
27 wildlife
28 cruise
29 sunscreen
30 playground
31 museum
32 exhibition
33 library

3
1 *tourist*
2 complaint
3 flight
4 cultural
5 insurance
6 requirements
7 affordable
8 Exploration
9 popularity
10 performance
11 economically
12 invasive

Vocabulary 2

1

1	*B*	6	A	11	C
2	A	7	B	12	D
3	D	8	D	13	D
4	B	9	C	14	A
5	C	10	A	15	C

2
1 *inhabited (NG)*
2 damage (T)
3 populations (F)
4 course (NG)
5 invasive (T)

3
1 *mammals*
2 amphibians
3 primates
4 invertebrates
5 Hybrids
6 marsupials
7 Organisms
8 Reptiles

4
1 *is indigenous to*
2 is submissive
3 is nocturnal
4 is invasive
5 is feral
6 is tame
7 is carnivorous
8 is dominant
9 is venomous
10 is asexual

5
1 *creatures*
2 scales
3 fossils
4 skeletons
5 giants
6 characteristics
7 migrations
8 packs
9 young
10 feathers

6
1 *dumping*
2 respiration
3 suffocation
4 disappearance
5 logging
6 deforestation
7 erosion
8 flooding
9 eradication
10 modification
11 cultivation
12 resistance

Vocabulary 3

1

1	*D*	7	A	13	B
2	B	8	B	14	A
3	A	9	D	15	B
4	B	10	C	16	D
5	B	11	A		
6	C	12	C		

2
1 *volcanoes*
2 tremors
3 magnitude
4 waves
5 destruction
6 construction
7 stress
8 statistics
9 factors
10 tsunamis
11 dams
12 bank
13 countryside
14 path
15 climate
16 typhoon
17 equator
18 speeds
19 hemisphere
20 eye
21 forecasts
22 warnings

3
1 *Timber*
2 Diamonds
3 Mud
4 Clay
5 Iron
6 Minerals
7 Crude oil
8 Calcium
9 Coal
10 Bamboo

4
1 *mineralogist*
2 cartographer
3 geologist
4 climatologist
5 volcanologist
6 glaciologist
7 oceanographer
8 seismologist
9 geographer

5
1 *tundra*
2 vent
3 plates
4 lightning
5 layers
6 latitude
7 bed
8 retreated

6
1 *classified*
2 recycled
3 makes
4 rises
5 pours
6 solidifies
7 trapped
8 crystallizes
9 weathered
10 ends up
11 transported
12 squeezed
13 melt
14 undergo
15 revert

Vocabulary 4

1

1	*D*	6	B	11	D
2	B	7	A	12	C
3	A	8	C	13	A
4	C	9	A	14	B
5	D	10	B	15	C

2
1 *abandoned*
2 collapsed
3 founded
4 invaded
5 spread

6 conquered
7 expanded
8 dispersed

3 1 *historian*
2 archaeologist
3 geneticist
4 genealogist
5 Egyptologist
6 etymologist
7 anthropologist
8 palaeontologist
9 geologist

4 1 *ancestors*
2 prehistoric
3 nomadic
4 trail
5 hieroglyphics
6 middens
7 carvings
8 skeleton

5 1 *golden age*
2 antiquity
3 era
4 decade
5 millennia
6 lunar calendar
7 prehistory
8 dynasty

6 1 *cradle*
2 dawn
3 heart
4 flaw
5 centre
6 key
7 mouth
8 birthplace

7 1 *e* 4 a 7 b
2 c 5 g
3 f 6 d

Vocabulary 5

1 1 *D* 5 C 9 A
2 D 6 A 10 C
3 A 7 B
4 A 8 C

2 1 A intellectual
B helpful
C operational
D instinctive
Answer: D
2 A weaken
B control
C determine
D understand
Answer: C
3 A told
B suggested
C responded
D disputed
Answer: B

3 1 *behavioural*
2 spatial
3 sensory
4 memorize
5 intuitively
6 perceptual

4 1 *prone to, susceptible to*
2 overcome, overwhelmed
3 an addiction to, a craving for
4 subconscious, involuntary
5 instinctive, innate
6 uncontrollable, compulsive
7 logical, rational
8 activate, stimulate
9 trait, attribute
10 mindset, mentality

5 1 *willpower*
2 hallucinations
3 obsession
4 IQ (intelligence quota)
5 disorder
6 dementia
7 well-being
8 amnesia
9 phobia
10 hypochondria

6 1 *consolidate*
2 convert
3 relate
4 stimulate
5 provoke
6 retrieve
7 modify
8 store
9 resemble
10 monitor

Vocabulary 6

1 1 *A* 6 B 11 B
2 C 7 A 12 A
3 D 8 C 13 C
4 A 9 B 14 B
5 D 10 D

2 1 *microchip*
2 feature
3 switch
4 console
5 gadget
6 device
7 wire
8 application
9 glitch
10 sensor

3 1 *state of the art*
2 commercially viable
3 durable
4 heat-resistant
5 waterproof
6 faulty
7 synthetic
8 handy
9 revolutionary
10 complex
11 mobile

4 1 *artificial*
2 automated
3 hydraulic
4 misaligned
5 overcome
6 navigate
7 terrain
8 recognition
9 perform
10 designed
11 logic
12 held
13 interaction

5 1 *data*
2 fingerprints
3 scanners
4 installation
5 image
6 irises
7 traits
8 hackers
9 databases

Vocabulary 7

1 1 *A* 7 D 13 D
2 C 8 A 14 C
3 B 9 B 15 A
4 B 10 A 16 C
5 D 11 B
6 A 12 D

2 1 *j* 5 e 9 h
2 c 6 g 10 b
3 d 7 a
4 i 8 f

3 1 *up (established)*
2 down (collapsed)
3 on (became a trend)
4 forward (anticipated)
5 with (resolved), off (postponed)
6 on (planned)
7 up (prepared)
8 for (received)
9 for/after (chose)
10 on (hired)
11 down (rejected)

4 1 *C* 5 B 9 C
2 B 6 B 10 C
3 A 7 B
4 A 8 A

5 1 *redundancies*
2 security
3 recruitment
4 applicants
5 management
6 employee
7 vacancy
8 selection
9 specialist
10 productivity
11 rejection

6 1 *campaigns*
2 billboards

3 catch
4 admen
5 audience
6 target
7 segment
8 brands
9 loyal
10 endorsement
11 promote
12 placement
13 logos
14 means
15 pop-ups
16 profiles
17 tailor

7 1 *revenue*
2 income
3 Tax
4 economic
5 margins
6 Sales
7 wealth
8 earnings
9 budget

Vocabulary 8

1

1	*D*	6	C	11	A
2	A	7	A	12	D
3	C	8	D	13	C
4	B	9	B	14	A
5	B	10	C	15	A

2 1 *anxiety (NG)*
2 beneficial (T)
3 exposure (F)
4 successfully (T)
5 similarity (F)
6 response (NG)

3 1 facts and events, phenomena
2 behaviour, actions
3 speculation, conjecture
4 data, information
5 breakthrough, advance

4 1 *underlying*
2 ground-breaking
3 controversial
4 empirical
5 reliable
6 feasible
7 biased
8 concrete

5

1	*A*	6	D	11	A
2	B	7	B	12	B
3	D	8	D	13	C
4	C	9	A	14	C
5	B	10	B		

Vocabulary 9

1

1	*B*	6	B	11	C
2	A	7	A	12	A
3	D	8	B	13	D
4	C	9	B	14	B
5	D	10	A		

2 1 technological/technical (NG)
2 cultural (T)
3 likelihood (F)
4 knowledge (T)
5 growth (NG)

3 Literature: *a memoir*, a metaphor, a poem, a genre, non-fiction
Music: a melody, rhythm, an orchestra, an instrument, rehearsal, improvisation, a composition
Sculpture: a blow-torch, bronze, an installation, design
Drawing and painting: canvas, a pigment, a portrait, a composition, charcoal, a sketch
Architecture: design, function, a builder, durability
Drama: a stage, a cast, a rehearsal, improvisation

4 1 *descriptions*
2 influential
3 ironic
4 predictable
5 impressive
6 exhibition
7 geometric(al)
8 visual
9 underrated/overrated
10 performance
11 literary
12 realism

5 1 *biography*
2 editorials
3 reviews
4 fiction
5 version
6 translations
7 plot
8 metaphors

6 1 *iconic*
2 urban
3 carved
4 heritage
5 awards
6 responsibility
7 function
8 concept
9 space
10 site
11 met
12 merits
13 facade
14 extension
15 wing
16 flaws
17 pulled
18 drawn

Vocabulary 10

1

1	*B*	6	D	11	A
2	A	7	D	12	B
3	C	8	A	13	A
4	A	9	B	14	B
5	C	10	A	15	A

2 1 *charity, aid*
2 shanty towns, slums
3 cycle, circle
4 starvation, malnutrition
5 discrimination, prejudice
6 underachieve, underperform
7 underprivileged, disadvantaged
8 campaign, crusade
9 anti-social, harmful
10 vulnerable, susceptible

3

1	*B*	4	B	7	C
2	D	5	A	8	B
3	C	6	A	9	C

4 1 *freedom*
2 censorship
3 disseminating
4 current
5 biased
6 impartial
7 investigative
8 agencies
9 broadsheet
10 superficial
11 published
12 demand
13 circulation
14 exposés
15 mass

5 1 *conference*
2 informative
3 correspondent
4 journalism
5 intrusive
6 coverage
7 influential
8 cultural
9 documentary
10 factual

Vocabulary 11

1

1	*B*	6	D	11	B
2	B	7	A	12	A
3	D	8	D	13	C
4	A	9	C		
5	C	10	B		

2 1 *lungs*
2 arteries
3 cells
4 bones
5 Tendons
6 hormones
7 muscles
8 veins
9 joints

10 metabolism
11 retinas
12 cochlear

3 1 *cardiovascular*
2 digestive
3 nervous
4 reproductive
5 respiratory
6 musculoskeletal
7 immune
8 endocrine

4 1 *inflammation*
2 breathing
3 inhalers
4 allergens
5 temperature
6 headaches
7 fatigue
8 specimen
9 quinine
10 thirst
11 damage
12 vision
13 exercise
14 fat
15 Insulin
16 cough
17 throat
18 Pneumonia
19 Vaccination
20 high-risk
21 antibiotics

5 1 *g* 4 a 7 h
2 e 5 f 8 d
3 b 6 c

6 1 *spreading*
2 Chronic
3 wrists
4 epidemic
5 eradicated
6 contagious
7 embryo
8 alternative
9 effect
10 insomnia
11 diagnosis

Vocabulary 12

1 1 *D* 6 B 11 C
2 B 7 C 12 D
3 B 8 A 13 B
4 C 9 B 14 A
5 A 10 A 15 C

2 1 *Opponents*
2 scant
3 dismisses
4 proof
5 campaigner
6 refutes
7 doubt
8 summaries
9 defended
10 rejected
11 contradict

12 denial

3 1 *common*
2 convincing/good
3 heated/widespread
4 implausible
5 anecdotal, empirical
6 incorrect
7 unanimous
8 good
9 prevailing

4 1 *e* 4 a 7 d
2 f 5 h 8 c
3 g 6 b

5 1 *taken aback*
2 leans towards
3 won over
4 written off
5 puzzled over
6 borne out
7 goes along with
8 rules out
9 point to
10 fathomed out

6 1 *against (D)*
2 with (A)
3 with (D)
4 between (A)
5 to (A)
6 to (U)
7 into (U)
8 out (U)
9 in (A)
10 into (D)

7 1 *criticism*
2 expectations
3 inconceivable
4 assumption
5 sceptical
6 Hypothetically
7 conviction
8 enthusiasm
9 agreement
10 influential
11 preoccupation
12 acknowledges

Vocabulary 13

1 1 *D* 8 C 15 B
2 B 9 A 16 C
3 B 10 A 17 C
4 A 11 C 18 D
5 C 12 A 19 B
6 B 13 B 20 C
7 D 14 A

2 1 *d* 5 l 9 c
2 i 6 a 10 b
3 h 7 f 11 e
4 g 8 j 12 k

3 1 *degree*
2 major
3 papers
4 prospectus
5 electives
6 programme
7 certificate
8 master's

4 1 *bibliography*
2 first draft
3 dissertation
4 case study
5 recommendations
6 thesis statement
7 project

5 1 *meet, extend*
2 undertake, carry out
3 attend, take part in
4 submit, hand in
5 amend, redo
6 sitting, taking
7 grades, marks
8 sample, subjects
9 proof-read, go through
10 seminar, tutorial

6 1 *extension*
2 submission
3 allocation
4 requirements
5 analysis
6 plagiarism
7 findings
8 assessment

Vocabulary 14

1 1 *D* 6 C 11 B
2 C 7 C 12 A
3 B 8 B 13 C
4 A 9 D 14 A
5 A 10 D

2 1 *go up*, climb, rise, grow
2 drop, fall
3 stay constant, hold steady
4 be unpredictable
5 shoot up, rocket, jump
6 dive, plunge, slump
7 reach a high point

3 1 *sharply, suddenly*
2 approximately, roughly
3 steeply, significantly
4 steadily, progressively
5 relatively, comparatively
6 somewhat, rather

4 1 *was a dramatic rise in*
2 has been a levelling out in
3 a slight fall in
4 was considerable fluctuation in
5 reached a plateau

5 1 *A* 4 D 7 C
2 B 5 C
3 D 6 B

6 1 *Whereas, Although, While*
2 Compared, In comparison
3 while, but, whilst
4 Regarding, Concerning, As for
5 All in all, Overall

7 1 *beginning to reject*
2 critical
3 becoming more likely
4 not included in
5 suddenly become more
6 become popular
7 predictable
8 future
9 How can we explain this change?
10 rare

Vocabulary 15

1 1 *recommended*
2 heed
3 Ensure
4 limited
5 impacted on
6 basic
7 key
8 further
9 reproduce
10 employ
11 paraphrase
12 required
13 allocated
14 identical
15 broad
16 appropriate
17 intended

2 1 *A* 2 A 3 D 4 D 5 A 6 A 7 D 8 A 9 A 10 D

3 1 *M* 2 C 3 C 4 M 5 M 6 C 7 C 8 C 9 M 10 M 11 M

4 1 *divisive, controversial*
2 complicated, multifaceted
3 assessing, weighing up
4 constantly, continuously
5 consider, bear in mind
6 certain, particular
7 improbable, unlikely
8 repercussions, outcomes

5 1 *depending, information*
2 impact, immense
3 elderly, anxious
4 construction, countryside
5 contentment/pleasure, afford, pleasure/contentment
6 the case, company, operate
7 question, reply
8 selection, violent

Vocabulary 16

1 1 *Consequently*
2 however
3 in terms of
4 so that
5 As for/In terms of
6 such as
7 yet
8 Despite
9 In the case of
10 even though
11 provided

2 1 even
2 In addition to
3 Not only, but
4 also/even

3 Ordering ideas: first of all, to begin with, secondly, finally
Introducing an idea: in terms of, as for, in the case of, concerning, regarding
Addition: also, not only/but, in addition to, moreover, furthermore, even
Contrast: but, however, yet, on the other hand
Concession: despite, even though, in spite of, while, having said that, nevertheless

4 1 *Nevertheless*/Having said this
2 Despite/In spite of
3 While/Even though

5 1 *First of all*/To begin with
2 in terms of/regarding/in the case of
3 in terms of/regarding/in the case of/as for
4 Furthermore/Moreover

6 Showing condition: provided, if, as long as
Showing result: consequently, subsequently, as a result, so, therefore, hence
Showing purpose: so that, in order to, so as to
Exemplification: for example, such as, like, for instance

7 1 a *hence*
b Therefore
c so
Sentence (b)
2 a for example,
b such as
c For example,
Sentence (a)
3 a as long as
b In order to
c so that
so as to: sentence (b)
if: sentence (a)

8 1 whereas
2 on the other hand
3 on the contrary
4 On the contrary
5 On the other hand
6 Whereas

9 1 *why*
2 because of/due to
3 for this reason/because of this
4 since/as
5 owing to/on account of

Vocabulary 17

1 1 process
2 theory
3 policy
4 sector
5 income
6 research
7 definition
8 response
9 estimate
10 benefit
11 legislation
12 authority

2 1 specific
2 similar
3 involved
4 major/significant
5 established
6 available
7 derived
8 economic
9 consistent
10 required
11 legal
12 significant

3 1 evidence
2 method
3 assessment
4 contract
5 principle
6 assume
7 data
8 export
9 individual
10 source
11 create
12 labour

4 1 procedures
2 environment
3 issues
4 factors
5 concepts
6 occur
7 per cent
8 variables
9 indicate
10 period
11 interpretation
12 structure

5 1 role
2 context
3 distribution
4 financial
5 approach
6 section
7 constitutional
8 area
9 function
10 analysis
11 identified
12 formula

6 1 Resident
2 chapter
3 purchase
4 text
5 assistance
6 evaluation
7 distinction
8 community
9 conclusion
10 survey
11 construction
12 computer

7 1 strategies
2 consequences
3 elements
4 resources
5 features
6 categories
7 regulations
8 range
9 injury
10 items
11 security
12 commission

8 1 complex
2 previous
3 perceived
4 relevant
5 positive
6 primary
7 restricted
8 traditional
9 normal
10 obtained
11 cultural
12 final

9 1 acquisition
2 impact
3 institute
4 consumer
5 participation
6 site
7 equation
8 journal
9 focus
10 potential
11 investment
12 region

10 1 design
2 administration
3 achieve
4 credit
5 maintenance
6 transfer
7 aspects
8 conduct
9 select
10 seek
11 affect
12 appropriate

Vocabulary 18

1 1 minority
2 validity
3 task
4 technique
5 proportion
6 reaction
7 criteria
8 core
9 contribution
10 philosophy
11 sex
12 compensation

2 1 registered
2 implied
3 illustrated
4 published
5 ensured
6 excluded
7 consented
8 demonstrated
9 removed
10 specified
11 shifted
12 commented

3 1 justification
2 outcome
3 convention
4 framework
5 constraints
6 deduction
7 Funds
8 reliance
9 partnership
10 location
11 link
12 coordination

4 1 sequence
2 scheme
3 instance
4 interaction
5 technology
6 immigration
7 component
8 emphasis
9 circumstances
10 layer
11 volume
12 document

5 1 alternative
2 negative
3 dominant
4 constant
5 physical
6 technical
7 initial
8 corresponding
9 maximum
10 considerable
11 sufficient
12 corporate

6 1 principal
2 internal
3 approximate
4 ethnic
5 annual
6 apparent/obvious
7 adequate
8 subsequent
9 Domestic
10 Prior
11 civil
12 obvious

7 1 emerged
2 attributed
3 retained
4 imposed
5 labelled
6 predicted
7 undertook
8 promoted
9 accessed
10 granted
11 contrasted
12 implemented

8 1 regime
2 integration
3 mechanism
4 parallel
5 hypothesis
6 conference
7 investigation
8 stress
9 option
10 commitment
11 summary
12 goal

9 1 project
2 occupation
3 sum
4 job
5 parameters
6 concentration
7 series
8 professional
9 code
10 output
11 phase
12 status

10 1 overall
2 Attitudes
3 statistics
4 cycle
5 communication
6 error
7 hence
8 implications
9 debate
10 despite
11 dimension
12 resolution

WORDS AND PHRASES ANSWERS

Words and phrases 1

1 1 *extended*
2 nuclear
3 divorce
4 remarried
5 blended
6 stepsister
7 only child
8 arranged marriage
9 ceremony
10 groom
11 first-born
12 siblings
13 kinship
14 upbringing
15 adoption
16 child rearing
17 single parent
18 institution
19 in-laws
20 relatives
21 emotional fulfilment

2 1 *debating, arguing*
2 contacted, approached
3 recommend, propose
4 interviewed, surveyed
5 teaming up, collaborating
6 coordinating, organizing
7 interact with, relate to
8 liaise, cooperate
9 mediate, arbitrate
10 contested, questioned

3 1 *fire*
2 decision
3 conclusion
4 surprise
5 contact
6 long way
7 across
8 down
9 criticism
10 together
11 against
12 down
13 up

4 1 *anti*
2 post
3 Pro
4 pre
5 pro
6 anti
7 pre
8 post
9 pro
10 Pre
11 pre

5 1 *case*
2 retrospect
3 addition
4 response
5 comparison
6 view
7 order
8 accordance
9 contrast
10 practice
11 advance
12 conclusion

Words and phrases 2

1 1 *(multi)cultural*
2 modernized
3 industrial
4 Suburban
5 extensive
6 financial
7 impressive
8 central
9 overpopulated

2 1 *stage*
2 layer
3 fragment
4 period
5 feature
6 phase
7 component
8 fraction
9 branch
10 quota
11 constituent

3 1 *uniqueness*
2 punishment
3 importance
4 reliance
5 Loneliness
6 awareness
7 improvements
8 happiness
9 intelligence
10 disappearance

4 1 *control*
2 nourished
3 eighteen
4 developed
5 law
6 review
7 privileged
8 estimate
9 staffed
10 lying

5 1 *rise*
2 encouragement
3 try
4 away
5 off
6 in
7 birth
8 grounds
9 credit
10 way

Words and phrases 3

1 1 *variety, sub-species*
2 subdivisions, sectors
3 classification, category
4 rank, status
5 breed
6 tribe, clan
7 personnel, workforce
8 class
9 strain, variant
10 colony, settlement
11 community

2 1 *measures*
2 course
3 hours
4 power
5 risk
6 responsibility
7 place
8 lead
9 account
10 dive
11 give

3 1 *provisional*
2 Current
3 simultaneous
4 previous
5 contemporary
6 historical
7 futuristic
8 temporary
9 prolonged
10 chronological

4

1	*g*	5	c	9	k
2	f	6	h	10	d
3	i	7	b		
4	a	8	e		

5 *coeducation* semi-circular, monopoly, biannual
1 *bi*
2 mono
3 semi
4 co
5 semi
6 mono
7 co
8 bi

6 1 *cover, ranges*
2 spread, stretches
3 converge, united
4 widened, diversified
5 rise, raise
6 multiplied, enlarge

Words and phrases 4

1 1 *ritual*
2 ceremony
3 festivals
4 anniversary
5 fasting
6 commemorate
7 pilgrimage

8 symbolizes
9 custom
10 occasion

2 1 *behalf*
2 agenda
3 point/verge
4 contrary
5 hand
6 average
7 basis
8 reflection
9 verge/point
10 loan

3 *triangle*, multinational, centimetre, pantheism
1 *pan*
2 centi
3 tri
4 multi
5 multi
6 centi
7 tri
8 pan

4 1 *at risk*
2 in control of
3 under pressure
4 at a disadvantage
5 an end to
6 another way
7 across/forward
8 down to
9 forward
10 off
11 through

Words and phrases 5

1 1 *pride*
2 (un)emotional
3 anger
4 envious
5 anxiety
6 assertiveness
7 intelligence
8 pessimism
9 conformist
10 impulsive

2 1 *h* 4 b 7 e
2 c 5 f 8 d
3 a 6 g

3 1 *inaccuracy*
2 inaccessible
3 insignificant
4 innumerate
5 indefensible/ inconceivable
6 inconvenient
7 inappropriate
8 inadvisable/ inappropriate
9 inconceivable/ indefensible

4 1 *time*
2 living
3 difference
4 perfect
5 progress
6 decision
7 suggestion
8 use
9 mistakes
10 gestures
11 adjustment

Words and phrases 6

1 1 *cyclists*
2 commuters
3 pedestrians
4 Urban planners
5 Passengers
6 An electric vehicle
7 A hybrid
8 A catalytic converter
9 Electronic fuel injection
10 *e*
11 g
12 c
13 f
14 a
15 h
16 b
17 d
18 *emissions laws*
19 product recall
20 speed limit
21 Traffic congestion
22 fuel efficiency
23 driver alertness

2 1 *both*
2 both
3 at random
4 both
5 posterity
6 outweigh
7 former
8 both
9 both
10 precursors
11 both

3 1 *effect, affected*
2 borrowed, lend
3 require, requested
4 reduce, declining
5 avoided, prevented
6 live, staying
7 find, find out
8 bring up, educated

4 1 *unpredictable*
2 unknowingly
3 unattainable
4 unjustifiable
5 unemployed
6 unrealistic
7 unqualified
8 unaffected
9 undeniable
10 uncertainty

5 1 *criteria*
2 obstacles
3 needs
4 deadline
5 opposition
6 standards
7 demand
8 halfway

6 1 *relatively*
2 controversial
3 unimaginable
4 excessively
5 investigative
6 commercially
7 debatable
8 managerial

Words and phrases 7

1 1 *tax*
2 packaging
3 recycling
4 disposable
5 biodegradable
6 leftover
7 accumulate
8 landfill
9 toxic

2 1 *pharmaceutical*
2 energy
3 dairy
4 aviation
5 textile
6 consumer electronics
7 construction
8 food processing
9 retail

3 1 *classified*
2 stabilized
3 solidifies
4 visualize
5 clarify
6 intensifying
7 liquefied/liquidized
8 symbolized
9 authorize
10 identify

4 1 *carry*
2 carries
3 holding
4 holding
5 carries
6 carry
7 hold
8 carried
9 hold

5 1 *Theoretically*
2 knowledge
3 statistical
4 inexplicable
5 inconclusive
6 feasibility
7 genetically
8 culturally
9 tendency
10 atmospheric

Words and phrases 8

1
1 *minor*
2 manslaughter
3 record
4 assault
5 lenient
6 hardened
7 capital
8 commit

2
1 *correct*
2 support
3 wrong
4 true
5 continued to say he was right
6 make the theory weaker
7 opposed
8 argued

3
1 *document*
2 extract
3 labour
4 aid
5 guarantee
6 conflict
7 input
8 project
9 subject

4
1 *strengthened*
2 loosen
3 widened
4 moisten
5 broaden
6 tightening
7 softened
8 straighten
9 shorten
10 harden

5
1 *cost of living*
2 standard of living
3 work–life balance
4 in living memory
5 way of life
6 in later life
7 make a living
8 claims many lives
9 living language
10 working life

6
1 *levels*
2 both
3 both
4 Admittedly
5 apparently
6 main
7 Generally
8 respects
9 means
10 both

Words and phrases 9

1
1 *cognitive*
2 translator
3 gesture
4 acquire
5 verbal
6 characters
7 mimic
8 indigenous
9 tongue
10 oral
11 dialect
12 rumours
13 anecdotal

2
1 *S* 4 A 7 S
2 A 5 A 8 A
3 S 6 S 9 S

3
1 *was instrumental in*
2 was symptomatic of
3 was indigenous to
4 was consistent with
5 was endemic to
6 was the epitome of
7 was a correlation between
8 was irrelevant to

4
1 *Craftsmanship*
2 adulthood
3 neighbourhood
4 scholarship
5 internship
6 likelihood
7 championship
8 livelihood
9 childhood

Words and phrases 10

1
1 *council*
2 anarchist
3 supervisor
4 democracy
5 minister
6 watchdog
7 regime
8 patriarchy
9 bureaucracy
10 principal
11 executive

2
1 *f* 5 c 9 b
2 h 6 d 10 e
3 j 7 i 11 a
4 k 8 l 12 g

3
1 *stability*
2 acquisition
3 exploitation
4 migration
5 individuality
6 justification
7 expansion
8 regularity
9 participation
10 assumptions
11 durability
12 comprehension
13 validity

4
1 *merely/basically*
2 barely
3 principally
4 reasonably/increasingly
5 predominantly/widely
6 radically
7 certainly/reasonably
8 widely
9 increasingly
10 inextricably
11 fully
12 marginally